Christopher Marlowe

MERMAID CRITICAL COMMENTARIES

MERMAID CRITICAL COMMENTARIES

Christopher Marlowe

Edited by
BRIAN MORRIS

HILL AND WANG · NEW YORK

Introduction

THIS IS THE RECORD of the first York Symposium, held at Langwith College, in the University of York, from 19 to 21 April 1968. The *New Mermaid* series of Jacobean dramatic texts has been expanding steadily since it began in 1963, and it was decided last year to enlarge the scope of the series by publishing collections of critical essays on the major dramatists, to accompany the editions.

Marlowe was the obvious choice for the first Symposium, since the series already had editions of *The Jew of Malta, Doctor Faustus,* and *Edward II,* with *Tamburlaine* in preparation, and nearly twenty leading scholars and critics from British Universities accepted invitations to come to the Symposium, and either read a paper to it or join in its discussions. The ideal behind the venture was that it might be productive if a small group of academics with special interests in Marlowe's work could live together for a long week-end, hear each other's work, and offer criticism, comment, and new ideas on it both publicly and privately. And something very close to this ideal did in fact take place. Private talk flourished in the Senior Common Room until late at night, and in the public discussions which followed each paper the attitudes ranged amicably from qualified approbation to civilised hostility, and the concerns were for everything from scholarly accuracy to mystic vision.

It emerged fairly clearly that the group wished to explore some areas of Marlowe's work more than others. *Tamburlaine, Dido,* and the Poems commanded a great deal of respect, while *Edward II* became at times almost an obsessive focus of interest: its influence on later plays, its naturalism, the homosexuality, the aptness of its justices, its religious orthodoxy, Brecht's adaptation of it—these were only a few of the aspects discussed. It may seem surprising that a volume of papers on Marlowe contains not one essay on *Doctor Faustus,* which many have regarded as his masterpiece. Both the papers and the discussions frequently referred to the play, but no one who was approached felt he wanted to offer a special study of it. It may be that Greg's vast labours on the text, together with the critical accounts given in recent years by Bradbrook, Brockbank, Brooke, Cole, Gill, Steane, and many others, have, for the moment, exhausted invention, and that we shall have to digest current judgements before creating new.

We found ourselves more interested in Marlowe's influence than in his inheritance. Harold Brooks anatomised his relationship with the early Shakespeare, Michael Hattaway linked him with Brecht, and Mulryne and Fender related him to the contemporary 'theatre of the absurd'. Source-hunting, once described as 'still an acceptable mode of conspicuous leisure', occupied no one, neither did we dispute questions of authorship, analogue, or date. It is perhaps an indication of critical health that the papers delivered were almost equally divided between the general and the specific: Gibbons, Morris, Smith, and Gill offered particular analyses, while Mulryne and Fender, Hattaway, Brooks, Palmer, and Merchant concerned themselves with wider issues. Although James Smith's paper was the only one which dealt intimately with problems of production and performance the sense of the theatrical life of the plays was a very present one, and frequently discussion turned upon the viability of a particular interpretation on the stage.

The papers are printed substantially as they were read. Certain revisions were made by authors as a result of discussion, but no editorial uniformity has been imposed. Thus, though most writers quote Marlowe from Tucker Brooke's edition (Oxford, 1910), some, for their own purposes, go elsewhere, and this inconsistency has been allowed to remain. Footnotes (many of them afterthoughts) have been regularised in presentation but seldom challenged in number or completeness.

The final impression given by the Symposium was of the continuing relevance of Marlowe's work. He has much to tell us about power, knowledge, greed, suffering, human dignity, and human worth. We have not learnt his lessons yet.

BRIAN MORRIS

Langwith College
York

Members of the Symposium

Professor M. C. Bradbrook, Girton College, Cambridge

Professor Philip Brockbank, University of York

Dr Harold F. Brooks, Birkbeck College, London

Dr Robert Cockcroft, University of Nottingham

Dr T. W. Craik, University of Aberdeen

J. S. Cunningham, University of York

Dr Stephen Fender, University of Edinburgh

Professor R. A. Foakes, University of Kent at Canterbury

Dr Brian Gibbons, University of York

Miss Roma Gill, University of Sheffield

Dr Michael Hattaway, University of Kent at Canterbury

Professor the Reverend W. Moelwyn Merchant, University of Exeter

Dr Brian Morris, University of York

Dr J. R. Mulryne, University of Edinburgh

D. J. Palmer, University of Hull

James L. Smith, University of Southampton

Professor Peter Ure, University of Newcastle upon Tyne

Keith Walker, University College, London

George Watson, University of Aberdeen

Contents

ix

The Jew of Malta *in the Theatre*

JAMES L. SMITH

The Jew of Malta *in the Theatre*

WHAT A CASE am I in, that am neither a good prologue nor cannot insinuate with you in the behalf of a good play! For Marlowe's *Jew* is surely the one play in the canon least likely to reduce academic blood pressure: indeed, such criticism that I have met seems agreed on only three points—that it is difficult, generically dubious, and theatrically effective. The quotations which follow, from Professor Bradbrook, Mr Steane, and Dr Craik respectively, sum up what I take to be orthodox opinion:

> *The Jew of Malta* is one of the most difficult of Elizabethan plays.

> Few plays have been given more names: tragedy, comedy, melodrama, farce, tragical-comical, farcical-satirical, 'terribly serious' or 'tediously trivial'; 'terrifying', it seems, cannot be too heavy a term, nor 'absurd' too light.

> *The Jew of Malta* is essentially a play for the theatre, and it is in the theatre that it must be judged, not according to preconceived notions of tragic dignity and tragic depth.[1]

Most scholars, however, seem very content to judge the play from the comfort of their study armchairs. I would like to suggest another approach—albeit a very unscholarly one. By examining the play's theatrical career, I hope to shed some light upon its dramatic genre and so clarify at least some of the problems encountered by more conventional critical enquiries. My main difficulty is, of course, a lack of reliable evidence. Of the original production, for example, very little is known. Henslowe presented the play some thirty-six times between 26 February 1591–2 and 21 June 1596 (and in 1601 bought 'thinges' to

---

[1] M. C. Bradbrook, *Themes and conventions of Elizabethan tragedy* (Cambridge, 1935), p. 156; J. B. Steane, *Marlowe: a critical study* (Cambridge, 1964), p. 166; T. W. Craik, ed., Marlowe, *The Jew of Malta*, The New Mermaids (London, 1966), p. xviii (all references to the play are to this edition).

keep its image bright in revival); and Barabas was played by the versatile
Edward Alleyn, then at the height of his powers, in a great false nose.[2]
How closely the acted text resembled that of the 1633 Quarto (which
appeared after Heywood's recent revival of the play at court and at the
Cockpit), and how sympathetically the Elizabethan audience viewed
Barabas and his bloodcurdling villainies, are still matters for fierce
debate and scholarly conjecture. Later revivals are, luckily, better
documented. And there have been more of them than one would at first
suspect. The play flashed briefly across the stage of Drury Lane in
1818 (24 April), and then promptly disappeared without trace for a
century. Williams College staged a revival—perhaps the American
premiere—in 1907, and the Phoenix Society presented it at Daly's
Theatre in London for two performances in 1922 (5–6 November). And
this, declared the programme of the Royal Shakespeare Company at
their quatercentenary revival in 1964, was the only 'recorded production
in London this century'. Actually, there had been at least six other
revivals in the interim, two of them in London, and two anticipating
the RSC by a matter of months. The Yale Dramatic Association
mounted one in June 1940, and the Marlowe Players of Reading
University another in 1954 (13–14 May)—a production which later
transferred to the Toynbee Hall, London, in the long vacation (1–3 July).
A third revival was staged by the Cambridge Theatre Group in 1957.
In 1960, the Tavistock Repertory Company presented the play at the
Tower Theatre in Canonbury Place (4–6, 10–12 March); in 1964 it was
given by the Marlowe Theatre at Canterbury (18–22 February), and the
Victoria Theatre, Stoke-on-Trent (10–28 March). Hot upon the heels
of the RSC revival at the Aldwych (1 October) came news of a Christmas
production by the Merseyside Unity Group; and finally the Aldwych
version, now almost totally recast, reappeared at Stratford during the
1965 Shakespeare season (14 April). The Toynbee Hall saw yet another
revival in 1966, when the play was mounted by the Marlowe Society of
Chislehurst, Kent (19–21 October).

All four professional revivals, with which I shall be most closely
concerned, seem to have been excellently cast and mounted. The
Drury Lane production[3] boasted Edmund Kean in a performance 'full

---

[2] See *Henslowe's Diary*, ed. R. A. Foakes and R. T. Rickert (Cambridge, 1961),
pp. 16–26, 34, 36–7, 47, 170; for Nashe's tribute to Alleyn, see E. Nungezer,
A Dictionary of Actors, Cornell Studies in English, XIII (New Haven and
London, 1929), p. 5; for his false nose, see William Rowley, *A Search for Money*
(London, 1609), p. 12.

[3] References here are to: *The European Magazine, and London Review*,

of striking passages' (T), well supported by Mrs Bartley, who played Abigail 'very respectably' (TI), and a large company of twenty-one speaking parts, eleven knights, three nuns, two ladies, and a 'Maid' played by Miss Carr. To judge from the playbill, the revival was lavishly mounted, 'With New SCENERY, DRESSES and DECORATIONS. The New Scenery designed by Mr GREENWOOD, and painted by him and Assistants'. A less partisan indication of the costumes (and characters) can be gained from a contemporary print of IV.iv. T. P. Cooke, who made the little part of Pilia Borza 'much more important' than the *Theatrical Inquisitor* had supposed possible, stands drinking in raffish doublet and hose with a Pistolian hat decked with tatty feathers; Harley, the 'original and impressive' Ithamore (EM), strikes a commanding gesture in a tunic belted and elaborately sashed; and Miss Boyce as Bellamira, resplendent in tiara and eardrops, necklace and pearl brace-let, sits at a rather modern card table in a high-busted flowing gown, looking like some decadent Mme Récamier. For the Phoenix Society, just over a century later,[4] Norman Wilkinson designed 'with taste and reticence' (BM), Baliol Holloway made a 'rich and picturesque' Barabas (DN), and Ernest Thesiger a ragged but 'remarkable' Ithamore (C); 'Miss Isabel Jeans was a charming Abigail and her early death a heavy loss' (T). At Stoke-on-Trent, the play was presented in-the-round, with a simple permanent setting which readily accommodated Marlowe's habit of changing location in mid-scene. Peter Cheeseman directed, with Bernard Gallagher as Barabas and the dramatist Alan Ayckbourn trebling as Machiavel, Del Bosco, and one of the three Jews. Costumes came from Stratford where, ironically, plans were already in hand for the RSC production—probably the most expensive revival since Heywood's.[5] The director, Clifford Williams, deployed all the resources of a large state-aided company. The Aldwych cast, numbering forty-one, was led by Clive Revill as Barabas, with Derek Godfrey as Machiavel,

LXXIII (1818), 429–32 (cited as EM); *The Theatrical Inquisitor, and Monthly Mirror*, XII (1818), 291–2 (TI); *The Times*, 25 April 1818 (T).

    [4] References here are to: *Blackwood's Magazine*, CCXII (1922), 833–4 (cited as BM); *The Curtain*, 7 November 1922 (C); *The Daily News*, 7 November 1922 (DN); *The Times*, 7 November 1922 (T).

    [5] References here are to: *The Manchester Guardian*, 2 October 1964 (cited as G); *The Illustrated London News*, 1 May 1965 (ILN); *The Observer*, 4 October 1964 (O); the RSC prompt copy for Williams' production (PC); the RSC programme for the Stratford revival (P); *Plays and Players*, December 1964, pp. 32–3 (Pa); *Plays and Players*, June 1965, pp. 32–5 (Pc); *The Queen*, 21 October 1964 (Q); *Theatre World*, May 1965, pp. 19–22 (TWb); *The Times*, 2 October 1964 (T); *The Times*, 17 April 1965 (Tb).

and Michael Bryant as Calymath (roles taken at Stratford by Eric
Porter, Tony Church, and Donald Burton). Both Ithamores captured
the grotesque lightness of the role. Ian Richardson, 'spell-binding' at
the Aldwych (T), presented 'a depraved Ariel, or a Puck smitten with
rabies' (T); Peter McEnery at Stratford 'a re-animated cadaver from a
cross of St Andrew' (TWb). The Bellamiras differed. Where Glenda
Jackson was 'delightfully predatory' (Pa), Patsy Byrne at Stratford
remained 'peevishly determined' (ILN); one offered a 'snake-haired
courtesan' (T) 'worthy of the highest professional fees' (Q), the other
'a down-at-heel Cleopatra' (Pc) who 'would have been a riot in the
Crummles company' (ILN). After a field-trip to Malta in search of
atmosphere, Ralph Koltai designed four free-standing rectangular
blocks, backed by an 'L' shaped wall and cyclorama. The stage floor
was covered by massive tiles which were scored with a herringbone
pattern and grooved to allow these blocks to slide sideways so that their
exposed faces presented whatever houses, windows, or walls the text
required, the walls themselves coloured and textured to create what
Koltai called 'the effect that heat and sunlight has on stone' (P). The
result reminded some critics of 'monolithic dominoes' (Pa) or 'slices of
festering Gruyère cheese' (G); but most praised Koltai's economic
evocation of 'glaring sun and heat-pocked walls' (Pa). The costumes,
designed in association with Nadine Baylis, were conventional Elizabethan breeches-and-tunic, but helpfully coloured to distinguish the
several factions. Del Bosco's Spanish armour set him apart from the
stiffly-uniformed Turks, 'blazing in white and red against the sombre
cloaks of the Maltese' (O), whose large decorative emblem on robes and
breastplates only fleetingly recalled that of the St John's Ambulance
men patrolling the theatre. Clive Revill played in a long gaberdine
braided down the front, and a brimless stove-pipe hat at least 18 inches
high. Pilia Borza, sporting a strip of Mexican blanket for a sash, still
looked very like T. P. Cooke, and indeed offered Ithamore one of his
bedraggled feathers for a quill (PC, IV.ii.66). But Bellamira remained
in both castings more truly 'a courtesan by her attire' (III.i.27) than
Kean's Miss Boyce. Glenda Jackson wore a 'Medusa wig and a costume
which, under Maltese skies, would inevitably render her a victim to
heartburn' (Pa); Patsy Byrne, by contrast, was 'lumpily sheathed in
black satin' (Tb), and trailed 'behind her a scarlet train that makes
snake-like exits of its own' (Tb). And, as a final extravagance, there was
a score by Guy Woolfenden which embraced a Turkish march for the
Bassoes, a Bellamira theme, bells for the nuns, and battle music to

cover Marlowe's bald 'alarms' between V.i and V.ii. This common professionalism apart, each production projected an individual image of the play which, as a theatre historian in search of the text's multi-faceted personality, it must now be my business to distinguish.

To begin then with Kean.[6] His revival of the play, 'after a total neglect of two centuries' (T), was generally regarded as a 'singular and hazardous experiment' (T) probably prompted by his flair for the striking gesture and his desperate search for new roles with which to woo a rapidly cooling public. (The suggestion that Kean was himself a Jew has been exhaustively refuted.[7]) After reading Richardson's reprint of the 1633 Quarto, *The Monthly Review* for April 1812 dismissed the play as a 'sanguinary composition' full of 'grotesque absurdities' with for hero a Jew who 'lives like Beelzebub upon earth, and dies blaspheming'. Clearly, this would never do for Kean. What he wanted was someone to continue the play in the heightened style of the first two acts. What he found was one Samson Penley, a comedian in the Drury Lane company, whose plagiarised farce *The Sleeping Draught* provided the afterpiece at Kean's first night. Although *The Jew of Malta* was carefully billed as 'founded on Marlowe's Tragedy', several critics declared the description 'very deceptive and disingenuous' (TI), and dismissed the alterations as 'inconsiderable' (EM) or 'trifling' (TI). They had clearly never read the play. The 'quaint and obsolete phraseology with which the original abounds was corrected and modernized' (H), vulgar expressions removed, and 'much of the rancour against the Jews which sully [*sic*] Marlowe's pages was expurgated' (H); Penley himself substituting for the Machiavelli prologue a personal *apologia* denying

> th' invidious aim
> To cast opprobrium o'er the Hebrew name;
> On every sect pernicious passions fall,
> And vice and virtue reign alike in all. (T)

The play was further emasculated. Instead of introducing us at once to

[6] References here, in addition to those of note 3, are to: *Blackwood's Edinburgh Magazine*, III (1818), 209–10 (cited as BM); J. Genest, *Some account of the English stage, from the Restoration in 1660 to 1830*, 10 vols. (Bath, 1832), VIII, 647, 677 (G); F. W. Hawkins, *The Life of Edmund Kean*, 2 vols. (London, 1869), II, 39–43 (H); Leigh Hunt, *Dramatic criticism, 1808–1831*, ed. L. H. and C. W. Houtchens (London, 1950), pp. 194–6 (LH); *The Monthly Review, or Literary Journal, enlarged*, LXVII (1812), 434; *The New Monthly Magazine, and Universal Register*, IX (1818), 444–5 (NM); B. W. Proctor, *The Life of Edmund Kean*, 2 vols. (London, 1835), II, 177 (P).

[7] See M. J. Landa, *The Jew in Drama* (London, 1926), pp. 311–14.

Barabas in his counting house, Penley invented 'a long and tedious scene between Lodowick and Mathias . . . in which each tells the other and the audience the story of his love for Abigail' (BM). *Blackwood's* commented tartly: 'Lodowick and Mathias are very uninteresting and intrusive people at best; and it is quite time enough to be troubled with them when the author wants them in order to heighten his principal character'. Even worse was to follow. To clean up the carnage, Penley

> very injudiciously left out all that relates to the poisoning of the nuns—in his 3d act, Abigail leaves the stage apparently in perfect health—a short scene of 35 lines ensues [III.v]—and then she is discovered on her deathbed, though it is impossible to divine what can have occasioned her death in so short a time. (G)

Barnardine is strangled off-stage by Ithamore (NM), Bellamira and company die through poisoned wine instead of poisoned flowers—'we think not for the better' remarked Leigh Hunt severely—and Barabas is 'blown up or rather fetched down from a gallery with shots, instead of being tricked into a burning cauldron' (LH), which Hunt conceded 'a piece of consideration certainly for our nerves, and extremely well managed'. *Blackwood's* remained censorious: 'we think the play, upon the whole, greatly injured by the alterations,' it declared, 'and see no reason for any of them.' They had, however, great point. The bloodiest spectacle had been cut, the more grotesque comedy curtailed, and the stage cleared for the entry of Kean's tragic hero, the honest Israelite unjustly victimised. Kean went to work with a great pail of whitewash. 'To illumine and render tolerable so dark a portrait' (T), he seized 'upon every passage that could diffuse an air of truth and probability around the character with instinctive discrimination' (H). The opening was magnificent. *The European Magazine* recalled no first act in which Kean had hitherto appeared which exhibited 'a more favourable and continued specimen' of his powers. 'His scene with the governor, when his wealth is so unjustly wrested from him, and his taunts at the quotations of Scripture, by which the latter seeks to justify his rapacity' were universally admired (TI); so too were 'his directions to his daughter where his treasure lay concealed' (EM). The soliloquy opening Act II had 'something very fine and sepulchral', and was later 'beautifully solemn and impressive' (BM). And 'when Barabas recovers the gold he has concealed, nothing could surpass the absolute delirium of drunken joy with which he gives the speech . . . beginning "Oh my girl! my gold!" &c' (BM, II.i.51–2). After such an emotional onslaught, no audience could deny Barabas its undivided sympathy, and Kean was able to continue the part in what Hunt called 'his very best taste of self-hugging revenge and triumphant Machiavelism' without forfeiting his hard-won stature as a tragic hero. This 'spirit of insatiable revenge' (EM) is finely caught in two contemporary prints. Cruikshank's etching for *The British Stage* (May 1818) shows Barabas, his right hand flung wide, advancing on his right foot to the audience, and fixing them with eyes which glare wildly from the corners of their sockets. The profile is noble, the nose loftily Arab, and the lips (framed with a small moustache and beard) are formed in a malevolent grin. The points of his white collar fall over the neck of his long gaberdine, which is decorated down the front and at the cuffs and fastened with a tassel and belt at the waist. West's *Theatrical Portrait* (11 June 1818), while preserving a more declamatory version of the same pose, removes the tassel and adds a tall Guy Fawkes hat. Even with this terrifying and commanding presence, however, Kean was anxious to avoid becoming merely monstrous. Dangerous patches of self-denigration were neatly skirted, but the greatest—Barabas' confession

> As for myself, I walk abroad a-nights,
> And kill sick people groaning under walls (II.iii.178 ff.)—

was too good to be cut. Instead, 'Barabas is made (aside) to feign that he has done all this, in order to try Ithamore's disposition' (BM), a 'happy thought' (BM) which to *Blackwood's* 'seemed to evince something that looked almost like genius'. Despite Kean's best endeavours, however, 'the applause, which was vehement in the first act, became more moderate as the play advanced' (EM); the third act, stripped of its nuns, flagged 'very much' (BM); but 'the heaviness of the fourth' (H) was, with some desperation perhaps, 'finely relieved by a song warbled by the tragedian in the disguise of a harper' (H). Executed 'in a sweet and florid style' (P), 'with considerable science' (NM) 'in the undertones and graces' (LH), it was 'rapturously encored' (EM)—though some critics considered the display a 'contemptible degradation' (BM) and 'a perversion of talent' (T). Thereafter, the performance rose to new heights, Kean acting with such 'breadth, grandeur, and terrible intensity' (H) that he saved the last scene 'from a laugh' (EM) and invested it instead with 'a high degree of tragic solemnity' (EM). His death occasioned 'a fine piece of pantomimic acting' (P); at the end of the performance, the applause 'broke out with all its former vehemence'

(EM), and the piece was 'given out for repetition . . . with universal approbation' (T). The production failed to take the town by storm. The play was dismissed as the most faulty composition of a dramatist whose genius was 'not strictly dramatic' (T), and the success of the evening placed squarely on the shoulders of the star. Loyally, but with flagging vitality, Kean nursed it through twelve performances, before it died on 30 May 1818 only to be resurrected for a single night the next season (14 November 1818) when Mrs West appeared as Abigail (G). The revival was not, however, without value. Kean was the first to cut the play loose from its Elizabethan context of Jew-baiting and Machiavellian policy. On the strength of the opening acts, he played all out for tragedy, the tragedy of a noble alien monstrously wronged and magnificently revenged, who falls victim to 'the united mistakes of persecution from without, and selfish subtlety from within' (LH). His loss, is that the play's multiplicity of tonal contrasts is denied, and the farcical wit of the later acts reduced to an unrelieved tragical sombreness. (In justice to Kean—and to Penley—it should be added that *Blackwood's* found this vice a virtue, and hailed *The Jew of Malta* as the first English play to embody 'dramatic unity,—that tending of all its parts to engender and sustain the same kind of feeling throughout'.) His gain, is that Barabas appears not as the bottle-nosed monster of Rowley's allusion but as a credible member of the human race twisted into a grotesque caricature of villainy by the pressures of society and his own deep-seated sense of injustice. This suggests a second gain: Penley's prologue argued for 'vice and virtue' in every sect, Gentile or Jew; and the sympathy which Kean demanded for Barabas in the opening acts must have implied antipathy to Barabas' oppressors, the hypocritical and mercenary Governor and his Christian knights. Now, *Blackwood's* had considered the play firmly moral because

> the characters are all, without exception, wicked . . . to compass their own short-sighted views, all set moral restraint at defiance, and they are all unhappy,—and their unhappiness is always brought about by their own guilt.

The final triumph of Ferneze laughs such shallow concepts of poetical justice out of court, and argues for the moral disenchantment of Marlowe—and of the more thoughtful of his audience. One final point: before we dismiss Kean's 'tragedy' as the inevitable distortion of a star actor in search of a role, it is well to remember that academic editors a century later were still operating from his premises; H. S.

Bennett saw the play as a 'misdirected masterpiece', a great tragedy gone awry, and C. F. T. Brooke noted with regret 'that the vigorous flow of tragic interest and character portrayal . . . wastes away amid what, for the modern reader, is a wilderness of melodrama and farce'.[8]

Revaluation was at hand. Eliot's influential essay of 1919 offered a brilliant reversal of this conventional view. Arguing from the last act backwards, he saw the play not as a tragedy but as a farce of 'terribly serious, even savage comic humour'.[9] Allan Wade, who directed the Phoenix Society revival three years later, seems to have profited from Eliot's suggestion.[10] Finding the fable incredible, the characters inhuman and their actions totally unreal (BM), he made some sense of the mess by presenting the play as 'a monstrous farce, a careless burlesque of human speech and human action' (BM). As in all good farce, the physical activity of the play was seized upon exultantly, the fighting underlined (G), and the whole presented at breakneck speed 'with an admirable slickness that left the audience gasping' (NS). Characterisation was of course cut to a minimum. Howard Rose hit 'the right robust manner' for Ferneze (G), but the three Jews were played with 'an air of intentional farce' (DN). Ernest Thesiger's Ithamore, a character *The Times* thought clearly 'intended for laughter', 'had some sublime moments' with Miss Margaret Yarde (NS), whose Bellamira was avowedly 'out for farce' (DN). 'The acting of the Jew spared . . . nothing of his brutality' (BM), but without reinforcement from the earlier scenes this only emphasised the character's 'superlatively vindictive' villainy (C). The audience regarded Barabas as no more than 'a monster of iniquity' (DN), a manifestation of 'sheer satanism' (G). In such a context, Baliol Holloway's fine acting (DC) went for nothing; unable to 'conquer the comic burlesque of the part' (DN), he merely 'howled in harmony with the lines allotted him' (C), and generated at his death 'nothing but a mild tremor of amusement' (BM). It was all, in fact, wildly amusing. The deaths of the

[8] *The Jew of Malta* and *The Massacre at Paris*, ed. H. S. Bennett (London, 1931), p. 19; *The Works of Christopher Marlowe*, ed. C. F. T. Brooke (Oxford, 1910), p. 232.

[9] T. S. Eliot, 'Christopher Marlowe', *Selected essays*, 3rd edn. (London, 1951), p. 123.

[10] References here, in addition to those of note 4, are to: *The Daily Chronicle*, 10 November 1922 (cited as DC); *The Manchester Guardian*, 7 November 1922 (G); *The London Mercury*, VII (1922–3), 199 (LM); *The New Statesman*, 11 November 1922 (NS); *The Sunday Express*, 12 November 1922 (SE); *The Sunday Illustrated*, 12 November 1922 (SI).

rival suitors, and the poisoning of the nuns, produced 'loud and unre-
strained' laughter (BM), and Jacomo's line 'all the nuns are sick, / And
physic will not help them' (III.vi.1–2) 'was greeted like the climax
of a successful farce' (T). To some extent, this is a legitimate reaction
to the play. Marlowe's text is mined with gags. Barabas' sportive asides
demand a curl of the lip and a wink at the house, and some of his direct
attacks have a breathtaking comic effrontery. Who would resist 'Some
Jews are wicked, as all Christians are' (I.ii.115), or his broad dissimula-
tion with Abigail (353–75) or the friars (IV.i.46–91)? But even here the
humour remains of Eliot's 'savage' and 'serious' kind, and this the
Phoenix Society did not attempt. Significantly, the quarrel between the
friars was 'not very funny' (DN), and Jacomo's line about the nuns
gained its farcical effect because Mr Homewood, sporting an excessive
beard (SI), 'spoke the words as if the unfortunate ladies were voyaging
in too stormy a Mediterranean' (T). Moreover, *The Times* noted that
'in this instance, the acting strained perhaps a little too far and not very
nobly'. But even when allowances have been made for the technical
inadequacies of Jacomo or the three Jews, it is clear that the production
as a whole sold out to the easy laugh, and thus failed to realise the truly
farcical potential of this 'terribly serious' play. Indeed, the serious
scenes, which an assured director would naturally heighten to offset the
farcical junketings of the rest, were made to render nothing but a
'delightful grotesqueness' (DN). *The Times* alone drew attention to the
death of Abigail, the mourning over the two dead suitors, and asked:
'were these intended to be as amusing as the Phoenix chose to make
them?' The answer surely is 'no'. As a result of this overall debasement
of Eliot's viewpoint, the production was a great success: it 'riveted the
attention' (LM), 'filled the house with laughter' (SE) and was generally
regarded as 'exactly right' (G). The play, on the other hand, was dismissed with contumely as an 'artless, feeble fabrication of horrors' (G),
'a tragedy of massacre and trumpets written in the nursery by a child
marvellously gifted with words' (T); at its worst 'extraordinarily bad'
(G), at its best merely excellent melodrama (NS). The Phoenix Society
it is clear did Marlowe a grave disservice. Kean squeezed all the tragedy
out of his partial reading of the play; the Phoenix left much of Eliot's
savage farce untouched. Neither production attempted to reconcile
within its prevailing mode the divergent tendencies of the play's structure, characterisation or tone. As a result, each revival achieved a limited
private success at Marlowe's expense. For in each case the performers
were justly praised, and the play unjustly damned.

The first attempt to weave together the play's contradictory elements into some significant pattern came, fittingly, from academic circles. The Reading University production of 1954 aimed less at farce than at satire. A programme note explained that Marlowe's play deliberately ridiculed while simultaneously exploiting the Elizabethan prejudice against Machiavels and Jews. This satiric intention was 'dramatically signalled by a trick played on the audience's expectations—the sudden, complete and violent reversal of a previously established mood'. Barabas' admittedly rapid transformation 'from a suffering and oppressed human figure into . . . "a prodigious caricature" ' is in this reading fully intended from the outset. The immediate introduction of 'such fantastic comic creations as Ithamore and Pilia Borza' is deliberately designed to underline this change of tone, and with result that 'the lurid events of the plot then unfold, not in ugliness and horror but with staggering and hilarious absurdity'. This ingenious interpretation made best sense at the crowning mockeries of Act V. As the programme justly observed, 'Barabas' successive disasters all, ironically, result from gross viola-tions . . . of cardinal precepts insisted on by Machiavelli in *The Prince*'. There a politic conspirer is warned

so soon as you impart your design to a discontented man, you supply him with the means of removing his discontent, since by betraying you he can procure for himself every advantage.

Barabas allows the newly discontented Ithamore to betray him, and acts so slowly in reprisal that his secret is revealed to Ferneze before the poisoned flowers finish their work. Even in this extremity, his 'sleepy drink' preserves him; yet having just betrayed the Christians to the Turks and become Governor, he at once betrays the Turks to the Christians, imparts his design to that most discontented of men the downcast Ferneze, and dies as a consequence. As the Reading pro-gramme remarks, 'the play therefore presents the spectator with the satirically posed problem: Who then are the real villains of the story, the true followers of Machiavelli?' And the answer, fumblingly antici-pated by Penley, must again be the Knights of St John and their hypocritical Governor—a man who obviously had his Machiavelli by heart, and well remembered that

A prudent Prince neither can nor ought to keep his word when to keep it is hurtful to him and the causes which led him to pledge it are removed.

The performance, billed as a 'Melodramatic Extravaganza', seems to have presented this interpretation with gusto. There were trumpeters and a lutenist (dubbing for Barabas in IV.iv ?), a generous display of complex doubling, and the prologue by Machiavelli re-instated and spoken by ' "?" '. Ian Calder, who was both Secretary and Treasurer to the Society, directed the play and also appeared in it as Barabas, playing the now intentional caricature of the villain with a fervour which *The Times* (14 May 1954) found not 'invariably intelligible' though it 'thoroughly sustained' the chosen comic line of the production. The outstanding merits of this revival lay in the unity of its conception and in its sustained effort to see the whole play—not merely the last part of it—as a satire in which farcical effects are utilised for larger and more savage ends. Its gravest defect was in supposing that in order to present this satire effectively it was necessary to make Barabas into Eliot's 'prodigious caricature'. Was it not possible to combine some element of Kean's sympathy with the Machiavellian savagery of the later acts, to unite the complex moods of the play into some satisfactory whole?

The problem remained unattempted until 1964, when both Cheeseman and Williams based their interpretations of the play on the realisation that Marlowe's method of juxtaposing tragedy and comedy, violence and humour, implied not primarily farce or satire but rather the *pantomime noir* of Orton or Giles Cooper.[11] Approaching the play in this spirit, Cheeseman found his company 'not in the least bewildered by its basic personality' (VP). Quite the contrary, in fact:

> this is just the kind of humour we can now encompass, the humour of the sick joke, and the black comedy. Its mood is extravagant. There is violence in the atmosphere, in the subject matter, and in the very switchback motion from tragedy to comedy within the joke itself. Poisoning a whole nunnery with a doped rice pudding is just such a gag. (VP)

And critics of the RSC revival, seeing Barabas' villainy as 'a huge and entirely deliberate joke' (T), hailed Marlowe 'a master practitioner of

[11] References here, in addition to those of note 5, are to: I. Brown, 'How bright a boy?' *Drama*, n.s. LXXV (1964), 27–9 (cited as D); *The Manchester Guardian*, 11 March 1964 (Gb); *The Daily Mail*, 2 October 1964 (M); *Punch*, 14 October 1964 (PN); *Plays and Players*, May 1965, pp. 10–11 (Pb); *The Sunday Times*, 18 April 1965 (ST); *The Daily Telegraph*, 2 October 1964 (TL); *The Daily Telegraph*, 15 April 1965 (TLb); *Theatre World*, November 1964, pp. 30–31 (TW); *Theatre World Annual, 1966* (London, 1965), pp. 64–5 (TWA); Cheeseman's programme note for the Victoria Theatre revival (VP).

black farce' (Tb), who disinfected his 'anti-human jibes' (G) with 'a grim sardonic humour' (TL). Time and again, Williams' production emphasised the prime tenet of 'black comedy': that laughter mounts in direct proportion to the threatened violence of the action it anaesthetises. Preparing the nuns' fatal porridge gave Ithamore's 'disarming zest for wickedness' (Q) immense comic opportunities. With farcical eagerness he snatches the pot away before it has been poisoned (III.iv.85), and to taste it 'takes a sip from spoon then starts to eat with his hands' (PC). 'Bar. grabs Ithamore's hair' (PC) and flings him aside (87), stirs in the poison with a terrible curse (95–104), and finally 'spits into pot' (PC) before Ithamore carries it off (112). As knockabout farce this sequence is—relatively—amusing; but when the tomfoolery centres on a poison-ous brew capable of causing the violent death of a whole nunnery the effect is grotesquely 'side-splitting' (TWb). And so completely had the audience forfeited by their laughter all claims to ordinary human sympathy and decency, that when the nuns later crossed the stage (III.vi.1) 'coughing and chocking' [sic] and 'clinging' to Jacomo (PC) the hilarity was redoubled. Lines like 'all the nuns are dead, let's bury them' (44) were greeted with such howls of uncontrollable laughter (T) that the audience risked 'laughing themselves into a coma' (Pa). As the friars were played by a 'knockabout team' (T) of vaudeville clowns, IV.i produced a similar effect. Ithamore, at a first-floor window, 'takes off girdle, throws out noose' (PC). Barabas 'bangs wall' (PC) to wake Barnardine (143), 'puts rope round his neck. Ithamore pulls up. Bar. holds his feet' (PC) and the friar is strangled (150). The body is leaned against the wall. It 'starts to fall forward. Bar. grabs him. Ithamore gets staff and leans it against Barn. (153). Both stand back and look at Barn.' (PC) with evident satisfaction (155). Jacomo enters, and executes a series of 'double takes' on seeing the body (163). Then he grabs Barnardine's staff (171), 'swings it round Right. Barn. drops down. Jacomo swings back' (PC), strikes the body as it falls, and 'looks down at Barnardine very pleased' (PC). As the scene continues, Itha-more 'smears "blood" ' (PC) on the corpse (175), 'shows head to Jac. Jac. drops stick' (PC), tries to escape, and is finally hustled off by Barabas and Ithamore who 'shake hands' (PC) behind the friar's back (202). Much of this scene depends upon the crudest slapstick and 'mugging'. But the hackneyed music hall routines are more than mere clowning, and the 'side-splitting' laughter derives its sadistic punch from the diabolical ingenuity of the villains and the gleeful irreverence with which a human body is thrown about the stage like a sack of potatoes. (The basic joke of Orton's play *Loot* embraces a similar assault on human dignity.) Even in the musician scene, Williams discovered a sick humour. Barabas appears in long cloak and wide-brimmed hat like 'Don Diego' from *The Alchemist*. 'A French musician' cries Bellamira triumphantly (IV.iv.28), and while he 'plays chords, sings Flamenco . . . stamps' (PC) the poisoned flowers are passed from hand to hand (37). Both musician and flowers are absurdly disguised and Bellamira is simultaneously deceived by them both. But one produces 'hilarity' (Pa), the other death. The combination is 'black comedy'.

Once this principle has been grasped, it becomes clear that the entire play is built upon the concept of the sick joke, and that what Cheeseman calls the 'switchback motion from tragedy to comedy within the joke itself' (VP) is reflected in the play's overall structure, as Marlowe deliberately sets out to yoke together the most violent extremes of action, character, and mood. The fortunes of the hero swoop and soar with breathcatching rapidity. Stripped of his wealth in one scene, he is master of millions the next; haled off to prison, thrown over the walls, and left for dead, he instantly revives, wins new allies, and becomes Governor of Malta. And then, at the very peak of his revenge, he is plunged down again straight into his own boiling cauldron. Much of the comic effect here springs from the swiftness with which these reversals tread upon each other's heels, 'short-circuiting the normal impediments to action' (Tb) and creating 'a legitimate dramatic shorthand . . . of black farce' (Pc), in which contradictory images of an action are projected onto the spectator's retina in such rapid succession that they seem to co-exist in absurdly exclusive independence. And Williams' rapidly paced production (135 minutes), aided by Koltai's smooth mid-scene changes of set (e.g. I.ii.217; II.iii.221; IV.i.128; V.i.60), made the point admirably. Marlowe often gains a similar effect by juxtaposing serious and comic scenes, or combining both elements within a single dramatic unit. In the interests of his *pantomime noir*, Williams brought out these contrasts, dutifully building up the serious formalities of power politics, religious ritual, or funeral procession and allowing the farcical action or satiric asides of Marlowe's text to do the rest. The political scenes were massively mounted in the best manner of the Stratford history cycle, which Williams had just co-directed. There were pompous group entries for the opposing factions, supported by standard-bearers and a Turkish march for Calymath. II.ii was presented as a summit conference, begun in mutual mistrust (3), continued with advisory whispers (8) and weighty pauses (9, 35), and concluded with a public handshake to seal the new alliance (47). For III.v there were Maltese and Spanish banners, formal bows formally acknowledged (1), and much upstaging as the area of conflict became defined (8). Yet these two scenes are followed without pause (thanks again to Koltai's adroitly manipulated setting) by the comedy of the slave market (II.iii) and the farcical retching of the poisoned nuns (III.vi). When contained within the unit of a single scene, these contrasts are even more striking. Williams' nuns enter their new house with elaborate formality. An antiphonal chant is heard off-stage (I.ii.307), then the Abbess appears carrying a large silvered crucifix and wearing a circular headdress so heavily starched it frames her face like a gigantic halo (TWA). Behind her comes a procession of chanting friars and nuns, who have smaller haloes (TWA). Abigail is admitted a novice by a ritual laying on of hands (339) and then amidst cries of 'Alleluia' (PC) the chanting and processing begin again—only to be shattered as Barabas 'breaks through between friars' (PC), 'jumps away L. on singing' (PC), and launches into his hilariously hypocritical rejection of Abigail (347), flinging her aside while whispering directions for locating the hidden cash (361) which is marked by a supreme irony with a cross (366). III.ii charts the reverse emotional course. The fatal duel between the rival suitors appears farcical in view of their mutual extermination and the gleefully ironic comments of Barabas from his lofty window above (6–9). But then the mood suddenly turns about. Ferneze and Katherine, cradling their dead sons in their arms (12), hurl bitter accusations across the stage (16–17), then join hands (38) as the knights form an elaborate *cortège* and exeunt to a funeral march. Marlowe thus asks his audience to consider the same event as both violent farce and poignant 'tragedy', all within the space of forty lines. It is a miracle of economy, and a model collision of those contradictory emotions which identify 'black comedy'. Occasionally, two characters create the same contrast. To offset the warmth and bustle of Barabas' opening soliloquy, Derek Godfrey's 'flint-eyed prologue' (T) was 'icily delivered' (PN). But Abigail was particularly useful here. Williams plotted her opening scene in a charmingly pathetic vein (I.ii.229–314). She enters 'weeping' (PC), runs to Barabas, puts her arms around him, 'sinks to floor sobbing' (PC), and so on. Her humanity is then deliberately contrasted with characters more farcically conceived. When Ithamore cheerfully informs her of her lover's death (III.iii.16) she 'swings round to hit Ith.' (PC) then 'sinks to the ground' (PC). As she dies, resting against

Barnardine's knee, she gives the friar her confession (III.vi.29). He 'opens
scroll drops Abig.' (PC). After her line 'And witness that I die a
Christian' (40), 'Barn. makes sign of cross on Abs head, Abigail dies'
(PC). 'Ay, and a virgin too, that grieves me most' (41) adds Barnardine
who then 'drops her with a bump' (PC). In each scene, the audience is
torn between its natural sympathy for the pathetic Abigail, and con-
vulsions of laughter at the complete callousness of the farcical characters
around her. Characterisation thus yields its own kind of *pantomime noir*.

In Williams' production, then, there were no alien elements. The
basic unit of the play was revealed as the sick joke, and the 'switchback
motion from tragedy to comedy within the joke itself' was shown to
extend to the overall action, to the sequence and structuring of individual scenes, and even to concepts of characterisation. As a result, the
audience accepted the play as a 'black comedy' and untroubled by
embarrassing uncertainties of *genre* were free to concentrate wholly on
Marlowe's dramatic purpose. As *The Times* remarked, the 'textbook
objections to the play's mixed form reflect no more than the theatrical
camouflage masking the play's real purpose' (T). And this, as all the
critics proclaimed, was no less than a vicious attack on the entire
Establishment, satirising 'the materialistic attitude of Christians and
Turks, as well as Jews' (TWb). Indeed, as one reviewer remarked,

> the only racial discrimination is against the human race. The Jew is a
> quadruple-dyed villain . . . the Muslims are paltry, extortionate,
> numskulls; the Christian gentlemen cowardly swindlers; the monks
> and nuns lecherous hypocrites. (Q)

The RSC revival brought out this bitter indictment in a variety of ways.
The religious orders were so roundly mocked by the 'black comedy'
itself, that Williams had very little need to chastise them further. The
nuns' 'fine sport with the friars' (III.iii.32) required only the memory
of their starched linen and processional ceremony to make its effect,
while Barnardine's treatment of the dying Abigail—and his grief at her
virginity—were sufficient indication of at least one friar's callousness
and lechery. Williams generalised the attack by having Jacomo welcome
her to the nunnery with ingratiating and effusive courtesy (I.ii.375).
In IV.i their vindictive and covetous hypocrisy was more harshly
treated. To buy off their damning evidence Barabas kneels to them (48)
professing conversion. Then as the hints of bribery reach home each
kneels to him (77–8), allowing Barabas to tout between them for the
better offer. Coming to blows, they 'fight on floor. Roll R. L. R.' (PC).

And when Jacomo later strikes Barnardine down, he looks at the body 'very pleased' (PC). The secular powers were satirised even more savagely. Cheeseman summed up the Maltese Knights as 'a crew of grasping Christian hypocrites' (VP), and found 'a marvellous sneer' (VP) in Calymath's line when, after watching the unfortunate Jew boiled to death in his own cauldron, he turns to the company and enquires: 'Tell me, you Christians, what doth this portend?' (V.v.92). Williams' production, which stressed 'all the anti-Christian values of Marlowe's play' (ST), scathingly exposed the Maltese powers as 'hypocritical opportunists' (Pc) 'trying to live off Barabas' money and wits, while persuading themselves that they are conferring a favour on him' (T). The Jew's 'chilly epigrams on Christian duplicity' (T) easily cut through this façade of evangelism, and the play's final couplet—in which Ferneze, lifting his sword 'on high hilt uppermost' (PC), attributes his treacherous victory to God—came across as 'an outrageous irony' (T). Even the Bellamira scenes supported Marlowe's satire, for as she flings Ithamore's gold aside with a fine gesture of flamboyant denial (IV.ii.124), she takes care that the bag falls into the outstretched hand of Pilia Borza as he departs on yet another expedition to wring money from the Jew (PC).

For much of this attack, Marlowe uses Barabas himself as his satiric spokesman. Yet as a Machiavel defeated by superior Machiavels, Barabas—as Ian Calder admitted—is himself satirised, and in this sense the play becomes, as more than one reviewer noted, an attack upon the entire human race. Here, Williams trod a middle path. He included in his programme those extracts from *The Prince* quoted earlier, but in his production cut several references to Barabas' 'policy' (e.g. I.ii.275–8; V.ii.123), and permitted the Jew a considerable measure of the audience's sympathy (TW). In short, he allowed that union of contradictory emotions which dictates the play's basic form to illuminate a balanced reading of the central character. Indeed, both 1964 revivals took as their point of departure a view of Barabas radically different from that of the Phoenix or Reading productions. Cheeseman and Bernard Gallagher agreed at the outset

> that it was no good playing the Jew as a pantomime devil, in a great villainous roaring performance. To win the real attention of the audience he must be a credible character, and a person whom the audience recognised. So Barabas begins as a cynical self-seeking businessman of intense energy and considerable pride, (VP)

whose opening speech celebrates commercial success 'with an attitude quite familiar to readers of *The Financial Times*' (VP). At Stratford, Williams discussed with Eric Porter what would happen if Barabas took Shylock out to dinner (Pb), and this led them to decide the Jew was essentially 'the big extrovert' (Pb), 'famous, cosmopolitan, influential and successful' (P), the kind of man who 'makes money as easily as breathing' (P). Porter presented this handsome 'Maltese magnifico' (Tb) 'with the proper extrovert relish' (ILN). Discarding Revill's gaberdine and stove-pipe hat, he played in an elaborate and rich gown, a mantle of thick-piled fur, a decoration round his shoulders, and large jewelled rings on each hand. Suavely groomed, the forelock tipped with silver, he radiated assurance and the self-satisfaction of the successful tycoon (Pc). This, however, was only a beginning. Both directors saw their anti-hero as psychologically disturbed: Cheeseman drew attention to his 'near paranoiac sensitivity and delusions of grandeur' (VP), and Williams talked of a 'will to dominate' which was 'pathological from the outset' (P). This Barabas clearly relished easy triumphs over pusillanimous victims. Porter drove the capitulating Jews in terror 'to back wall' of the set (PC) at I.ii.81, and in II.iii dragged Ithamore around the stage 'holding on to his ear' (PC, 171), set his 'foot on Ithamore's back' (PC, 203), and later made to throttle him 'with both hands' (PC, 217). Since Barabas is committed to this struggle for power in a society where money is all and morality nothing, he rapidly degenerates into what Cheeseman calls a 'kind of half crazy gangster' (VP) whose grip upon an audience's sympathy depends largely on the manifest injustice of Ferneze's extortions in I.ii. This established, declares Cheeseman,

> When Barabas makes the fateful decision to do evil to those who did [it to] him, we are right behind him. After such an emotional conversion the battle for our sympathies is won. (VP)

The conception is as stubbornly sympathetic as Kean's, but the performance failed to do it justice. Noting this 'inconsistency' *The Guardian* judged Gallagher's Barabas as 'a magnificent caricature . . . sweeping a black cloak around like a vulture, cackling like Dracula, licking his chops in exultation as he succeeds in poisoning an entire nunnery with a mess of pottage'. It is 'genuinely funny' (Gb) but more a 'bloody farce' (Gb) than the 'black comedy' Cheeseman intended. Williams was more subtle. Realising that the logic of Marlowe's 'gangster epic' (P) was itself dangerously 'seductive' (P), he defended Barabas' atrocities by explicit

reference in the programme to the comic, violent, world of Bonnie and
Clyde and the Chicago bootleggers described by Kenneth Allsop:

> To achieve self-advancement the bootlegger used methods—murder
> and violence—which the ordinary citizen stopped a long way short
> of, yet his attitude to life, his beat-your-neighbour tactics, his triumph
> in the competitive system at its most ferocious extreme, had a kind
> of romantic rightness. . . . There for all the United States to watch
> was the way the profit motive worked when no holds were barred,
> and it was difficult for anyone bred in and breathing the atmosphere
> of a dollar civilisation, taught that ruthlessness and aggression were
> requisites for success, to do the mental somersault needed to see
> Capone and his gangsters as evil. (P)

The critics took the point. The play was greeted as 'a kind of *ur-Gold-
finger*' (PN) 'showing the emergence of a clear-sighted opportunist
within a society that would act in the same way if it dared' (T); even the
Jew's inhuman villainies seemed no more than 'a desperate defensive
action against the stupid and pig-headed Maltese establishment' (TW).
Here was Kean's whitewashing technique brought up to date by reference to an entirely modern morality. To strengthen the interpretation,
Williams gave the fearful crimes of his romantic gangster 'an aura of
wholesomeness in contrast to the hypocrisies of the Church and the
mealy-mouthed tyrannies of the State' (Pa). Ferneze's more aggressive
lines were switched to the military firebrand Del Bosco (e.g. III.v.30–4;
V.i.1–2), and the Governor downgraded into a whimpering weakling,
browbeaten by Del Bosco (II.ii.41) and Katherine (III.ii.31), who
cringed and backed into corners before the all-dominating Jew (V.v.20).
By contrast the demonic gusto of Barabas carried all before it. Here was
no paltry criminal but a 'grand-scale artist in crime who finds it hard to
tolerate the unsophisticated villainy of his slave accomplice' (Tb).
Barabas hands Ithamore the feigned challenge from Lodowick (II.iii.
374). Ithamore 'moves in to take letter. Stops' (PC). ' 'Tis poisoned, is
it not?' he asks (376). 'No, no' snaps Barabas (377), 'out of patience at
such a cliché' (Tb). Such satanic professionalism radiates its own
perverse glamour; there remains a certain 'magnificence about his evil'
(Q), 'something praiseworthy in the way in which he uses whatever
weapon comes to hand, be it treachery, apostasy, deceit or murder'
(TW). And when the resulting villainies 'are so preposterous that one
cannot take them as anything but a huge and entirely deliberate joke'
(T), the audience is left laughing at the victims, admiring the devilish

cunning with which they are deceived, yet morally condemning a
gangster whose descent into crime is so sympathetically motivated that
despite all scruple 'one grows a good deal more fond of him than of
any other character' (T). Both Revill and Porter were able to convey
this compound of Richard Crookback and Macbeth. Playing with
miraculous 'control' (Pa) and 'restraint' (Pc), both remained simultaneously sinister and funny (M, ILN), credible yet grotesque. With one
hand Revill 'gave us an almost credible person and with the other the
outrageous, unbelievable, and comical fiend' (D), while Porter's Grand
Guignol caricature (TWb) had such 'villainous dignity' (TLb) that
Barabas remained 'a worthy and potentially tragic representative of a
stricken and persecuted race' (ST). As a result, Barabas' painful death
(well managed with a pivoted trap which allowed him to hang over the
smoking cauldron to the last gasp) was violent, hilarious, yet strangely
moving. The grotesque monster was grotesquely boiled, the wronged
magnifico wrongly tortured. Shaw, reviewing a melodrama in which
the heroine is inadvertently locked in a ship's boiler when the heat is
turned on, describes the audience 'half white with its purgation by pity
and terror, and half red with a voiceless, apoplectic laughter'.[12] The
effect is entirely relevant to *The Jew of Malta*. But what in *True Blue*
was a disastrous miscalculation is in Marlowe's play wholly intentional.
Barabas, no less than the rest of the play, is deliberately conceived (and
executed) in the vein of the best 'black comedy'.

Every age carries on an uneasy commerce between the old and the
new. The classics give substance to contemporary work by setting it
within an enduring frame of reference, and contemporary attitudes
sometimes illuminate and sometimes obscure works conceived in an
earlier culture. Kean distorted the play to make Barabas into a Romantic
and tragic hero, and for the Phoenix Society in the brittle twenties it
remained nothing but a quaint though meaningless archaism. In 1964
things were different. Bernard Levin to be sure thought the RSC revival
a futile attempt to breathe life into a 'preposterously bad' play (M) and
ended his review: 'For goodness' sake put Marlowe back in his grave
for another 400 years' (M). But the majority of critics recognised in
Marlowe's 'moment to moment changes between pantomime, horror,
and wintry calm' (T) a *pantomime noir* (PN) 'as merciless as Genet and
as heartless—not to say hilarious—as Feydeau' (Pa). One reviewer even
went so far as to welcome 'Mr Marlowe (is this a pseudonym?)' (Pa) as

[12] George Bernard Shaw, *Dramatic Opinions and Essays*, 2 vols. (New York,
1916), I. 369. (I am indebted for this reference to D.)

'a new writer of promise' (Pa) whose anti-hero was clearly an Angry Old Man based on Jimmy Porter and designed like him to satirise the entire Establishment. And the parallelism is not wholly without point. It is, in fact, difficult to resist the suggestion that Marlowe's play was more at home at the Aldwych in 1964 than at any London theatre since Henslowe's day. No one will ever regard *The Jew of Malta* as an easy play to come to terms with;

> it inhabits a rare dramatic zone where farce and melodrama meet, and which comes to life in the theatre and nowhere else. Among other things the production [by the RSC] is a classic demonstration of how far a play's theatrical impact can differ from the impression it makes on the page. (Tb)

The Marlowe of the theatre is terrifyingly modern. Can the Marlowe of more academic critics boast as much?[13]

[13] I would be pleased to hear of any other productions of *The Jew of Malta* not mentioned in this article on the play.

Unstable Proteus:
Marlowe's The Tragedy of Dido
Queen of Carthage

BRIAN GIBBONS

Unstable Proteus:
Marlowe's The Tragedy of Dido
Queen of Carthage

THERE IS NO RECORD of a performance of *Dido Queen of Carthage* in Marlowe's lifetime, and the date and occasion of its composition remain uncertain. The title page of the 1594 edition states that it was played by the Children of the Chapel, and adds the name of Nashe as part-author. In the Oxford edition of 1910 Tucker Brooke recorded the view—not yet unanimously rejected—that 'the dramatic looseness' of *Dido* marks it as immature work, although he did admit that 'much of the blank verse shows very considerable finish and fluency', that Nashe's connection seems very uncertain, and that the first draft, supposedly composed before Marlowe left Cambridge in 1587, must have been revised sometime during the years 1591–3, the period of *Hero and Leander*.[1]

Tucker Brooke confessed that he could not fit *Dido* into Marlowe's dramatic career after *Tamburlaine*, since *Dido's* subject-matter and structure seemed at variance with his conception of Marlowe's 'pretty definite line of development'. More recent critical approaches have emphasised the serious limitations of this idea that Marlowe's separate plays are advances one upon another in a coherently developing sequence, and find rather that each is a structure different in kind from the others: the plays are experiments in separate modes of theatre.[2]

[1] *The Works of Christopher Marlowe*, ed. C. F. Tucker Brooke (Oxford, 1910), pp. 387–90. All quotations from Marlowe are from this edition.

[2] This is lucidly argued by Nicholas Brooke, 'Marlowe the Dramatist', in *Elizabethan Theatre* (Stratford-upon-Avon Studies 9, London, 1965). There is a chapter on *Dido* in J. B. Steane, *Marlowe: a critical study* (Cambridge, 1964) which is rather general but appreciative. Clifford Leech discusses *Dido* briefly but suggestively in 'Marlowe's Humour', reprinted in *Marlowe: Twentieth Century Views* (Englewood Cliffs, N.J., 1964), and Ethel Seaton, 'Marlowe's Light Reading', in *Elizabethan and Jacobean Studies Presented to F. P. Wilson* (Oxford, 1959) is interesting on the relation of popular romances to *Dido*. I am

Very little attention has so far been paid to *Dido* from this point of view, however, partly because of the problems I have mentioned and partly because of the really daunting question of the nature of Elizabethan court drama and boys' acting. It is therefore with some sense of trepidation that I raise the subject of Marlowe's *Dido* considered as a *play*, but I seek reassurance, or at least encouragement, from recent reappraisals of court drama and boy actors by Professor G. K. Hunter,[3] from a conviction that *Dido* was composed with court performance in view, and certainly with a lively awareness of the conventions of court drama and boys' acting style, and finally from a belief that the play is essentially Marlowe's throughout, and is fine enough to deserve the closest and most sympathetic critical attention.

Dido, as Marlowe's only known experiment in court drama for boy actors, must appear a distinct and unique play even in the canon of Marlowe's extraordinarily diverse works. There is a profoundly Protean quality in his creative genius, adopting in swift succession a wide diversity of poetic and dramatic forms, yet investing each with a new potency and expressive range: and with an awareness of his original and creative achievement in other modes of theatre, we must ask how far *Dido* exhibits new and enriched potential in the drama of the court and the acting of the children's companies. The question, if finally too complex to answer, remains fresh, and not least because *Dido* was written during the years which, as G. K. Hunter has remarked, witnessed the transition from earlier Elizabethan court drama to the more independent plays of the nineties and after. Professor Hunter writes that 'many, if not most of the plays which were performed at the court of Elizabeth remained strongly affected by this tradition, strong in the context of the court. It is impossible to imagine an independent play like *Othello* being performed at court before the 'nineties of the sixteenth century.'[4]

From the narrow point of view of dramatic form, Marlowe's *Dido* is in this sense an independent play; for if we compare it with *The Arraignment of Paris* (1583) we notice that in the conclusion of Peele's court play the golden ball is finally presented to Eliza, queen and governor of Elizium, acknowledged freely by Diana, Venus, Pallas, and Juno to be of 'peerles excellencie', her kingdom

---

not aware of other *useful* discussions of *Dido* apart from the condensed, acute comments of Harry Levin in *The Overreacher* (London, 1954). H. J. Oliver's *Revels* edition (1968) has just appeared.

[3] In *John Lyly* (London, 1962), chapters III and IV, and in editions of Marston's *Antonio & Mellida* and *Antonio's Revenge* (London, 1965).

[4] G. K. Hunter, *John Lyly*, p. 90.

> An aunciant seat of kinges, a second *Troie*,
> Ycompast rounde with a commodious sea:[5]

whereas by contrast the tragic catastrophe of Marlowe's *Dido* comes
with the heroine's suicide, stabbing herself and leaping into the flames
with the cry

> Liue false *Aeneas*, truest Dido dyes,
> *Sic sic iuuat ire sub umbras.* (1720–1)

The dramatic illusion remains intact, the play-world may even rival
the real world of the court in splendour and hyperbolic pride. If we are
concerned to relate *Dido* to a tradition which includes *Othello* and
Antony and Cleopatra, Phèdre, and the tragic opera of Verdi and Wagner,
then Dido's challenge to Elizabeth as the focus of splendour, beauty,
and sublimity may be seen as almost revolutionary. Of course such a
suggestion is only playful: the spectacle also mirrored the magnificence
of monarch and court: but in this last scene Marlowe's Dido attains a
state of high exaltation: she transforms tragedy into triumph. A fate
like Semele's is for Dido a consummation devoutly to be wished, but
she cannot wait passively for 'flaming *Iupiter*'. She is as rash as Phaeton,
proud and aspiring as Icarus, and in her ardent imagination Icarus
himself becomes a symbol of supreme erotic ecstasy:

> Ile frame me wings of waxe like *Icarus*,
> And ore his ships will soare vnto the Sunne,
> That they may melt and I fall in his armes: (1651–3)

The sublime hyperbole begins in a witty and paradoxical conceit,
however, and in this sense is reminiscent of Marlowe's renowned piece
of non-dramatic court art, *Hero and Leander*.

It is important to consider *Hero and Leander* in relation to *Dido*
because the poem reflects qualities in the play which have not always
been appreciated justly. The Mock Heroic mode was brilliantly suited
to Marlowe, of course, but it is also to be noticed how well it suited the
spirit and nature of Elizabethan English. In *Hero and Leander* Marlowe
is lyrical and heroic, yet indulges the wilful exuberance and playful
indecorous spirit in the language: he wittily elicits latent—and often
unexpected—energies. In this Marlowe is anticipated by Arthur
Golding, his precursor in the art of Englishing Ovid. In Golding the

[5] George Peele, *The Arraignment of Paris*, ed. H. H. Child (London, 1910),
lines 1049–50.

wider characteristics of Elizabethan court art are also apparent: a delight in multiplicity, not only as an informing aesthetic but as a continuous local effect in the tone, texture, and manner of poetry. Professor Hunter notes the prevalence of multiple presentation of ideas in Lyly's court plays, and goes on to note that Ovid's influence was largely due to his 'unclassical' qualities—'his lack of reticence, his copiousness, his facile wit, his command of a polished and complex surface texture and of an easily imitable rhetoric'. If we turn to a passage in Golding full of pre-echoes both of *Hero and Leander* and *Dido*, we can find rich illustrations of such effects achieved through a sensitive awareness of such natural potentialities in English, and we should also begin to appreciate a mode of writing significantly different from the rhetoric of Marlowe's tragedies written for adult actors on the popular stage.

Golding's translation of the story of Phaeton, from the second book of the *Metamorphoses*, begins in spectacular heroic terms:

> The Princely Pallace of the Sunne stood gorgeous to beholde
> On stately Pillars builded high of yellow burnisht golde,
> Beset with sparckling Carbuncles that like to fire did shine.[6]

Despite his typical tendency towards seeming naiveté, the poet's excitement expresses itself in the vitality of the verse and the lively diction: and it is not long before the scene comes to life with Vulcan's picture, wrought on the silver doors, of the sea and sea gods:

> Loude sounding *Tryton* with his shirle and writhen Trumpe in hande:
> Unstable *Protew* chaunging aye his figure and his hue,
> From shape to shape a thousande sithes as list him to renue:
> *Aegeon* leaning boystrously on backes of mightie Whales
> And *Doris* with her daughters all: of which some cut the wales
> With splaied armes, some sate on rockes and dride their goodly haire,
> And some did ryde uppon the backes of fishes here and theare. (12–18)

Golding delights in this scene, a sublime if ornate Renaissance masque, for its elaborate, detailed and rich artifice; but his verse fills the scene with life and movement—'Unstable *Protew*', '*Aegeon* leaning boystrously'—and syntax combines with rhythm to release unexpected exuberant youthful energies in the last line. Unexpected, also, is the modulation in tone from the directly admiring description of Triton to the genially

[6] Arthur Golding, *The. XV. Bookes of P. Ouidius Naso, entytuled Metamorphosis, translated* (London, 1567; repr. and corr. W. H. D. Rouse, 1961).

light mockery with which Doris' children are indulged. Wit, self-conscious sophistication, a keen yet mercurial and genial sensibility, a serious intelligence: such are the qualities which the poet as Elizabethan spectator brings to his appreciation of court art.

The description of Phoebus and his palace forms only the introduction to a long episodic account of Phaeton's career; and despite the self-indulgent copiousness of the narrative, and Golding's frequent prolixity, it contains insistent pre-echoes of Marlowe in its instability of tone and texture. The feelings of gods are exhibited with full hyperbolic power but Golding also conveys, through shifts into vernacular vocabulary and domestic tone, their fitness as subjects for humour and mockery. So Phoebus replies to the entreaties of his son Phaeton:

> Thou fondling thou, what dost thou meane with fawning armes about
> My necke thus flatteringly to hang? Thou needest not to dout.
> I have alreadie sworne by *Styx*, aske what thou wilt of mee
> And thou shalt have.

Phoebus' chariot is described with great splendour, rivalling the finest pageant cars recorded in Renaissance paintings and drawings;[7] yet, similarly, our sense of its scale and richness fluctuates as the language modulates from the sublime to the vernacular.

In the narrative as a whole the swift and Protean changes of attitude and tone do not confound all response: the effect is rather to render the detailed, subtly unstable texture underlying the sublime experience of awe, fear, wonder, or desire. Golding often conveys such ambivalent effects with an ease and a force that invites comparison with Marlowe. In Golding the harnessing of the steeds for the Chariot of the Sun is colourfully described, the rhythm becomes strong, dramatic, commanding:

> He had the fetherfooted howres go harnesse in his horse.
> The Goddesses with might and mayne themselves thereto enforce.
> His fierifoming Steedes full fed with juice of Ambrosie
> They take from Maunger trimly dight: and to their heads doe tie
> Strong reyned bits: (158–62)

This prepares for the full magniloquent power of rhetoric at the start of the ride:

[7] For example, Denis van Alsloot, *Isabella's Triumph* (1615), a painting in the Victoria and Albert Museum, London.

They girded forth, and cutting through the Cloudes that let their race,
With splayed wings they overflew the Eastern winde a pace. (209–10)

Yet there is an abrupt release of irrepressible, youthful, humorous
delight in the actual moment when Phaeton mounts the chariot: Golding's tone, his choice of verb, both are Marlovian:

> for *Phaeton* both yong in yeares and wit,
> Into the chariot lightly lept, (97–8)

Phaeton's act is playful but dreadful, his rashness absurd and ominous;
so Golding's line conveys both levity and weight. In *Hero and Leander*
the nature of erotic passion is expressed in an image at once brilliant
and dark, vital yet destructive;

> as a hote prowd horse highly disdaines
> To have his head control'd, but breakes the raines,
> Spits foorth the ringled bit, and with his houes
> Checkes the submissiue ground:

the effect of the image, applied to Leander, is directly exalting and
humorously mock heroic, in Mercutio's vein: and indeed the decisive
act of Leander is described in a memorable couplet where we respond
simultaneously to absurd, ominous, admiring, and lightly mocking
tones:

> With that hee stript him to the yu'rie skin,
> And crying, Loue I come, leapt liuely in.

Implicit here also is Marlowe's abiding concern with extremes: even
in his comedy hyperbole, violence and shock are central elements, and
passion is his theme. Augustan and Romantic categories are too rigidly
exclusive to account for the mode in which Golding describes the sea
gods, or Marlowe Leander, but that is something of a guide to the mode
of *Dido*, where stylisation, declamation, and rich artifice do not inhibit
the play's expressive resources and theatrical vitality. It may now be
appropriate to consider the specifically dramatic context of the play,
for such claims need some substantiation.

*   *   *

An Elizabethan court play or masque, in the Great Chamber, was
expected to be performed with sufficient splendour and assurance to
reflect something of the splendour and dignity of the royal audience.

Court entertainment mirrored the notably theatrical nature of the court itself, where costume and role were also conventional, and where ritual continually imposed emblematic tableaux about the monarch and throne. By Elizabeth's time pageants, masques, and plays involved the use of elaborate, though still deliberately emblematic, stage scenery and furniture, including rocks and mounts, fountains, chariots, a palace, an arbour, a wood, great hollow trees; while in *Dido Queen of Carthage* Marlowe required a cave, trees for a wilderness, a pavilion, clouds, a throne, a city, and a pyre.

Many of the spectacular elements in Elizabethan court drama are found in a play of particular interest in relation to *Dido*: Richard Edwardes' *Palamon and Arcite*, performed before Elizabeth in the hall of Christ Church in 1566. In *Palamon and Arcite* the gods descend in person, and Mars and Venus dispute on the stage their claims to power. The death of Arcite is marked by subterranean fire sent by Saturn from below and apparently presented by 'special effects'. The hunting scene offered a boisterous contrast to such sublime and awesome spectacle, and 'at the cry of the hounds in the [quadrangle] upon the train of a fox, in the hunting of Theseus, when the boys in the windows cried, "now, now"; "o excellent!" said Elizabeth, "those boys are ready to leap out at windows to follow the hounds" '. The tragic catastrophe seems to have included a degree of alienation, for as G. K. Hunter recalls, it is recorded that when Perithous cast a rich cloak into the funeral pyre for Arcite, one spectator seeing this 'would have stayed [him] by the arm with an oath' whereon Elizabeth remarked 'go, fool! he knoweth his part'.[8] The pleasures of conspicuous expenditure are fused with those of spectacle at once heroic and absurd.

An account of William Gager's *Dido*, which was performed in 1583 at Christ Church at the entertainment of Count Alasco of Poland, further illuminates the special quality and atmosphere of court theatre, by turns spectacular and playful, stirring, lyrical, absurd, heroic. In Gager's *Dido* there was 'a goodly sight of hunters with full cry of a kennel of hounds, Mercury and Iris descending and ascending from and to an high place, the tempest wherein it hailed small comfits, rained rosewater and snew an artificial kind of snow; all strange, marvellous and abundant'.[9] We can only speculate about the influence of Gager's tempest on the subsequent tempest in Marlowe's *Dido*, which marks the consummation of the love of Dido and Aeneas:

[8] Hunter, op. cit., pp. 112–13.
[9] Ibid.

It haild, it snowde, it lightned all at once, (1067)
. . .
There was such hurly burly in the heauens:
Doubtles *Apollos* Axeltree is crackt, (1069–70)

As this scene of Marlowe's suggests, a degree of sophisticated humour in the audience and self-conscious artistry in the dramatist may be taken for granted in court drama, where clouds can descend, flowers open, mists rise, rain and snow fall, nymphs be metamorphosed into rocks, birds, roses, or trees. Nevertheless, a scene lit with great numbers of candles and torches would be brilliant and shimmering as spectacle; flames in darkness could be impressive and sublime; while music and song significantly enriched the expressive resources of the court theatre's dramatic language.

This becomes even clearer when we recall the tradition of gorgeous costuming. The astonishing richness and sensuousness in fabric and colour of the early Elizabethan court masque costumes is almost enough to explain why Marlowe turned his attention to court drama, 'feigning bawdy fables gathered from the idolatrous heathen poets'. It may be appropriate to cite just two examples from the wealth of descriptions, to bring the point home. First, in the winter of 1559–60 was performed the exquisitely sensuous masque of Moors; they had apparel of cloth of gold and blue velvet, with sleeves of silver sarcenet and 'bases' of red satin. On their heads they wore curled hair made of black lawn and wreathed with red gold sarcenet and silver lawn. Their limbs and faces were of black velvet, and they carried darts of 'Tree and paste-and-paper gilded'. The torchbearers were eight Moorish friars with headpieces of crimson satin. In the pastoral tradition, and directly relevant to *Dido*, a mythological masque of 1560 showed Diana in purple, three pairs of Huntress Nymphs in carnation purple and blue respectively. Actaeon and six fellows wore purple with orange buskins and gilt boar-spears and were accompanied by eight Maidens in purple with various coloured kirtles, eight Hunters in yellow with murrey buskins, and twelve hounds. Actaeon's garments were 'all to cutt in small panes and steyned with bloud'.[10]

In this perspective, the frequent emphasis on costume in Marlowe's *Dido* takes on its true significance. When Aeneas first enters he is dressed 'like a Fisher swaine' (Dido's description in Act V, line 1570)

[10] E. K. Chambers, *The Elizabethan Stage*, i. 156–7.

and he and his men meet Illioneus and his companions; Illioneus tells
how Dido

> clad vs in these wealthie robes we weare. (360)

Dido's first act on meeting Aeneas is to dress him splendidly:

> Warlike *Aeneas*, and in these base robes?
> Goe fetch the garment which *Sicheus* ware: (374–5)

The hunting costumes of Venus and Dido are emphasised; Venus has a
purple costume and a bow and quiver, and describes her sisters as
dressed in leopard skins, while Dido's hunting costume is evidently
splendid, if the ambiguous syntax may be trusted:

> My princely robes thou seest are layd aside,
> Whose glittering pompe *Dianas* shrowdes supplies
> . . .
> Faire Troian, hold my golden bowe awhile,
> Vntill I gird my quiuer to my side: (913–14, 917–18)

Cupid as Ascanius, a tender juvenal, presents a miniature, mock heroic
foil to the principals, like Moth armed for Hercules in *Love's Labour's
Lost*,

> in his pompe,
> Bearing his huntspeare brauely in his hand. (942–3)

When Dido gazes in wonder at Aeneas crowned with a diadem and
bearing a golden sceptre in his hand, she cries in joy

> Now lookes *Aeneas* like immortall *Ioue*, (1251)

which confirms the splendour of the play's opening scene, where Jove
is enthroned with Mercury at his feet. We may suppose that Venus
wore a costume representing her emblem the dove, while she was
apparently accompanied by live doves, since she offers Ascanius

> A siluer girdle, and a golden purse, (601)

and tells how

> These milke white Doues shall be his Centronels: (615)

Juno presumably wore a peacock coloured robe, possibly incorporating
peacock feathers. She may have been attended by live peacocks (though
in view of the haughty temperament of the bird this seems uncertain)

and if so the emblematic union of Venus and Juno could have been represented in III.ii:

> Fancie and modestie shall liue as mates,
> And thy faire peacockes by my pigeons pearch: (868-9)

Finally, as Dido prepares for death, she casts into the flames the rich garment she presented to Aeneas at their first meeting; so Marlowe recalls the memorable gesture of Perithous in *Palamon and Arcite*.

If we wish to reconstruct the original conditions under which *Dido* might have been performed, we should note that the staging was probably contrived as E. K. Chambers suggests,[11] one side being *en pastoralle*, representing the wood, and also the cave, and with space for Jove's throne and its curtain, while the other side, representing Carthage, evidently had a 'house'—an open loggia—a wall and gate. It would appear that the centre of the stage was clear, and backed by trees.

In a banqueting house or decorated Great Chamber,[12] Dido's exalted erotic invitations to Aeneas would have been accompanied, reflected, and repeated in hangings, ornaments, and costumes, seductive in the subtle brilliance of candlelight. Marlowe's music is rich:

> Ile giue thee tackling made of riueld gold,
> Wound on the barkes of odoriferous trees,
> Oares of massie Iuorie full of holes,
> Through which the water shall delight to play: (750-3)

the harsh manly world of Aeneas the mariner is metamorphosed into court art: the speech creates a wonderfully wrought artefact, a rare, elaborate example of Elizabethan jewellery or, magnified, a mythological masque in which

> Seaborne Nymphes shall swarme about thy ships,
> And wanton Mermaides court thee with sweete songs, (763-4)

[11] Chambers, op. cit., iii. 35-6.
[12] Cf. the banqueting house erected in 1581, described by Holinshed, which had 'two hundred ninetie and two lights of glasse ... in the top of this house was wrought most cunninglie upon canuas, works of iuie and hollie, with pendents made of wicker rods, and garnished with baie, rue, and all maner of strange flowers garnished with spangles of gold, as also ... strange fruits, as pomegranats, oranges, pompions, cucumbers, grapes, carrets ... Betwixt these ... great spaces of canuas, which was most cunninglie painted, the clouds with starres, the sunne and sunne beames, with diuerse other cotes of sundrie sortes belonging to the queenes maiestie, most richlie garnished with gold.'— *The Elizabethan Stage*, i. 16.

but in the first place it is a passionate expression of Dido's wholly erotic being, which creates, transcending these, far other worlds, and other seas, in the very moment on stage in which she reacts to Aeneas' feelings. The court drama's resources of costume, scenery, and spectacle are absorbed into the richer and fuller life of poetic drama so that they have metaphoric significance; so Marlowe reveals the fuller potential of this dramatic language.

Furthermore the style is suited to the resources of boy actors. The boys' companies seem to have been noted for their skill and grace in movement and speech, particularly in declamation, dialogue, and complex patterns of exchange. Their clear voices may have lacked emotional colour, but their training as choristers meant that music and song could express emotions beyond their acting range, if the dramatist lacked Marlowe's poetic and rhetorical genius. The boys were emphatically not amateur, their style was disciplined, formal, and elegant, while their youth—some of them at least must have been of rather diminutive stature—must have made them suited to perform plays in which there was a multiple presentation of attitudes, ideas, and feelings, where their appearance expressed the drama's concern with simultaneously heroic and mock heroic effects, as in the stage direction '*Here the Curtaines draw, there is discouered* Iupiter *dandling* Ganimed *vpon his knee, and* Mercury *lying asleepe.*'

Marlowe can take for granted the spectacular impact of costume and tableau here, and can set up a counterpoint of attitudes and moods in the dialogue and action, confident that genuine heroic rhetoric will have immediate effect whenever it appears. So Ganymede complains of the 'shrewish blowes' given by jealous Juno, in terms which deftly and wittily parody the 'mighty line' yet express direct physical shock:

> She reacht me such a rap for that I spilde,
> As made the bloud run downe about mine eares. (7–8)

Jupiter's reassurance to Ganymede reveals simultaneously the absurdity of the god's decadent erotic tastes and the awesome rashness of his divine power:

> I vow, if she but once frowne on thee more,
> To hang her meteor like twixt heauen and earth, (12–13)

The emotions of the gods are extreme, sudden, and volatile; in their lives hyperbole is the normal mode, as paranoia is the appropriate and usual condition; and Marlowe's emphasis in this opening scene prepares

us for wider themes in the play. This Jupiter, who for his sport plucks a
feather from Hermes' wing and in his turn is twitted by Venus for his
lecherous perversion (he, a middle-aged married god) is recalled to his
loftier role by the magnificent speech of Venus, who pleads for Aeneas'
release from war and tempest in verse full of violent movement, enacting
the elemental conflict and the inner storms of passion which threaten
Aeneas:

> Poore *Troy* must now be sackt vpon the Sea,
> And *Neptunes* waues be enuious men of warre, (64–5)

This imagery suggests the radically damaging physical and psychological
effect of such extended and extreme suffering: Aeneas' sanity, his very
identity, are in peril:

> . . . the waues doe threat our Chrystall world,
> And *Proteus* raising hils of flouds on high,
> Entends ere long to sport him in the skie. (75–7)

In the passage as a whole the resources of rhetoric are orchestrated to
enact the passionate movements of the sea, beginning with a swell,
rising to full tempest and then calming in the lines

> Disquiet Seas lay downe your swelling lookes,
> And court *Aeneas* with your calmie cheere, (122–3)

The storm ends with a recollection of the birth of Venus

> That erst-while issued from thy watrie loynes,
> And had my being from thy bubling froth: (128–9)

Here, in verbal music, suggestions of playful strife among the wavelets
on the calm shore are evoked; 'bubling froth' recalls Golding precisely
because the seemingly gauche, naive phrase seems self-consciously
humorous, intended to suggest child-like innocence, a harmless echo
of the tempest's savage energy.

The speeches in this scene are in a sense formal and declamatory, the
actors have few movements or gestures: but the dramatic life is intense,
emotional conflict violent, the range of action wide, indeed extreme.
Here it is appropriate to point an analogy with opera, particularly in
view of Marlowe's central interest in extreme emotional states and the
violent trajectories of disordered passion and consciousness. The
point may be demonstrated in the supposedly 'undramatic' speech of
Aeneas, one hundred and sixty or so lines long, at the end of which he
himself remarks, not without irony, 'sorrow hath tired me quite'.

THE TRAGEDY OF DIDO QUEEN OF CARTHAGE

Marlowe's style is initially close to that of Racine in *Phèdre*, as a comparison shows. First, the opening of Théramène's great speech in Act V:[13]

> A peine nous sortions des portes de Trézène,
> Il était sur son char; ses gardes affligés
> Imitaient son silence, autour de lui rangés;
> Il suivait tout pensif le chemin de Mycènes;
> Sa main sur les chevaux laissait flotter les rênes;
> Ses superbes coursiers, qu'on voyait autrefois
> Pleins du'une ardeur si noble obéir à sa voix,
> L'oeuil morne maintenant, et la tête baissée,
> Semblaient se conformer à sa triste pensée.

Now Marlowe's Aeneas:

> The Grecian souldiers tired with ten yeares warre,
> Began to crye, let vs vnto our ships,
> *Troy* is inuincible, why stay we here?
> With whose outcryes *Atrides* being apal'd,
> Summoned the Captaines to his princely tent,
> Who looking on the scarres we Troians gaue,
> Seeing the number of their men decreast,
> And the remainder weake and out of heart,
> Gaue vp their voyces to dislodge the Campe,
> And so in troopes all marcht to *Tenedos*: (421-30)

There is more activity in Marlowe, he is less concise, less intent on noble simplicity than Racine; and yet the sense of impending, colossal disaster, the dimensions of the tragic action, the invocation of woe and wonder; all these he does achieve. It is the more interesting, then, that as Aeneas proceeds with the narrative we detect increasingly strong fluctuations in tone and style: wildness and excess increase, hyperbole, horror, and absurdity proliferate and mount. For, in the act of recollecting his experience of the Fall of Troy Aeneas relives the terror, he suffers such perturbation that his tale turns into a nightmare both profound and appalling, dominated by obsessional images of slaughter and blood:

> kill, kill they cryed.
> Frighted with this confused noyse, I rose,

---

[13] Racine, *Phèdre*, V.vi.11-19, in *Théâtre Complet*, ed. Maurice Rat (Paris, 1960).

And looking from a turret, might behold
Yong infants swimming in their parents bloud,
Headles carkasses piled vp in heapes, (485–9)

This echoes, surely significantly, his earlier vow to a disguised Venus:

this right hand shall make thy Altars crack
With mountaine heapes of milke white Sacrifize. (201–2)

The excessive degree of hyperbole is disturbing, carries suggestions of hysteria and distorted eroticism.

The situation Aeneas describes is terrible on an epic scale, truly fit for hyperbole, yet also deeply absurd, farcical. Aeneas, shuddering, relates how the 'franticke' queen hung by her nails in Neoptolemus' eyelids until

At last the souldiers puld her by the heeles,
And swong her howling in the emptie ayre,
Which sent an eccho to the wounded King:
Whereat he lifted vp his bedred lims,
And would haue grappeld with *Achilles* sonne,
Forgetting both his want of strength and hands,
Which he disdaining whiskt his sword about,
And with the wind thereof the King fell downe: (542–9)

The disturbing mixture of shocked compassion and insane humour is deliberate, and the ludicrous figure 'want of strength and hands' has a savage effect with parallels elsewhere in Marlowe, for example the psychopathic glee of Ithamore:

I, Mr. he's slain; look how his brains drop out on's nose.

(*Jew of Malta*, l. 1687)

Surely, too, the deft frivolity of the verb 'whiskt'[14] intensifies the grimly

---

[14] In discussion this reading was queried, and it was suggested that there was nothing unexpected or ambivalent in Marlowe's use of 'whiskt' in this context. It is true that the usage by Barbour in 1375, recorded in the O.E.D. ('The king . . .Vatit the sper . . . And with a wysk the hed of-strak') suggests that the verb in medieval epic lacked frivolous resonances; but the O.E.D.'s examples from the period closest to Marlowe's *Dido* clearly also do connote playfulness and frivolity: *Stanyhurst*, 1577: 'Sodaynly it (a salmon) fetcheth such a round Whiske, that at a trice it skippeth to the top of the rocke' and *Lyly*, 1589: 'To give them a whiske with their own wand'. It is entirely consonant with Marlowe's purposes in this speech in *Dido* to offer implicit ironic comment on simplistic or traditional responses to valour, war, and violent death. His purpose is complex, this is not simply 'funny'.

bathetic last line. This rhetoric, indeed, carried to the utmost degree of extremity, this intense parody of hyperbole, is also the true language of madness, a profoundly serious response to the horror:

> *Marcus* Why dost thou laugh? it fits not with this hour.
> *Titus*   Why, I have not another tear to shed:
>
> > (*Titus Andronicus* III.i.265–6)

As Aeneas concludes his narrative of the Fall of Troy a kind of absurd levity of tone, an almost dismissive curtness, seems to betray the intensified stress in a mind unable to accept, or face, the final sequence of disasters and humiliations. Indeed we may detect the pressure of hysteria in the strikingly curt description of his failure to protect first his wife, then Cassandra, then Polixena, and there is a pathetic *and* absurd evaporation of feeling in the couplet at which he breaks down: Polixena, he relates,

> Was by the cruell Mirmidons surprizd,
> And after by that *Pirrhus* sacrifizde. (582–3)

We learn from Achates that Aeneas, when he saw this happen, 'swomme quickly backe' to the ship; and so the scene comes to rest in an air of strained, nervous farce.

The apparent hero, ancestor of the British race, loyal defender of Troy, founder of Rome, breaks down and betrays his guilty cowardice! It is, we may think, characteristic of Marlowe to treat Aeneas, a very *type* of the Renaissance hero, with sardonic irreverence; but this is not mere caricature. Aeneas' account of the Fall of Troy combines Virgilian grandeur and range with medieval details of horror and violence which derive from popular romances, especially the well-known *Troy Book* of Lydgate; and this must remind the audience that the Aeneas of medieval legend was a notorious villain not an epic hero. Aeneas knows the frightful details of Priam's death because he and Antenor had led Pyrrhus to the king's place of refuge and stood by, consenting, as he was murdered.[15] By interweaving Virgil and Lydgate Marlowe fuses contradictory attitudes to Aeneas, and Aeneas himself is consequently radically unstable, Protean: a hero, a wretched and impotent coward, a tragic victim of destiny.

*   *   *

[15] See Ethel Seaton, 'Marlowe's Light Reading', in *Elizabethan and Jacobean Studies Presented to F. P. Wilson*, ed. H. Davis and Helen Gardner (Oxford, 1959), p. 27.

The texture of Aeneas' long speech is significantly different from that of Thérimène in *Phèdre*; but the main similarities between the two plays are important nevertheless. In *Dido* images of the sea and ship's tackling, of storm and fire, have a central dramatic function as leit-motivs. In *Phèdre* the iteration of key thematic images, 'sang', 'monstre', 'le fond des forêts', 'rivages sombres', 'infernales ombres', intensifies the depiction of Phèdre's profound and violent obsession:

> Mes homicides mains, promptes à me venger
> Dans le sang innocent brûlent de se plonger.
> . . .
> Où me cacher? Fuyons dans la nuit infernale. (IV.vi.58-9, 64)

The monster which rises from the disrupted surface of the sea to destroy Hippolyte is an appalling hyperbolic image of destructive passion. By contrast, Marlowe's play ends with the assumption of the heroine into the element of fire itself: and this is the supreme image of love.

The heroic love theme in *Dido* is related to the theme of Aeneas' suffering at the command of the gods. The organic relationship between the storms at sea, the storms of war, and the stormy force of passion, is apparent in the personal confession Aeneas makes to Dido, when he tells her his ships are unrigged, his sails all rent in sunder, oars broken, tackling lost,

> Yea all my Nauie split with Rockes and Shelfes: (742)

Dido takes up these implicit metaphors of Aeneas' sense of physical and sexual dereliction, and transforms them with fresh erotic energy:

> Ile giue thee tackling made of riueld gold, (750)

The consummation of their love is symbolised by an enchanted storm which enriches the harmony:

> The ayre is cleere, and Southerne windes are whist, (1084)

Hence, later, Aeneas embraces Dido with the cry

> This is the harbour that *Aeneas* seekes,
> Lets see what tempests can anoy me now. (1265-6)

and Dido magnificently recalls it with the lines

> O that I had a charme to keepe the windes
> Within the closure of a golden ball,
> Or that the Tyrrhen sea were in mine armes,

> That he might suffer shipwracke on my breast,
> As oft as he attempts to hoyst vp saile. (1305–9)

The power and depth of Dido's emotion are dramatically realised in what we are accustomed to think of as a uniquely Shakespearean manner; and in fact it is essentially the *dramatic* power of *Dido* which influences Shakespeare in *Antony and Cleopatra*. In Shakespeare's play Marlowe's theme of tragic love is re-enacted. Shakespeare's protagonists face the same situation, their relationships and actions are reminiscent of their Marlovian ancestors, and above all the quality and dramatic effect of Dido's sublime erotic rhetoric informs the inner life and movement of Cleopatra's poetic imagination. The connections are essentially dramatic. Thus Cleopatra's alternating warmth and coldness to Antony recalls Dido's behaviour to Aeneas, both in the comic episode in the cave and in the final scene of their parting; Cleopatra's unpredictable capriciousness recalls the comedy of Dido's treatment of Iarbus (III.i.641–89) and, in fiercer mood, the situation where the messenger brings news of Antony's marriage to Octavia corresponds to that in *Dido* when the Nurse brings news of the disappearance of Ascanius (V.i. 1620–32) and suffers savage punishment.

In Shakespeare's play, as in Marlowe's, the sea and ships have both literal and metaphoric significance, and thematic images of sea-tempest and fire relate the wider historical narrative to the chief heroic protagonists. Dido and Aeneas, like Antony and Cleopatra, are continually associated with the elements, and the dramatic poetry exalts them to divine proportions. When Dido appears in the costume of Diana, in which Venus herself has already appeared, the exaltation is made emblematic, and later in the play Aeneas is enthroned as splendidly as Jupiter in the opening scene, and doubtless on the same throne. Shakespeare's Enobarbus tells how Cleopatra did lie in her pavilion

> O'er-picturing that Venus where we see
> The fancy outwork nature.

Antony becomes a god in Cleopatra's imagination:

> His face was as the heavens, and therein stuck
> A sun and moon, which kept their course, and lighted
> The little O, the earth . . .
> His legs bestrid the ocean, his rear'd arm
> Crested the world: his voice was propertied
> As all the tuned spheres, (V.ii.79–81, 82–4)

So, as the pressure of desire mounts, Dido exalts Aeneas to divine
proportions:

> *Prometheus* hath put on *Cupids* shape,
> And I must perish in his burning armes: (1016–17)

in her erotic hyperbole Dido also unconsciously predicts her own
tragic destiny; but the flames of her funeral pyre refine as they consume,
and in death she experiences apotheosis. Cleopatra meets the same fate
as Dido, not in real flames but in sublime metaphor:

> I am fire and air: my other elements
> I give to baser life. (V.ii.288–9)

and Cleopatra's real tragic destiny is unconsciously predicted also, in the
imagery associating her with the serpent. The lines

> He's speaking now,
> Or murmuring, 'Where's my serpent of old Nile?'
> For so he calls me. Now I feed myself
> With most delicious poison. (I.v.24–7)

are recalled in the final moments of the play when a real serpent feeds
her its poison, and the experience is exalted by a final superb erotic
hyperbole:

> The stroke of death is as a lover's pinch,
> Which hurts, and is desir'd. (V.ii.294–5)

Thus Dido's bitter image of disappointment and rejection

> O Serpent that came creeping from the shoare,
> And I for pitie harbord in my bosome,
> Wilt thou now slay me with thy venomed sting, (1573–5)

is transmuted to become an emblem of supreme fulfilment:

> Peace, peace!
> Dost thou not see my baby at my breast,
> That sucks the nurse asleep? (V.ii.307–9)

* * *

Yet although, like Cleopatra, Dido attains a state of divine exaltation,
Aeneas cannot be compared with Antony. If Aeneas is in a sense the
prisoner of the fates, we cannot ignore the almost pathological quality
of his passiveness. There is something shocking in Aeneas' abrupt,

immediate, and total capitulation to the command of the gods to leave Carthage[16] (IV.iii) and on this and the later occasion (V.i) his radical change of tone, his cynical indifference to Dido, suggests the disintegration of his personality with his collapse into impotence. Indeed there is pathos, but also farcical comedy, in his subsequent welcome to Dido's embrace as *maternal* protection. Aeneas seeks in Dido's arms an escape from destiny; but once more destiny calls him and once again he capitulates instantly. Dido now subjects him to the full fury of her passion—which she expresses in metaphors of sea-tempest—the waves crash over Aeneas, and then at last they cease abruptly as Dido offers herself up to him in a supreme gesture:

> if thou wilt stay,
> Leap in mine armes, mine armes are open wide (1587-8)

Aeneas impotently retreats, in implicitly ironic contrast to the aspiring leaps of Phaeton and Leander, for this time his will is utterly crushed, fragmented. He expresses his condition in an image of hopelessness and tragic passivity:

> What, would the Gods haue me, *Deucalion* like,
> Flote vp and downe where ere the billowes driue? (1465-6)

Marlowe's *Tragedy of Dido Queen of Carthage* may conclude in the exaltation of the heroine, but the play is not a unified heroic tragedy; we must see it, rather, as a counterpoint of varying kinds of erotic experience and attitudes to passion. It is this multiplicity which we are called on to appreciate and which finally determines the special quality of Marlowe's achievement.

Marlowe employs comedy as a means of counterpointing the themes of active and passive passion. The central comic figure is Cupid, himself an appropriately multiple character, by tradition profoundly serious as well as profanely playful: a witty and bawdy youth, certainly, but also a god of love, associated in pagan mysteries with the god of death,[17] just as that other comic figure Ganymede traditionally represented the

---

[16] Clifford Leech briefly notices the comic aspect of this episode in his article 'Marlowe's Humour' referred to above, note 2.

[17] In James Shirley's masque *Cupid and Death* (1653) Death wields Cupid's dart in a manner very like Marlowe's Cupid in *Dido*. In his edition of *Cupid and Death* in *A Book of Masques in Honour of Allardyce Nicoll* (London, 1967) Bernard Harris gives an account of the relation between the two mythological figures, referring to Edgar Wind, *Pagan Mysteries in the Renaissance* (London, 1958) and Erwin Panofsky, *Studies in Iconology* (London, 1939).

baseness of physical desire, but was interpreted also in neo-Platonic terms as the *mens humana*, beloved by Jupiter: that is, the Supreme Being: and abducted to heaven by means of the eagle to a state of enraptured contemplation, divorced from the body and free of corporeal things.[18]

In *Dido* the costumes of Cupid and Ganymede immediately assert this emblematic significance, against which the subsequent bawdy episodes are set. The implicitly serious meaning of the emblems is never erased. The stylised pattern of stimulus and response when Cupid strikes Dido, and later the Nurse, though abruptly, cruelly, and farcically bawdy, also demonstrates the divine, absolute, sudden, and mysterious power of passion, through which man may be exalted, or rendered absurd, hysterical, pitiably impotent. The seemingly disjunctive abruptness of the dramatic counterpoint is surely not a sign of Marlowe's immaturity or irresponsibility as a dramatist, but rather an appropriate and a powerful means of expressing the profound duality of man.

Cupid's absolute power corresponds to Jupiter's as mock heroic to heroic, and this implies the potential ambivalence in both, since Jupiter can be ridiculously comic, Cupid sublime and serious. So too Dido's response to Cupid's stimulus suggests the element of absurdity in her extreme eroticism, and might imply that hysteria contributes to her final state of exaltation. This multiple irony, in a play for boy actors, is perhaps most unsettling, profound, and witty, when the ugly, aged servant woman woos Cupid with an erotic invitation which echoes not only that of Jupiter to Ganymede, in the opening scene, but that of Dido to Aeneas in one of the most sublime moments of the play.

So, in *Dido*, Marlowe creates from the conventions of court drama a dramatic language through which he explores the inner complexities of the sublime and the heroic, and the Protean nature of personality and identity under the stress of passion.

[18] See Erwin Panofsky, *Studies in Iconology*, pp. 213 ff., and figs. 158, 169, and *Renaissance and Renascences in Western Art* (Uppsala, 1960), p. 78 n.

Marlowe and the 'Comic Distance'

J. R. MULRYNE and STEPHEN FENDER

Marlowe and the 'Comic Distance'

THERE IS A MOMENT in *Dido Queen of Carthage* when Aeneas, newly arrived from Troy, sees outside Carthage a statue which he takes to be a statue of Priam. Achates briefly shares his delusion:

> I cannot choose but fall upon my knees,
> And kiss his hand. O, where is Hecuba?
> Here she was wont to sit; but, saving air,
> Is nothing here, and what is this but stone? (II.i.11–14)

Aeneas cannot adjust so quickly to matter-of-fact reality:

> Achates, though mine eyes say this is stone,
> Yet thinks my mind that this is Priamus;
> And when my grieved heart sighs and says no,
> Then would it leap out to give Priam life.
> O, were I not at all, so thou mightst be!
> Achates, see, King Priam wags his hand;
> He is alive; Troy is not overcome! (II.i.24–30)

Achates, in his common-sense role, returns him to the facts:

> Thy mind, Aeneas, that would have it so
> Deludes thy eyesight: Priamus is dead. (II.i.31–2)

We call attention to this episode at the outset of our paper because we think it provides a convenient paradigm for some of the things we want to say about our reaction to Marlowe's plays. Unlike Ovid's Pygmalion, invoked in the speech we've omitted, Aeneas cannot give his statue life; unlike Shakespeare's Leontes, Aeneas cannot 'awake his faith' and have it rewarded by the redemption of past time. In Marlowe, the mind is at odds with the facts, while the heart oscillates baffled between two kinds of knowledge:

> Yet thinks my mind that this is Priamus;
> And when my grieved heart sighs and says no,
> Then would it leap out to give Priam life. (II.i.25–7)

In a very 'modern' way, Marlowe invites us to share Aeneas' psychology, and see the stone Priam made flesh, yet with another side of our consciousness we are equally sure of what we might call a more detached, 'objective' view: that the supposed Priam remains stone. We call this a paradigm because it is only one of many instances in Marlowe in which contradictory views of experience are brought together and left unresolved: the ideal and the common sense; the hint of a comprehensive order and the rejection of all order; the socially concerned and the individualist; the moral and the libertine; metaphor and fact. Such conjunctions as these have been the source of most of the critical disputes centring on Marlowe's plays. Our contention is that, to use Raymond Williams' phrase, the 'structure of feeling'[1] in Marlowe is one that *requires* such opposites, and involves a genuine ambivalence (not an ambiguity) of feeling. Ultimately, we will argue, his work provides models of an absurd universe. Camus might have been speaking of Marlowe when he wrote:

> These perpetual oscillations between the natural and the extra-ordinary, the individual and the universal, the tragic and the every-day, the absurd and the logical, are found throughout his work and give it both its resonance and its meaning. These are the paradoxes that must be enumerated, the contradictions that must be strengthened, in order to understand the absurd work.[2]

We want in the following pages to explore the 'ambivalence' of Marlowe, principally in two plays: *Tamburlaine* in the comic mode and *Edward II* in the historical. Very little of our evidence is original; all we hope to do is to provide an affective or philosophic approach that excludes less than usual of the full range of meaning of a Marlowe play, and that by its very nature avoids most of the familiar critical disagreements.

To return to *Dido Queen of Carthage* for a moment. The treatment of Aeneas in the scene just mentioned involves a certain deflation of the hero; in his delusion he becomes for the moment comic. Our regard for him remains undiminished; the feelings his delusion expresses are entirely natural and entirely praiseworthy. But there enters into our relationship with him a distance that is also an uncertainty. And this is

---

[1] Raymond Williams, *Modern Tragedy* (London, 1966).
[2] Albert Camus, 'Hope and the Absurd in the World of Franz Kafka', in *Kafka: A Collection of Critical Essays*, ed. Ronald Gray (Englewood Cliffs, N.J., 1962), p. 148.

a minor example only of the way in which Marlowe uses what we shall have to call, for want of a better word, 'comic' devices, to unsettle our response to the various characters. Even as the play opens we find it difficult to adjust to the mixture of tones. Jupiter's talk with Ganymede is jocular, its subject the petty squabbles of very undignified gods; and yet Venus' speech about Aeneas, and Jupiter's piece on the founding of Rome, seem intended to impress us as serious and weighty. A few lines later, Venus congratulates herself on the safe arrival of Aeneas ('how art thou compass'd with content, / The while thine eyes attract their sought-for joys'); and yet she undermines the dignity of his entrance by concealing herself in a bush, and predicting his laments:

> Here in this bush disguised will I stand,
> Whiles my Aeneas spends himself in plaints,
> And heaven and earth with his unrest acquaints. (I.i.139–41)

The effect is to make the audience detached, even half-mocking, in their attitude to Aeneas' desperate adventures. As Venus hints, the whole thing may be over-acted. And yet the burlesque intention doesn't hold. Aeneas' speech, when it comes, is direct and unposturing:

> Pluck up your hearts, since fate still rests our friend,
> And changing heavens may those good days return
> Which Pergama did vaunt in all her pride. (I.i.149–51)

We react once more in his favour; until Marlowe again makes our responses somersault. Achates answers Aeneas:

> Brave Prince of Troy, thou only art our god . . .
> Do thou but smile and cloudy heaven will clear,
> Whose night and day descendeth from thy brows. (I.i.152–6)

Aeneas, we know, is the gods' plaything; and we know what the gods who play are like. The switchback of attraction and withdrawal continues. How are we to take the behaviour of gods and men for the rest of the play?

The use of 'comic' devices in *Dido* has long been recognised. Some critics simplify the play by thinking it intended to be funny throughout: Trollope called it 'a burlesque on Dido's story as treated by Vergil'.[3] For

[3] Quoted in *'Dido Queen of Carthage' and 'The Massacre at Paris'*, ed. H. J. Oliver (London, 1968), p. xix. We use this edition to quote from *Dido*, and quote *Tamburlaine* from the edition in the Regents Renaissance Drama Series.

Clifford Leech, in the most balanced and useful essay yet published on Marlowe's humour, 'the dominant tone' in *Dido* 'is that of a gentle and delighting humour: the affairs of men and gods are seen as a spectacle engagingly absurd'.[4] J. B. Steane, on the contrary, wishes to discount the comedy altogether; in his judgement Marlowe is too 'unstable' to succeed 'in dramatising this essentially tragic story as a tragedy'.[5] The comic treatment of the gods, he thinks, is quite simply a blunder on Marlowe's part, and wholly unintegrated with the rest of the play. Where disagreement such as this can exist among sensitive and honest critics, some rather different approach to this play, and by extension to others in the Marlowe canon, may be tried.

Our own belief is that *Dido* fails, not because an intrusive humour spoils the essentially tragic story, nor because the play is not consistently humorous (as it manifestly is not: Aeneas' description of the fall of Troy, to take a single example, must be classed among Marlowe's most powerful, and most savage, dramatic writing) but because the structure of feeling represented by the sympathy/withdrawal alternation of the first scene is not consistently maintained. Marlowe's subject in *Dido* was the not entirely un-Virgilian one of men who choose, but do not choose, their destiny. Aeneas is at once the noble leader of a people and the victim both of a destiny chosen for him and of the wayward impulses of his own fancies and those of others. The gods reflect his ambivalent situation by being themselves powerful and petty, dedicated to noble causes and to trivial appetites. The situation is an absurd one in that contrary estimates of every action are possible and patently self-cancelling. To have dramatised this myth satisfactorily would have required a very deft control of an audience's responses, switching them back and forth between the twin perspectives of the hero and the victim. Inexperience, and the difficulties presented by translation, prevent Marlowe in this case giving consistent dramatic expression to what he has to 'say'.

Where *Dido* fails, *Tamburlaine* succeeds. Not that it involves the reader in an extended switching of attitudes; its method is largely evolutionary: the polarities of our response become explicit over the play's two parts.

We want to call *Tamburlaine* 'comic' not because we wish to place it in a formal category—such categories were, after all, very fluid in the

[4] Clifford Leech, 'Marlowe's Humor', in *Essays on Shakespeare and Elizabethan Drama in Honour of Hardin Craig*, ed. R. Hosley (London, 1963), p. 71.

[5] J. B. Steane, *Marlowe* (Cambridge, 1964), p. 46.

late sixteenth century—but because the name of comedy helps us to
locate, much more accurately than 'tragedy' or 'history', what we take
to be the essential nature of our response to this play. We have insisted
on ambivalence of feeling; when ambivalence is specified as theory, it
becomes paradox, and paradox is written into the history of comic
theory. Aristotle, who defined the ridiculous as a sub-species of the
ugly, qualified his definition, and opened the door to paradox, by
insisting that the ugliness concerned must be such as did not wholly
repel. When Aristotle's ideas were taken up by Roman authors, his word
for ugly (αἰσχρός), was translated as *turpis*, producing the more remarkable paradox of a baseness that could somehow also attract. A similar
paradox finds its way into Renaissance literary criticism in, for example,
Madius, who in his *De Ridiculis* (1550) added to the standard *turpitudo*
as a source of laughter another source which he called *admiratio* or
wonder, astonishment. The dual sources must exist together; if
admiratio ceased, the comic disappeared. Sidney too, though this was
not among his major concerns, recognised in comic experience the
kinship-in-difference of 'delight' and 'laughter'.[6] What each of them
acknowledges, in other words, is the inherent and essential ambivalence
of (at any rate) major versions of comic experience. This we insist
reflects very well the doubleness of a sensitive response to *Tamburlaine*:
our attraction to the magnificence of Tamburlaine's concepts and
achievements is stressed against our growing awareness (implicit from
the beginning) of the monstrosity of all that he does. Neither impulse
dominates or gives way to the other; each coexists with the other to
produce in the audience a state of mind that is at once contradictory and
yet profoundly true of thinking and feeling about the play's central
topic, the fulfilment of will. Writing of Kafka, Eliseo Vivas explains
very accurately the nature and moral bearings of the 'comic' response,
in the way we wish to use the term:

> Generally speaking, a comic grasp of the world rests on the perception
> by the writer of a moral duality which elicits from the reader a
> 'comic' response as the only means of freeing himself from the
> conflict towards values to which he is attached and yet towards which
> he cannot justify his attachment satisfactorily.[7]

[6] For a useful survey of the history of comic theory see Marvin T. Herrick,
Comic Theory in the Sixteenth Century (Urbana, Illinois, 1964).

[7] Vivas, 'Kafka's Distorted Mask', in *Kafka: A Collection of Critical Essays*,
op. cit., p. 144.

Critical dispute about the play, too familiar to summarise, centres round whether we 'blame' or 'sympathise with' the hero. The more subtle ethical position outlined by Vivas more truly represents our own response to the play and makes a good deal of the disagreement redundant.

It is unnecessary to outline all the ways in which Marlowe develops and sustains an ambivalent attitude to Tamburlaine. We may represent them by noting two examples of the important theme of 'hyperbole into fact'. For Tamburlaine's claim on our attention is that he can realise hyperbole or 'conceit':

> These lords, perhaps, do scorn our estimates
> And think we prattle with distempered spirits.
> But since they measure our deserts so mean,
> That in conceit bear empires on our spears,
> Affecting thoughts coequal with the clouds,
> They shall be kept our forced followers
> Till with their eyes they view us emperors.

As they do. And the audience becomes accustomed to charting Tamburlaine's magnificent progress by the ease with which he makes good his most optimistic boasts. He promises to make Bajazeth his footstool and compel the kings of Trebizon and Soria to pull his chariot. It is his glory that he actually carries out his vaunt, and the power of his will is made the more dazzling by contrast to that of Bajazeth, who, for all his threats to turn Tamburlaine into a 'chaste and lustless eunuch' and make him 'in my sarell tend my concubines', himself ends up in a cage. But there is another aspect to the realisation of hyperbole. For Tamburlaine's word—in both senses of 'word'—becomes a kind of cage too, and the price he pays for making good his hyperbole is the kind of ridiculousness that comes of trying to turn metaphor into fact. Equally powerful as our wonder at his ability to make good his threats is our sense of the ridiculousness of hyperbole enacted. His behaviour is, after all, curiously literal. We might have expected to take all his talk about making Bajazeth his footstool, or harnessing the kings of Trebizon and Soria, as figures of speech for his assumption of their political power, or as metaphors for any number of ways in which he might humiliate them. But what the audience gets is Tamburlaine *really* using Bajazeth as a footstool, *really* making the kings pull his chariot, and again and again. His relentless turning of metaphor into fact is both glorious and ridiculous. His ability to carry out his word emphasises his power and suggests its limitations, in that it forces him to carry out his promises literally. And we cannot resolve this ambivalence by choosing to interpret or produce the play in one way or another. The ambivalence is built into the text.

The second example reminds us, in a simpler way, of the distance Marlowe maintains—and progressively widens as the play develops—between hyperbole and fact. Tamburlaine's language is at its most intoxicating (as well as its freest and most flexible) as he anticipates the conquest of Babylon:

> Thorough the streets, with troops of conquered kings,
> I'll ride in golden armour like the sun,
> And in my helm a triple plume shall spring,
> Spangled with diamonds, dancing in the air,
> To note me emperor of the three-fold world.

The energy of the verse, the strong alliteration helping, combines with the evoked scene to assure us of the magnificence of the deed. And Tamburlaine does what he promises. But the facts attaching to his conquest are either petulant or sickening: the murder of a stubborn man, and the wholesale slaughter of innocent citizens:

> I have fulfill'd your highness' will, my lord.
> Thousands of men, drown'd in Asphaltis' lake,
> Have made the water swell above the banks,
> And fishes, fed by human carcasses,
> Amaz'd, swim up and down upon the waves,
> As when they swallow asafoetida
> Which makes them fleet aloft and gasp for air.

Such, on a detached estimate, is the reality corresponding to hyperbole. Once more, our attitude to Tamburlaine swings through a wide arc, responding to the greatness of vision and the triviality of fact. As Camus expresses it:

> There is in the human situation (and this is a commonplace of all literatures) a basic absurdity as well as an implacable nobility. The two coincide, as is natural.[8]

The coincidence in *Tamburlaine* is maintained throughout.

On such a reading as this, there are obvious analogies to be made between Tamburlaine and other hero-villains of the Elizabethan drama.

[8] Camus, op. cit., p. 149.

Volpone, for example, excites in us just such an ambivalent response as does Tamburlaine. But if we ask where the differences lie, it becomes clear why we prefer to call *Tamburlaine*, in the technical sense, absurd. *Volpone* in its satirical aspect always refers us back to orthodox moral premises. Even when there are hints that orthodoxy may be little observed—the *avocatori* are corrupt, Volpone's money goes to a hospital for the *incurabili*, Celia and Bonario are weakly drawn—orthodox principles nevertheless stand as a moral base, one of the polarities of our ambivalent judgement. In *Tamburlaine*, the appeal is rarely to orthodox moral ideas, and we certainly do not find a comprehensive moral framework behind the action as a whole. Our judgement of Tamburlaine, though it may on occasion appeal to basic humanitarian instincts, normally acts through a sense of proportion, a recognition of extravagance and triviality which is morally neutral. The only lesson that the death of Tamburlaine teaches is the existential one of man's common mortality:

> Shall sickness prove me now to be a man,
> That have been term'd the terror of the world?

It's from just such a basic proposition—the ultimate meaninglessness of endeavour—that the absurdist position springs. Tamburlaine seeks to evade death by finding immortality through his son, and the echoes of the familiar theme of Elizabethan poetry are set in motion. But ironically the emblems that attach to Amyras are those of Phaeton and Hippolytus: charioteers who (as the verse is at pains to tell us) could not control their charges. Tamburlaine's inheritor we may expect to prove, as Yeats would have it, a mouse. The sway of mortality is complete. The ambivalent judgements end in nothing:

> For earth hath spent the pride of all her fruit,
> And heaven consum'd his choicest living fire.

*   *   *

In two plays, *The Massacre at Paris* and *Edward II*, Marlowe puts what we have called his characteristic structure of feeling to the test, not of legend or the liberties of the imagination, but of history. We wish to suggest that in *Edward II* Marlowe presents another but consistent version of unreconciled ambivalence.

Edward II has aroused a good deal of puzzlement. Critical debate divides over whether the play seriously tries to attract the audience's attention to general truths about the behaviour of individuals, or social groups, or the state itself. The argument has been over the extent to which the specific events on the stage lead out to more 'public' issues, as they do, for instance, in Shakespeare's history plays. Those who doubt Marlowe's seriousness in this respect include E. M. W. Tillyard, J. C. Maxwell, and J. B. Steane:

> In spite of [the] two political themes *Edward II* shows no prevailing political interest: no sense of any sweep or pattern of history. What animates the play is the personal theme.[9]

> The problem of the king and his 'favourites', which is primarily a political one for Shakespeare, assumes a disproportionate and independent psychological interest for Marlowe.[10]

> *Edward II* is narrowly personal: the people are small, and beyond them is nothing greater.[11]

On the other hand, Irving Ribner argues that:

> [In *Edward II*] the ends of tragedy and those of history [are] entirely fused, for Edward's sins are sins of government, the crisis he faces is a political one, and his disaster is not merely death but the loss of his crown and the ruin of his kingdom by civil war.[12]

And Professor Moelwyn Merchant has just published an introduction to the play, in the New Mermaid series,[13] which tries to show that *Edward II* is, after all, the history play which Tillyard says it is not. His most important and interesting point is that the action is given both thematic unity and wider relevance by the play's emblematic technique. Thus, the three anonymous men who meet Gaveston at the beginning show in a schematic way what values he represents; when Edward meets the mower (a conventional emblem for death), he 'proceeds to closer insights, both of his friends and of his own pitiful state' (p. xx);

---

[9] E. M. W. Tillyard, *Shakespeare's History Plays* (Peregrine Edition, 1962), p. 108.

[10] J. C. Maxwell, 'The Plays of Christopher Marlowe', in *The Age of Shakespeare*, ed. Boris Ford (Penguin Guide to English Literature No. 2, revised ed. 1956), p. 175.

[11] Steane, op. cit., p. 222.

[12] Irving Ribner, *The English History Play in the Age of Shakespeare* (Princeton, 1957), p. 124.

[13] *Edward II*, ed. Merchant (New Mermaid series, London, 1967), introduction. Other citations appear in the text.

Edward's death, the nature of which is suggested by Lightborn's prescription for a hot spit, recalls Edward's life: 'That suffering and death should bear an appropriate relation to sins committed is a commonplace of medieval thought, theological, literary or aesthetic' (p. xxi); Brecht is criticised for a 'notable failing' in his adaptation, where the death is 'evasively laconic' (p. xxi), in that Lightborn merely stabs Edward.

Professor Merchant's approach to *Edward II* roughly parallels what Professor Battenhouse did with *Tamburlaine*. One way in which he supports his argument that in *Tamburlaine* Marlowe was making a sustained, serious comment on the folly of ambition, is by showing that Marlowe added certain emblematic actions to criticise Tamburlaine. Tamburlaine throwing off his shepherd's clothes would suggest to the Elizabethan audience, which idealised the shepherd's existence and took seriously the type of Abel (as the first shepherd), and of Christ (as the Good Shepherd), that Tamburlaine was casting aside the lowly, meek, and good life. Tamburlaine tempting Theridimas with treasure would remind the audience of Satan tempting Christ with the kingdoms of the world.[14] Professor Merchant's approach to the emblems in *Edward II* is very interesting. If we take it that emblematic techniques tend to ritualise action—that is, to give it wider implications through providing a visual comment on it—then Merchant's discovery of a fabric of emblems in *Edward II* would give the play a consistency of authorial attitude never before established.

We should say here that we consider Professor Merchant's reading of the play to be one-sided, but that we think his point about the emblems in *Edward II* is irrefutable. In fact, we would like to take the point even further and construct a version of the play viewed, for the time being, exclusively through its emblematic, and other symbolic, events. The synthesis would go something like this:

Edward, as husband and king, has broken faith with God by slighting the two sacraments (public and private) in which he is involved: his kingship and his marriage. Gaveston, the reason for Edward breaking both these sacraments, gives an indication of his values when he meets the three men and, as a symbolic gesture, accepts the services of the traveller 'to wait at my trencher and tell me lies at dinner time' (I.i.31) but rejects the soldier and rider. In the course of the action Edward regains authority as both husband and king—but temporarily. When he

---

[14] Roy Battenhouse, *Marlowe's Tamburlaine, A Study in Renaissance Moral Philosophy* (Nashville, 1964), p. 151.

persuades Isabel to get Gaveston's deportation repealed, he is so grateful to her that he promises 'A second marriage 'twixt thy self and me' (I.iv.334), and when he makes war on the barons, and succeeds partially in punishing them for having killed Gaveston, he declares: 'Edward this day hath crowned him king anew' (III.iii.75). But both assertions are heavy with dramatic irony. In the first case because his very promise to Isabel celebrates the renewal of the cause of dissension between them, and in the second case because the success over the barons is muted by the thought of the queen still at large in France, and Mortimer's confident feeling that his hope still 'surmounts his fortune far' (III.iii. 73). The real truth is expressed—again, emblematically—by the barons' 'devices' prepared for the triumph which Edward plans to welcome Gaveston back from Ireland: the 'lofty cedar' with 'kingly eagles' on top with the canker creeping up the bark, the motto *Aeque Tandem*, and the bird seizing the flying fish, the motto *Undique mors est* (II.ii.15-28). Edward's decline has the inevitability of fate, which reinforces our impression that his downfall is the unavoidable effect of his political and moral failings; hence, the action is given a 'meaning' by being tied together causally in this way. He is betrayed by a mower, an emblem of death (IV.vi.46), his beard is shaved off in ditch water, as a visual statement that he is not a man, he is finally killed in a manner recalling his life-long perversion, and his assassin's name—fitting for one killing the anointed of God—is English for Lucifer.

So to summarise this scheme: the 'theme' of the play is the quality of Edward's attention to the sacraments of marriage and kingship: he fails by neglecting them; when he recovers his power temporarily, his revival is expressed in terms of the sacraments newly reassumed; when he dies, he is killed by a sort of anti-Christ in a ghastly anti-sacrament reminiscent of the sin and crime by which he broke both the sacraments he was sworn to uphold.

Yet we have only to outline such a synopsis to see how far short it falls of a complete description of our response to *Edward II*. The problem is that alongside the emblems and symbolic action, which indicates one kind of authorial attitude in one way, there are more realistic events which suggest other attitudes in other ways. It needs to be said here, though, that the mere mixture—by itself—of symbolic and realistic action is not what makes Marlowe's procedure so odd. Shakespeare does it in *1 Henry VI*, for instance, when a father who has killed his son and a son who has killed his father unite in a formal, antiphonal statement about the woes of civil war. But in Shakespeare the emblematic action reinforces the realistic action; both the symbolic and the realistic methods of exposition point to roughly the same 'meaning'. What distinguishes Marlowe's technique from Shakespeare's in this respect is that in *Edward II*, at least, the realistic and symbolic modes display different—even opposing—authorial attitudes to the action, so that if we attend exclusively to the symbolic action, we get one quite complete meaning, like the scheme outlined above, but if we pay attention to the more realistic action, we get a very different 'meaning'— or perhaps no meaning at all.

One cannot deny the Maxwell-Steane-Tillyard view of the play any more than one can deny Professor Merchant's account. The ambivalence of the barons' motives (very different from the ambiguity of Boling-broke in *Richard II*) is an important indication of Marlowe's double view. They are motivated both by concern for the good of the realm and by pride. Whenever they voice their concern for the country, the audience finds its attention directed to historical themes, but concern for their own status immediately deflects our attention away from these themes. Similarly, despite what the emblems may suggest of a 'meaning', what Edward actually makes of experience tends to undo any meaning. Marlowe does not choose to exploit the scenes in which Edward relinquishes his crown, or Edward is on the point of death, in the way that Shakespeare was to do with Richard II on similar occasions. When Richard is made to resign the crown he vacillates, and even displays some traces of childish posturing, but 'Ay, No, No ay' (as Miss Spurgeon reminds us) means much more than Yes, No, No yes. In the context, the double meaning suggests that Richard is being converted into a 'nothing' and raises the question of whether Richard can take decisions of this magnitude if he is nothing. At his death Richard is allowed the dignity not only of a fighting finish, but of full anagnoresis, in which he conceptualises the sins and crimes which led to his humilia-tion. By contrast Edward on resigning his crown merely vacillates, and the imminence of his death moves him to the realisation of nothing more than that he has to die, and even *that* fact he tries to defer, pathetically attempting to buy off Lightborn with a jewel. Hence our attention is riveted firmly on his personal predicament, and not, as in the case of *Richard II*, drawn to public themes.

Finally, the realistic action seems to conflict with what the emblems tell us in the matter of how Edward dies. This is rather tricky. The first point to note is that the 'punishment-fitting-the-crime' aspect of his death is not an invention of Marlowe's to add thematic unity to the play, but the literal truth as recorded in the chronicles. In other words, the taste for grim metaphysical appropriateness was that of Edward's murderers, not Marlowe, who softened the death at least to the extent of having Lightborn mention the hot spit only once and appear to concentrate his attention on the table, when he actually does the deed.

But the scene is horrible enough, even so. Later editors felt the need to soften it by adding a stage direction to the effect that Edward is killed by having a table placed over him, and Brecht and Feuchtwanger, as Professor Merchant notes, further soften the death by having Lightborn merely stab Edward. But is this natural-enough tendency to soften the death necessarily an evasion? It all depends on what is being evaded. It *is* an evasion of the oppressive 'realism' of the scene, but is the realism itself not confusing, both emotionally and intellectually?

Aristotle explains what he means by *mimesis* by reminding us that if we see 'obscene beasts' or 'corpses' in real life, we are horrified; if we see pictures of them, or other representations of them, we are delighted, to the extent that the art in question has represented the object accurately (*Poetics*, IV.3, Loeb, p. 13).[15] Our pleasure is that of relating thing and thing compared—in seeing the particular episode or object in the work of art related to life as we know it. But this is very different from seeing life itself. We come out of the theatre after having seen a tragedy saying not 'how horrible' but 'how true'. As Aristotle says, 'a poet's object is not to tell what actually happened but what could and would happen either probably or inevitably' (ibid., IX.1, Loeb, p. 35). This is also true of the history play, which is closely related to tragedy (as titles like *The Tragedy of King Richard the Second* suggest) since the facts of history, as known by all, are the 'tragic plot' of the history play, and any notions the audience gets about the historical process (in Shakespeare's histories, at least) are very like the general rules about fate with which the audience at a tragedy is presented.

If Brecht wanted to make *Edward II* into a play embodying a statement about the dialectic of history—as seems likely—then he may have sensed that at the end of *Edward II*, as Marlowe wrote it, we come out saying not 'how true' but 'how horrible'. This may have been his reason for changing the nature of the murder. Clifford Leech says that Brecht's changes in Marlowe's play (giving the barons credible motives

---

[15] We are not trying to 'judge' Marlowe in any other way against the canons of classical tragedy; Aristotle merely provides a convenient vocabulary for expressing our sense of how Marlowe differs from his contemporaries in this respect.

and softening Edward's death) 'diluted the sense of gratuitous, but profoundly intelligible horror'.[16] Exactly so. But *gratuitous* horror (i.e. inexplicable horror) is not the province of the history play (or the tragedy, as Aristotle knew it), in both of which *genres* the events must be related to an intelligible process of history or fate.

So we return to the old argument: the conventional view that *Edward II* concentrates on 'personal' events and cannot be called a history play, as Tillyard defines the term, opposed to the approach of Professor Merchant (similar to Professor Battenhouse's, but in regard to *Edward II*) that there is, after all, a consistent historical and public theme in the play, conveyed at least in part by the conceptualising emblems and other symbolic action. What we suggest is not that one or the other of these views is wrong, but that both have been so well demonstrated as to be irrefutable. The emblems are there, but we misunderstand them if we look for them to perform as similar techniques do in early Shakespeare history. That is, they do not ratify the realistic action. Instead, they act as false leads, promising a falsely comforting 'meaning' which is then discomfited in the realistic action. This is very different from saying that the play has no meaning beyond the personal stories of Edward, Isabel, and Mortimer. The undeniable presence of the emblems, together with their undeniable negation in the realistic action, poses a special case: it suggests a tone at once more pessimistic than Professor Merchant has suggested, and more universal, more general, than the conventional view holds. Here are all the guidelines by which a more conventional dramatist would indicate a meaning. Marlowe, however, shows us the clues only to negate the meaning. In this way he dramatises a gap between (on the one hand) all the official positions, the public motives, the apparent universal order, and (on the other hand) all the private prejudices, the selfish motives, the real universal chaos.

In *Tamburlaine* the emblems are sometimes posed more conventionally, but even there the author seems to invite his audience, at times, to view conventional associations with a certain detachment. Can we agree with Professor Battenhouse that the iconography of the Good Shepherd indicates a definite authorial attitude, when the characters in the play themselves play conventions off against one another as part of their argumentative tactics? When Cosroe hears that Tamburlaine is marching against him, he says:

[16] *Marlowe: A Collection of Critical Essays*, ed. Clifford Leech (Englewood Cliffs, N.J., 1964), p. 11.

> What means this devlish shepherd, to aspire
> With such a giantly presumption
> To cast up hills against the face of heaven,
> And dare the force of angry Jupiter?
>   (*I Tamb.*, II.vi.1–4)

The moral force of this remark, citing as it does a conventional emblem
for cosmic order, is neutralised not only by the realistic action (in this
case, Cosroe's own history as a usurper), but by Tamburlaine's blithe
use of the same emblem to suggest the opposite meaning, only a few
lines further on:

> The thirst of reign and sweetness of a crown,
> That caus'd the eldest son of heavenly Ops
> To thrust his doting father from his chair,
> And place himself in the imperial heaven,
> Mov'd me to manage arms against thy state.
> What better precedent than mighty Jove?
>   (Ibid., II.vii.12–17)

Even the powerful tableau of the dead Bajazeth and Zabena invites more
than one response. Zenocrate moralises the emblem as a *memento mori*,
reinforcing the lesson with her repeated 'Behold the Turk and his great
empress!' But she is answered by Anippe:

> Madam, content yourself, and be resolv'd,
> Your love hath fortune so at his command,
> That she shall stay and turn her wheel no more,
> As long as life maintains his mighty arm
> That fights for honour to adorn your head.
>   (*I Tamb.*, V.i.374–8)

From any objective standards of good rhetoric and sound moral values,
Anippe's case is the weaker; furthermore, she does not answer the
burden of Zenocrate's argument—that all men must die. Yet she does
have the last word in the discussion, which to an audience in the
theatre, hearing the speeches serially, gives some counterbalancing
weight to her interpretation of the emblem.

The 'emblem' of Bajazeth and his wife remains on stage through the
rest of Part I as a backdrop against which is viewed Tamburlaine's
victory over the king of Arabia, the Soldan and his daughter reunited,
and 'divine' Zenocrate is crowned queen of Persia. But what does the

mute emblem do—undercut the temporal glories by reminding us of the end of all mortal activity, or reinforce them by emphasising the distinctions between Tamburlaine's strength and other kings' weakness? It all depends on whether you choose to believe Zenocrate's or Anippe's interpretation.

This use of the emblem is surely different from Shakespeare's in the early histories. In Marlowe the distinction between metaphor and fact is sometimes blurred; Tamburlaine really harnesses the two kings to his chariot; the mower is not only a *memento mori*, but the actual instrument of Edward's arrest; at the end of *The Jew of Malta* our attention is drawn both to the emblem of Barabas in the cauldron, and the ropes and pulleys by which the device operates. In Shakespeare the division is clear: when Henry VI joins the lamenting father and son, he ceases to speak as he does in the more realistic parts of the play and instead fits his language to the almost liturgical pattern of proposition and response which gives the scene its special status as formal comment. Perhaps this is why, in Shakespeare, the emblem communicates directly to the audience a certain truth about the action (as is conventional), whereas in *Tamburlaine*, at least, the emblem is distanced from us to the extent that we can see others (the characters in the play) discussing it, manipulating it, becoming another audience, as it were, between us and the emblem itself.

If in *Tamburlaine* the emblem gains a certain neutrality by being distanced in this way, in *Edward II* it provides a false lead promising a consistent authorial attitude which is then negated. Both processes—in *Tamburlaine* and *Edward II*—are methods of distancing the emblem, and hence of neutralising meanings which the emblem would conventionally convey. In each case the audience's response is balanced in uncertainty between opposing attitudes: in *Tamburlaine* because it cannot react 'for' or 'against' the hero, in *Edward II* because it is forced to undergo a process of expectation and disappointment. In each case ambivalence is unresolved; the plays function as models of absurdity.

Marlowe and Early Shakespeare

HAROLD F. BROOKS

Marlowe and Early Shakespeare

ANYONE WHO UNDERTAKES to talk about the relation between early plays of Shakespeare and the plays of Marlowe, is entering a discussion which is of long standing, and bound to continue. I do not pretend to have read all the relevant contributions on Marlowe, and who will claim to have done the like for Shakespeare? Even so far as my own thinking is concerned, most of this paper will be an interim report. If anywhere it is something more, that will result from my special interests in types of drama with differing conventions; in medieval drama; in *Richard III*; and in the Restoration period. My subject is not easily separable from a bigger one, the place of Marlowe in the English dramatic tradition; and I shall attempt some comments on both.

Round about 1930, the young Oxford student, Harold Brooks, knew quite well the place of Christopher Marlowe in the English dramatic tradition. If means existed by which he might have learned better, he was not aware of them. His one doubt (recently acquired, and with a bit of a shock) was whether perhaps *The Spanish Tragedy* might not have preceded *Tamburlaine*. That left him uncertain whether Marlowe had indeed been the first to take blank verse on to the public stage, and to make of it a dramatic vehicle less inflexible than it had been in *Gorboduc*. With the possibility that Hieronymo came before Tamburlaine, the young man should have extended his doubts to another of Marlowe's priorities, but he did not. It was agreed, he continued to suppose, that Marlowe had rediscovered the true secret of giving unity to a serious drama, by restoring the supremacy of one character, the protagonist, as it had existed in the practice and Aristotelian theory of Greek tragedy. As W. D. Briggs wrote in his introduction to *Marlowe's Edward II* (1914), Marlowe in Tamburlaine 'not merely provided a central figure, but actually centralized the interest' (pp. xcii f.). This was particularly needful because one of the chief types of play at the time, the English chronicle history, was virtually an amorphous affair, and remained so up to *Edward II* itself. Among these amorphous plays were the three parts of *Henry VI*, and the sources of the second and third parts: *The . . . Contention betwixt the two famous Houses of Yorke and Lancaster*, and *The true Tragedie of Richard Duke of Yorke*. 'Poets', says Briggs,

> coming fresh to the dramatisation of their country's history, appeared [not to feel] the necessity . . . of attempting to introduce more than a semblance of order into the chaos of dramatic material supplied by the chronicles, [or] of looking below the surface of events.

Edward II, then, was what Tucker Brooke had already called it, 'the first considerable history play in the English language'.[1] It was the first, one was encouraged to think, in which the facts as given in the chronicles were re-arranged and even altered in order to create a coherent drama. Before then, one was led to assume, the playwrights had merely taken the events of a king's reign or comparable period, and presented these in a succession of scenes governed only by the chronological sequence of the chronicle-source. They made, in their ignorance, a mistake resembling in principle the one stigmatised by Aristotle in 'all the poets who have written a *Heracleid*, a *Theseid*, or similar poems' and who supposed 'that, because Heracles was one man, the story also of Heracles must be one story'.[2] They never asked themselves whether the reign of their chosen king had unity of action. Ignorant of Aristotelian principles, some of which Marlowe divined for himself, these dramatists would have scoffed at Sidney's, if they had had the chance to read in manuscript his strictures on the 'mungrell Tragy-comedie'[3] of their immediate predecessors. They continued the line of the 'play in two tones', with its ill-synchronised double action of kings and clowns. But *Edward II*, even more completely than *Tamburlaine*, banished

> . . . such conceits as clownage keepes in pay.

In those plays of which he was sole author, Marlowe demonstrated that even when written for the public stage, serious drama could dispense with the low comedy so much favoured by the barbarous taste of the popular audience. That taste was still very much what it had been in the middle ages; and the medieval drama of mistery cycles, saints' plays, and moralities, with its successors the Tudor moral interludes,

---

[1] *The Works of Christopher Marlowe* (Oxford, 1910), p. 308. I shall quote Marlowe from this edition.

[2] *Poetics*, Bywaters' translation, ed. W. Hamilton Fyfe (1940), p. 24.

[3] Sir Philip Sidney, *An Apologie for Poetrie* (1595, written *c.* 1580), ed. E. S. Shuckburgh (1891), p. 54.

belonged (so one gathered) to the prehistory of English drama, before its real history began in the age of Lyly, Peele, Greene, Kyd, and Marlowe himself.

For the neo-classical French critic, 'Enfin Malherbe vint'.[4] In the university of my youth, from men of classical education, I got a strong impression that, as regards plays other than comedies, 'Enfin Marlowe vint'.[5]

Nowadays, the picture we form is different. To begin with, *Edward II* does not keep its old pride of place; the history of the chronicle-history play has been rewritten. Earlier, those who traced it, F. E. Schelling (*The English Chronicle Play*, 1902) as well as Briggs among them, were badly handicapped by knowing nothing of Bad Quartos. They could not take into account the memorial transmission and re-vamping which evidently intervened—and at any time up to the date of publication—between the lost original texts and the extant printed versions of such plays as Peele's *Edward I*, or the anonymous *Famous Victories of Henry V*, *True Tragedy of Richard III*, and *Troublesome Reign of King John*.[6] Worst of all, since they could not recognise as such the Bad Quartos of *2* and *3 Henry VI*, they naturally regarded them as independent compositions, collaborations by several authors, subsequently revised into a partly Shakespearean form as printed in the First Folio. Alexander's proofs, in 1929, that they were derivative versions of *2* and *3 Henry VI*,[7] opened the way to a new placing and a new understanding of those plays, and *1 Henry VI* with them. Thanks to Harold Jenkins' article, 'Shakespeare's History Plays: 1900–1951',[8] I need not recapitulate how the opportunity was taken. Two observations will serve our purpose.

The first goes back to the evidence brought by Charlton and Waller, in 1933, to support what was then 'the almost revolutionary suggestion'[9] that *Edward II* was influenced by Shakespeare. In 1946, the case was furthered by Rossiter's argument that Marlowe's play owed something to *Woodstock*, and *Woodstock* to *2 Henry VI*.[10] F. P. Wilson, in *Marlowe and the Early Shakespeare* (1953), authoritatively endorsed the newer

[4] Boileau, *L'Art Poétique*, i.131.
[5] I am conscious that the impressions sketched may not always have been what my mentors hoped to convey.
[6] Cf., e.g., L. Kirschbaum, 'A Census of Bad Quartos', *R.E.S.*, XIV.
[7] *Shakespeare's Henry VI and Richard III*.
[8] In *Shakespeare Survey*, 6 (1953), especially pp. 4–11.
[9] Jenkins, op. cit., p. 7.
[10] A. P. Rossiter (ed.), *Woodstock[:] A Moral History* (1946).

view (p. 105), so that Nicholas Brooke, writing eight years later in *Shakespeare Survey*, can assume general acceptance of the judgement that Marlowe learnt from *Henry VI*, and Shakespeare reclaimed the debt in *Richard II* (No. 14, 1961, p. 34).

Meanwhile—and this is my second observation—the *Henry VI* plays themselves had been revalued. Those of us who saw them staged by Sir Barry Jackson[11] in the early 'fifties, at the Birmingham Rep. or the Old Vic, were left in no doubt of their theatrical impact and dramatic unity. And already in *Shakespeare's History Plays* (1944), E. M. W. Tillyard, garnering the fruits of study by himself and others,[12] had re-estimated for a wide public not only the *Henry VI/Richard III* cycle, but also the sources and tradition behind it. One could no longer suppose, with Briggs, that the materials on which the dramatist worked were chaotic. Behind *Henry VI* lay the shaping concepts of Hall's Chronicle and *The Mirror for Magistrates*, and the form of the Tudor Morality plays on religious politics. Attention once focused on these Tudor Interludes,[13] it became easy to see that, like them, Shakespeare's cycle was a drama of ideas. The recognition was helped, no doubt, by our familiarity with the modern drama of ideas in Ibsen, Shaw, and the rest. It corrected Briggs' error when he found in *1 Henry VI* no 'looking beneath the surface of events'; Shakespeare is, in fact, much more concerned with political thinking than Marlowe is in *Edward II*. Another result was to explode the notion that the history-play was waiting for Marlowe to rediscover the grand central protagonist, and so at last to give it unity. For an idea, protagonist or no protagonist, can obviously constitute the unifying centre of a play. Examined without prejudice, *1*, *2*, and *3 Henry VI* are found to have the unity of a pattern (quite a common sort of pattern) in which the centre is un-occupied, but is unmistakable because the parts that make up the design are all balanced about it. In creating this pattern, and turning history into drama, Shakespeare from the start no less than Marlowe after him, takes liberties with the facts as he knew them. Finally—the point is a very familiar one—it looks as if Marlowe's modification in *Edward II* of his prevailing manner were in response to Shakespeare. Even while drawing inspiration from *Tamburlaine*, Shakespeare, as W. H. Clemen has said, knew how to tone down the extravagance of its

[11] 'On Producing *Henry VI*', *Shakespeare Survey*, 6 (1953), pp. 49–52, is his own commentary on part of this experience.
[12] For whom see Jenkins, op. cit., pp. 7–9.
[13] As by A. P. Rossiter, *English Drama from Early Times to the Elizabethans* (1950), ch. VIII; see especially pp. 115, 122.

forceful utterance.[14] And the symmetric structure so vital to his drama depended on his ability to dispose characters in groups and to exploit the groupings. It is in these directions that *Edward II*, like *Henry VI*, differs from *Doctor Faustus*, and even *The Jew of Malta*; and most of all from *Tamburlaine*. Edward was not written for Alleyne; the play was destined for Pembroke's Men, a company then perhaps Shakespeare's. That may be a principal reason why Marlowe did not build it almost wholly on the protagonist, who here depends closely on the support (dramatically speaking) of the groupings of secondary characters, a number of them well developed.[15] Concordantly, with a few exceptions, the vehemence of style is diminished, even to the muting of Marlowe's poetry.

In itself, *Edward II* is still to be admired no less than before; but its place as supposedly the first considerable English historical drama belongs in truth to *Henry VI*. F. P. Wilson went so far as to wonder whether in the earliest of the *Henry VI* plays Shakespeare did not begin the genre, and its vogue (to which Nashe bears witness in 1592), on the popular stage. In doubting Shakespeare's priority, I am not going to raise the ghost, so well laid by Wilson and Rossiter, of the ill-made chronicle-history play.[16] No dramatist put, or was likely to put, a mere chronological sequence of scenes upon the stage. To say nothing of precedent in the medieval dramatisations of narrative and the Tudor political Interlude, theatre and its patrons require more. And like the Bad Quarto of *Edward I* (which may be contemporary with *Henry VI*),[17] the extant texts of the *Famous Victories* and *The True Tragedy of Richard III* are not safe guides to the original defects of those works, considerable as they no doubt were. But if Tarleton, clown of the Queen's Men, made a hit in the *Famous Victories*, then it existed in some form before his death in 1588.[18] *The Troublesome Reign of King John* and the anonymous *Richard III*, were also Queen's plays. Several passages of the first and one scene of the second, surviving in the Bad Quartos, are in fourteeners or the remains of fourteeners, and belong presumably to early versions, quite likely prior to *Tamburlaine*.

---

[14] *English Tragedy before Shakespeare*, tr. T. S. Dorsch (1961), p. 125.
[15] P. Alexander, op. cit. (see index under 'Pembroke's Men'); and his *Shakespeare's Life and Art* (1939), pp. 55–7, 82.
[16] Cf. F. P. Wilson, op. cit., pp. 105–8; A. P. Rossiter (ed.), *Woodstock*, pp. 9 f.
[17] Irving Ribner, *The English History Play in the Age of Shakespeare* (1957), p. 89.
[18] F. P. Wilson, op. cit., pp. 106 f., comments however on the shakiness of the evidence.

Was *Edward II*, though following *Henry VI*, written before Shakespeare completed his tetralogy with *Richard III*? If so, it might be responsible for Shakespeare's new plan of combining a Marlovian protagonist with the method he had so far favoured. On the contrary, *Edward II*, I believe we can show, was indebted to *Richard III*.[19] The most cogent argument for the priority of *Henry VI* was that 'the two passages in Part II and the one in Part III which resemble passages in *Edward II* were . . . suggested to Shakespeare by the chronicles for the reigns of Henry VI and Edward IV, whereas there are no corresponding passages in the chronicles of Edward II's reign which might have suggested these passages to Marlowe' (Wilson, p. 105, citing Rossiter). Similarly, certain features of *Edward II* have no source unless in some account of Richard's usurpation. Outside Marlowe, Mortimer is not styled Protector, nor spoken of as a possible threat to the life of young Edward. Marlowe clearly knew the speech in *3 Henry VI* where Margaret sees the new-made Protector, York, as a threat to the life of Henry; and the like is falsely alleged of Duke Humphrey, Protector in *2 Henry VI*, by his enemies.[20] It is neither of these Protectors, however, but the Protector Richard of Gloucester, whom Mortimer resembles in Marlowe's play but not in the chronicles, in taking supreme power only after pretended reluctance. Again, the sources know nothing of the boy king's protest when Mortimer condemns his uncle Kent; but the boy Edward V's protest when Richard arrests Rivers and Grey, his 'uncles', is historical.[21]

As belonging to Richard's history, all these features were available to Marlowe in More's narrative, printed in Holinshed and elsewhere. But what chiefly complicates the argument is their presence in *The True Tragedy of Richard III* (1594) so that Marlowe might have found them in the pre-Shakespearean play, provided that to this extent the Bad Quarto affords true evidence of what it contained. Some link certainly exists between the *True Tragedy* and *Edward II*. Its version of Edward V's protest at the arrest of Grey is closer than any to Edward III's protest at the arrest of Kent—much closer than Shakes-

---

[19] The suggestion has been made in A. S. Cairncross (ed.) *1 Henry VI* (1962), xxxvii. Note Irving Ribner's opinion, op. cit., p. 127 n. 3, that in *Richard III* 'there is . . . little Marlovian quality . . . which cannot be attributed to the influence of *Tamburlaine*'. I should add *The Jew of Malta*.

[20] *3 Henry VI*, I.i.237 ff. (see below, p. 76 citing *Edward II*, 970); *2 Henry VI*, I.i.162–4, III.i.20–37, 173–5, 248–56 (new Arden edns.).

[21] Cf. *Edward II*, 2387 ff., 2423 ff.; *Richard III* (New Cambridge Shakespeare), III.vii.45–236; III.i.6–16.

peare's version; and there is a clear verbal parallel. Edward V's words (in prose):

Well since I cannot command I wil intreat[22]

may be the source of Edward III's lines:

and yet me thinkes I should commaund,
But seeing I cannot, ile entreate for him.
(Edward II, 2429 f.)

Alternatively, the compilers of the Bad Quarto may have caught it up from Marlowe, and indeed have followed him in the whole passage. In view of the fragments from Marlowe (including *Edward II*) incorporated in the reported text of *2 Henry VI*, and perhaps in the vamped-up *Troublesome Reign*,[23] and from *Edward II* in the Bad Quarto *Massacre at Paris*, this seems the likely explanation.

But whether or not *Edward II* draws on the pre-Shakespearean *Richard III*, there is little doubt that it draws on Shakespeare's. The crucial lines are Mortimer's, describing how he became Protector:

They thrust vpon me the Protectorship,
And sue to me for that that I desire,
While at the councell table, graue enough,
And not vnlike a bashfull puretaine,
First I complaine of imbecilitie,
Saying it is, *onus quam grauissimum*,
Till being interrupted by my friends,
Suscepi that *prouinciam* as they terme it,
And to conclude, I am Protector now.
(Edward II, 2387–95)

For our purpose, the crucial phrase is the comparison to 'a bashfull puretaine'. The mock Puritan Richard exists, I believe, nowhere but in Shakespeare's *Richard III*, where, for example, he plays the saint with the help of Scripture maxims, claims the unworldly innocence of a new-born infant, and thanks his God for his humility. More drew Richard as a play-actor, and gave the hint to Shakespeare when he called him 'a

[22] Malone Society Reprint, ed. W. W. Greg (1929), ll. 747 ff., 754.
[23] See A. S. Cairncross (ed.) *2 Henry VI* (new Arden), pp. 184 f.; P. Alexander, *Shakespeare's Henry VI and Richard III*, pp. 93 ff.; H. 'J. Oliver (ed.), *Dido Queen of Carthage* and *The Massacre at Paris* (1968), lv–lx, especially lvi f., and Rupert Taylor, 'A Tentative Chronology of Marlowe's and some other Elizabethan Plays', *PMLA*, 51 (1936), 643 ff. (to be used with caution).

deepe dissembler, lowlie of countenance'. He also told of Richard's attempt to give a providential air to the pre-arranged moment of his arrival at Dr Shaa's sermon.[24] There is nothing of any such traits in *The True Tragedy*; even when the Page reports that Shaa's sermon 'hath pleased my Lord', nothing is said of the bungled plan for a 'Providential' incident.[25] In *The Mirror for Magistrates*, Shakespeare would read a general reflection on the wickedness of the world as illustrated by the fatal council to which Hastings was summoned by Richard and Buckingham:

> Religions cloake some one to vyce doth chuse,
> And maketh god protectour of his cryme.
>
> (ed. L. B. Campbell, 1938, p. 282)

Here, and in More, is almost all the prompting Shakespeare seems to have had for his depiction of a sanctimonious Richard. I say 'almost', because he may have been encouraged by *The Jew of Malta*: the pretended conversion of Barabas (l. 1557 ff.) was precedent for a display of false piety by a Machiavellian. The precedent was there, even more obviously, for Marlowe: and may well have encouraged, in turn, the assimilation of Mortimer to Shakespeare's Richard. But is it not, then, possible that Mortimer owes his touch of the 'bashful Puritan' wholly to Barabas, his lineal predecessor? It seems most unlikely: Barabas' 'conversion' does not strike that particular note. Still less can one suppose that from the tenuous hints in More and the *Mirror*, which unlike Shakespeare he had no special reason to ponder, Marlowe added to Mortimer's self-description a characteristic which is never illustrated in the play, and never mentioned again. The natural conclusion is that Mortimer's lines reflect in epitome the climax of Richard's posing; the scene where, standing between two Bishops, he is pressed by his friend Buckingham to accept the crown, says nay, and takes it (III.vii.94–236; cf. 46–51).

The priority of *Richard III* being now, I hope, granted, Marlowe's epitomising from this scene can be shown. Richard begins by affecting to reject the 'sovereignty', the 'yoke' which the deputation, he protests, 'would here impose on me'. 'They thrust upon me the Protectorship', crows Mortimer, whose 'first' feigned objection was, like Richard's, his own 'imbecilitie' or incapacity. 'My desert', Richard bashfully avers,

Unmeritable shuns your high request.

[24] Holinshed's Chronicle (1587), III.712 b, l. 13; 727b–728a.
[25] ed. cit., ll. 908 ff.

Again and again he returns to this disclaimer. He is 'a bark to brook no mighty sea', his 'defects' are 'so mighty and so many', his 'poverty of spirit' is 'so much', that he is 'unfit for state and majesty'; he lacks a great deal of what it would require to help the king's lieges. Mortimer's second objection, that the Protectorship would be '*onus quam grauis-simum*', corresponds to another of Richard's, repeated more than once; kingship is a 'load', a 'burthen', a 'yoke', a 'care' that it is proposed to 'heap' on him, or 'buckle' on his back. Richard avows that

> . . . God he knows, and you may partly see
> How far I am from the desire of this.

Mortimer too can congratulate himself on having dissimulated his desire: 'They . . . sue to me', he tells us, 'for that that I desire'; and this, of course, is what the deputation do to Richard:

> *Mayor:* Do, good my lord, your citizens entreat you.
> *Buckingham:* Refuse not, mighty lord, this proferr'd love—

with Catesby chiming in:

> O, make them joyful, grant their lawful suit![26]

Again, in the scene in *Richard III* where the boy-king protests at the arrest of his uncles, Richard a little later twice comments on his precocity:

> So wise so young, they say, do ne'er live long

and

> Short summers lightly have a forward spring (III.i.79, 94)

The comments, in view of Richard's schemes and the boy's fate, are extremely pertinent; and while they are not in the sources, their point depends on the historical situation which the sources gave. Presumably they suggested to Marlowe Isabel's foreboding for her son, not closely germane to the situation at the moment in his play, and not fulfilled:

> A boye, this towardnes makes thy mother feare
> Thou art not markt to many daies on earth. (l. 1387 ff.)

Not that the borrowing is idle. It helps authenticate Isabel's affection; provides dramatic irony, since her son's rapid maturing is to be her

[26] The Shakespearean quotations are from III.vii.146 f.; 154 f., 159-62, 166, 205; 146, 204, 228-30; 235 f.; 201-3. At 235 I prefer the Quarto reading.

downfall, not his; and anticipates his own fears for his safety when Mortimer condemns Kent, the crisis which prepares his decisive revulsion at his father's murder. Both Marlowe and Shakespeare, of course, are utilising proverbs,[27] which they would know independently: but this does not affect the argument; it is not in doubt that one of them knew the other's play, and hence had met with this use of the proverbial notion there.

In considering parallels, the difference of criteria appropriate to different situations is not always sufficiently recognised. Apart from the parallels themselves, there may be no evidence of any connection between the two works. The severest of criteria must then be satisfied. So too with evident debts which might be in either direction. But if debt and its direction has once been established, then a class of parallels unusable before becomes useful: the parallels which bear in themselves no sign of which author was the borrower, but now this is known, testify to more of his borrowings. Finally, while ideas and expressions very familiar at the time can constitute no good evidence of indebtedness, yet if we can be sure our author knew a particular work, his employment even of the same commonplaces is not negligible. For that is at least one relevant place where he had met them. In *Edward II* Marlowe has at least two widely familiar images he had met with in Shakespeare's tetralogy. Lamenting the murder of the two Princes, their mother, in *Richard III*, complains:

> Wilt thou, O God, fly from such gentle lambs,
> And throw them in the entrails of the wolf? (IV.iv.22 ff.)

In the scene where Edward II resigns the throne, he thinks of his son, in the power of Mortimer, as 'a lambe, encompassed by Woolues' (l. 2027). But here Marlowe, there is little doubt, is recollecting *3 Henry VI*, where the king, having resigned his heir's right to the throne and submitted to make York Protector, is described as a 'lamb environed with wolves'. For that line follows next but two after

> Stern Falconbridge commands the narrow seas,
> (I.i.246, 249, new Arden edition)

the accepted source of Marlowe's

> The hautie *Dane* commands the narrow seas.
> (*Edward II*, 970)

---

[27] M. P. Tilley, *A Dictionary of the Proverbs in England in the Sixteenth and Seventeenth Centuries* (1950), L 384, F 774.

Possibly Marlowe's lamb is 'encompassed' not 'environed', because he
conflated 'the lamb environed with wolves' and the 'bear, encompass'd
round with dogs', a few scenes later in Shakespeare's play (II.i.15).
My second instance is an emblematic image: Mortimer's device of the
cedar, the eagle, and the canker. Cedar and eagle, the recognised
sovereigns of the evergreen trees and the birds, are coupled both in
Richard III:

> Our aery buildeth in the cedar's top (I.iii.264)

and *3 Henry VI*:

> Thus yields the cedar to the axe's edge,
> Whose arms gave shelter to the princely eagle: (V.ii.11 f.)

compare Mortimer's cedar

> On whose top-branches Kinglie Eagles pearch. (l. 819)

The eagles and the stock variant for the canker, the drone, are in
2 Henry VI: 'Drones suck not eagles blood', alluding to the story that
they did, for which see Lyly's *Endimion* and Mouffet's *Theater of
Insects* (cited by E. A. Armstrong)[28] and *The Mirror for Magistrates*.[29]
    Adjustment of priority between *Edward II* and Shakespeare's four
plays does not upset the dates to which in orthodox opinion they can
be assigned. It merely helps to fix *Richard III* in 1591. Along with
Henry VI, *Richard III* draws on the 1587 editions of Holinshed and
The Mirror for Magistrates; while *3 Henry VI* aroused Greene's
jealousy before his death on 3 September 1592. About the same time,
Nashe expressed his enthusiasm for Talbot scenes which are probably
those of *1 Henry VI*.[30] It is interesting that so many of the lessons he
found in the drama, and above all (it appears) in history-plays, could
have impressed him particularly in *Henry VI*, *Richard III*, and
Edward II: the 'stratagems of warre' in *1 Henry VI* (though also in
Tamburlaine and *The Jew of Malta*); 'the ill successe of treason' in the
rest; 'the miserie of ciuill dissention' in them all,[31] and 'the fall of hastie
climbers' likewise, but especially in Mortimer's speech on Fortune's
wheel (ll. 2627 ff.). 'All cunning driftes ouer-guylded with outward
holinesse' may even refer specifically to Richard, unless Nashe had in

---

[28] Cf. A. S. Cairncross's edn., IV.i.108 n.
[29] ed. cit., p. 274 (Hastings, l. 166).
[30] Cf. A. S. Cairncross (ed.), *1 Henry VI* (new Arden), p. xxxi.
[31] Not forgetting Lodge, *The Wounds of Civil War* (? 1587/8).

mind the aliases assumed by Vice-characters in the Moral Interludes, or Barabas and his 'conversion'.[32] However this may be, within the wider limits of 1587 to summer 1592, Shakespeare's tetralogy most probably falls in 1590–1, after the publication of *The Faerie Queene* Books I–III in 1590, and before that of the vamped text of *The Troublesome Reign* in 1591, which seems to have picked up phrases from *Richard III* as well as *2, 3 Henry VI*.[33]

No one doubts that *Edward II* came late in Marlowe's career, cut short on 30 May 1593.[34] His career in the drama perhaps did not continue beyond January, when *The Massacre at Paris* was 'ne' for Henslowe. During the rest of his life, the theatres were closed because of plague; one imagines him working at *Hero and Leander* rather than for the paralysed London stage. The *Massacre* most likely was new when Henslowe produced it; in the well-considered opinion of its most recent editor, 'Proof of a 1592 date is impossible: the presumption is strong'.[35] If *Doctor Faustus* also belongs to 1592, being composed (as Greg concludes probable) after the first edition of its source came out about May,[36] there is not much room for *Edward II* later than spring of that year. A date then of very late in 1591 would fit the influence upon Marlowe's play of Shakespeare's tetralogy, and the influence which, in turn, it is reasonably supposed to have had on Kyd's *Solyman and Perseda* (registered for publication 20 November 1592). Shakespeare himself owed a debt to the dramatisation of Edward's sufferings when he narrated the vengeance on Pinch in *The Comedy of Errors*. Marlowe read in Stowe's chronicle how Edward was shaved, under duress, 'with a basen of colde water taken out of the ditch'. In the play, Edward protests:

> . . . what will you murther me,
> Or choake your soueraigne with puddle water? (2294–5)

Matrevis demands 'Why striue you thus?' and '*They wash him* [so runs

---

[32] *Pierce Penilesse his Supplication to the Divell* (1592); published *c.* 8 September, written June/August—so R. B. McKerrow, *The Works of Thomas Nashe* (1904–10), IV.77 f.; text, I.213. Nashe's references are not merely general: 'to prove every one of these allegations could I propound the circumstances of this play and that play'.

[33] A. S. Cairncross (ed.), *3 Henry VI*, xliii–xlv.

[34] e.g. Charlton and Waller (edd.), *Edward II* (1933), p. 20, argue for composition in autumn 1591, first London production December 1592.

[35] H. J. Oliver, op. cit. (1968), p. lii.

[36] I am not wedded to this date for *Doctor Faustus*. Cf. Harold Jenkins' review of Greg, *MLR*, XLVI (1951), 85–6.

the stage-direction] *with puddle water, and shaue his beard away'*. Later, in his dungeon, Edward declares he has had to stand 'in mire and puddle' (2507). Shakespeare employs a messenger to report the assault on Pinch,

> Whose beard they have sing'd off with brands of fire,
> And ever as it blaz'd, they threw on him
> Great pails of puddled mire to quench the hair.
>
>   (V.i.171–3, new Arden edition)

The fire appears to come from a threat in the *Menaechmi* (at least in Warner's version)[37] to put out the wife's eyes with a burning lamp; but Shakespeare's regular sources for the *Comedy* gave him no other cue, and certainly nothing about 'puddled mire'. Besides, he has remembered the same episode from Marlowe at the point where Pinch gave the offence which is thus revenged. At Pinch's instance, *'three or four'*, says the stage-direction, *'offer to bind'* Antipholus the husband; *'he strives'*, and cries out in the same words as Edward, 'What, will you murder me?' (IV.iv.104, S.D., 107). The phrase is a commonplace; but in this collocation, evidential. Shakespeare's indebtedness provides a valuable check on the earliest date for the *Comedy*; and as there is a good though not watertight case for actually placing the *Comedy* late in 1592,[38] it harmonises with our hypothesis of 1592 or the end of 1591 for *Edward II*.

When we leave *Edward II* and the history-play, what I took in my youth for the established views on Marlowe stand, perhaps, in less need of correction. I shall not be suggesting Shakespearean influence on *Tamburlaine* and *The Jew of Malta*. I regard their impact, and that of *The Spanish Tragedy*, on Elizabethan drama and not least on Shakespeare, as something it would be hard indeed to exaggerate. Still, one has to bear in mind that Marlowe's influence co-existed with others, that of *The Spanish Tragedy* among them; though I am pleased to see that Philip Edwards is urging us not to date Kyd's play too early.[39] A historian has no business, of course, with hopes, where unknown facts are concerned; but I hope *The Spanish Tragedy* is close to *The Jew of Malta* and prior to *Titus Andronicus*: say in 1589. To take an obvious example of the sort of multiple influence I am speaking of: *Titus*

---

[37] R. A. Foakes (ed.), *The Comedy of Errors*, V.i.183 n.
[38] R. A. Foakes, op. cit., pp. xviii–xx.
[39] He favours 1590, but early enough for *3 Henry VI* to borrow from it—see his Revels edition (1959), pp. xxvi f.

Andronicus as a tragedy of revenge, and the theme of vengeance which is vital to *Henry VI* and *Richard III*, have behind them, no doubt, *The Spanish Tragedy, The Jew of Malta*, Seneca, and Ovid.

Further, Marlowe's influence itself does not consist simply in his innovations. He is also transmitting influences from more than one tradition: from the classics on the one hand, for example, and from the native medieval drama on the other. E. M. Waith and others before him have rightly related Tamburlaine to the hero of Seneca's *Hercules Oetaeus*;[40] no less rightly he is recognised as a descendant of the Herods, Pilates, and Caesar Augustuses of the Mistery Plays. Harry Levin makes a particularly happy comparison of him to the Herod of the Wakefield Master, whose entrance is prepared by a vaunt stuffed with the names of countries and cities marking the extent of his dominion.[41] If I were seeking the antecedents of Marlowe's high astounding terms, I should explore Seneca and Lucan, Ovid and Virgil, but also the aureate diction concentrated by fifteenth-century poets out of Chaucer. Here, in one of those self-introductory gabs of which the type is continued by Richard III and the Guise, is Saul before he became Paul:

> Most dowtyd man I am lyuyng upon the ground,
> goodly besene with many a riche garlement.
> My pere on lyue, I trow ys nott found,
> thorow the world, fro the oryent to the occydent,
> my fame ys best knowyn vnder the firmament;
> I am most drad of pepull vnyuersall,
> they dare not dysp[l] ease [me] most noble.

> Saul ys my name, I wyll that ye notyfy,
> which conspyreth the dyscyplys with thretes and menaces;
> be-fore the prynces of prestes most hye and noble,
> I bryng them to punyshement for ther trespace . . .

> By the god bellyall, I schall make progresse
> Vnto the princes both Caypha and Anna,
> wher I schall aske of them in suernes,
> To persue thorow all dammask and lib[y]a . . .[42]

---

[40] *The Herculean Hero* (1962), pp. 63–85 *passim*, especially 63 f., 82–5.

[41] *Christopher Marlowe: The Overreacher* (1954, 1965), p. 49; A C. Cawley (ed.), *The Wakefield Pageants* (1958), p. 65.

[42] *The Conversion of St. Paul*, ll. 15 f. in *The Digby Plays*, ed. F. J. Furnivall, E.E.T.S.e.s. LXX (1896, 1930), pp. 27 f.

Besides the geographical and other proper names, the polysyllables at the end of lines and the occasional 'Gallic inversion' (as in 'pepull vnyuersall') are features of Marlowe's soaring style. For a brief example of his polysyllables, take this from *Tamburlaine*:

> Vntill the Persean Fleete and men of war
> Sailing along the Orientall sea,
> Haue fetcht about the Indian continent:
> Euen from *Persepolis* to *Mexico*,
> And thence vnto the straightes of *Iubalter*:
> Where they shall meete, and ioine their force in one,
> Keeping in aw the Bay of *Portingale*.

In the same scene he has the 'Gallic inversion' 'Serpents venomous'.[43] I am fortunate in my instance, for T. W. Craik points out to me that the identical piece of heightened diction is used by Robert Henryson, the fifteenth-century Scots Chaucerian, in *Orpheus and Eurydice*:

> Scho strampit on a serpent vennemus.[44]

Speeches of particular kinds, such as the schemer's soliloquy employed by Barabas, Guise, Lorenzo, Aaron, Richard III, Iago, and Edmund, or the soliloquy of inner conflict or agony (though not at the pitch of Faustus' last hour) have their precedents in Seneca and Ovid.[45] But the same two types of soliloquy, naturally enough, are the earliest in English drama. Here in York were spoken the soliloquies of Christ in Gethsemane, founded on the Agony in Scripture, and the typical villain's soliloquies of Diabolus before tempting him in the wilderness, and of Judas deciding to betray him.[46]

Some important dramatic motifs in Shakespeare and Marlowe are specifically from the medieval tradition. Richard II's image of death, who 'with a little pin Bores through (the) castle wall, and farewell King';

[43] Part I, 1350–6; 1203 cf. 'truce inviolable', *2 Tamburlaine* 2467, 'League Inviolable', *3 Henry VI*, II.i.30.

[44] l. 105, repeated *verbatim* at 124.

[45] Types of set speech, and their history in Elizabethan drama up to the advent of Shakespeare, are a central subject of W. H. Clemen's invaluable *English Tragedy before Shakespeare* (1955, tr. 1961). For Seneca, see his index. Dryden (*Essays*, ed. W. P. Ker, I. 15, 53) actually thought Ovid, among the Latin poets, would have made the best dramatist: chiefly on the strength of his skill with inner conflict, and with conflicts of two passions at a time (as in a Love and Honour play).

[46] *York Plays*, ed. L. Toulmin Smith (1885), pp. 242–5, 179 f., 225 f. Agony and Betrayal are by the 'York Realist'; Temptation perhaps by the 'Metrist'. The set speech of inner conflict was not 'a new motif in English drama' when it appeared in *Gismond of Salerne* (Clemen, op. cit., p. 81).

Mercade with his news of the royal father's death, at the end of *Love's
Labour's Lost*; the death of Tamburlaine's Zenocrate, which marks the
limit to his aspiring love; and of Tamburlaine himself, which with
its strict arrest sets the limit to his aspiring conquests, are all of them in
direct line from Death, God's Messenger in *Everyman* and *The Castel of
Perseverance* and *The Pride of Life*, and from the Danse Macabre.
Muriel Bradbrook has shown, most excitingly, the precedent for *The
Jew of Malta* in *The Croxton Play of the Sacrament*, which thus takes its
place in the genealogy of *The Merchant of Venice*. The Croxton Play
illustrates admirably, too, the continuity in stage-business and the use of
properties. The hand of Jonathas drops off and Professor Bradbrook
has compared to this both the *disjecta membra* of Faustus found by his
scholars, and the false limb and head he sheds in earlier scenes.[47]
Shakespeare made use of the severed hand gambit in *Titus Andronicus*;[48]
and before the hand of Jonathas there were the two hands of impious
Fergus in the York Burial of the Virgin,[49] the notorious stage-effect to
which the audience responded rather too uproariously for the gilds
charged with that pageant.

Neither the medieval drama nor the Tudor Interlude[50] can safely be
neglected when studying the characteristics or features by which plays
of Marlowe's may have influenced his successors. When we observe
how Richard III's opening survey of the situation,

> Now is the winter of our discontent
> Made glorious summer. . . .
> Now are our brows bound with victorious wreaths . . .
> And now, instead of mounting barbed steeds . . . (etc.)

resembles the survey, also with its repeated 'Now's', at the beginning
of Tamburlaine's

> Blacke is the beauty of the brightest day . . .

we should also be aware that such summaries, similarly phrased, are a
convention of the Moral Interludes.[51]

[47] *English Dramatic Form* (1965), pp. 54 f., 52.
[48] III.i.150ff.; cf. also *Selimus* (Malone Society Reprint), 1429–38; and Webster,
The Duchess of Malfi, IV.i.41 ff.
[49] Not extant. See Toulmin Smith, op. cit., pp. xxvii and n. 1, xlix, n. 3;
V. A. Kolve, *The Play Called Corpus Christi* (1966), pp. 130 f. and nn.
[50] See T. W. Craik's standard investigation, *The Tudor Interlude* (1958).
[51] *2 Tamburlaine* 2969–85; W. H. Clemen, op. cit., pp. 52, 98, 285, notes this
speech-type; E. A. Honigmann (ed. *King John*, IV.iii.145, etc., n.) its frequency
in the Moralities.

Indeed, to treat the Interludes, Moralities, and Mistery Cycles as belonging to a prehistory of the English drama, instead of as a full part of it, falsifies quite seriously the picture of Marlowe's advent. Had my mentors not undervalued the medieval tradition, they could hardly have given me the idea that he brought with him, at last, a proper means of dramatic unity. Dramatic unity was as old in England as the great cyclic dramas. Latterly, some of their component plays, like the *Secunda Pastorum*, or groups of plays like the Passion group organised and largely re-written by the York 'Realist', began to be developed as unified dramas on their own account; but even so, at least at York and Chester the cycle as a whole remained the full drama to which unity belonged. It has one dominant person, God (Father and Son); one action, of God's Providence in the redemption of His faithful; one conflict, with the Devil and those whom the Devil enlists to combat God's Will; a conflict having its spaced climaxes in the Fall, the Incarnation, the Passion and Resurrection, and the Second Coming at Doomsday. It conducts this conflict by alternation of fortune, and this action with alternate tightening and slackening of tension. It is mistaken to say of such a drama, as so great a dramatic historian as Allardyce Nicoll has said in his time: 'the plays are chaotic in construction' and that they 'cannot be judged critically on any standards such as are applicable to other dramas'.[52]

Again, a more sympathetic awareness of medieval and early Tudor drama[53] might have assisted interpretation of Marlowe's attitude to the play in two tones, of which one is broad comedy or even farce. I do not remember to have been corrected for taking the summons

> From such conceits as clownage keepes in pay

to mean that Marlowe, if left to his own taste, would have written all his plays without sub-plots and as plays in one tone. *Edward II* is such a play. I supposed that but for the public and his collaborator, Marlowe would fain have had *The Jew of Malta* and *Doctor Faustus* wholly serious, and that not merely the content and the writing but the very presence of the comic scenes was something for which he took no responsibility. But in the scenario there must presumably have been for *Doctor Faustus*, were comic scenes forced on a protesting Marlowe by a

[52] *British Drama* (1925), pp. 31, 39; cf. Rupert Brooke, *John Webster and the Elizabethan Drama* (1916), pp. 35 f.: 'We cannot understand them now. . . . They are far from our ideas of drama', etc.

[53] e.g. the Wakefield Master's *Mactacio Abel* as well as *Secunda Pastorum*, and Medwall's *Fulgens and Lucres*.

collaborator? A devil-play such as, after all, *Faustus* is, if it had had no comedy would have been very untraditional indeed. As for *The Jew*, comic as well as serious villainy is inherent in the whole conception of Barabas. Just as the Shavian drama of ideas helped us to reinterpret and revalue *Henry VI*, so what Yeats called 'that tragic farce we have invented' no doubt helped T. S. Eliot's characterisation of *The Jew of Malta* as farce of 'terribly serious, even savage comic humour'.[54] Yet the analogy of *The Playboy of the Western World* or *The Wild Duck* is not really so helpful as it is to recognise the actual heritage of Barabas, and *Doctor Faustus* too, from the Vice and the medieval Devil, figures in whom menacing terror or malice is combined with the comic. Neither *The Jew of Malta*, nor *Titus Andronicus*, nor *Richard III*, has a sub-plot (though *The Jew* has subsidiary intrigues), but in each of them either a villain-hero or a villain contributes the comedy or the chief part of it. Barabas and Aaron belong to the character-genre which, apropos of *Richard III* and *Don Giovanni*, Bernard Shaw styled 'Punch' (*Our Theatres in the Nineties*, ii.104, 285): the humorous, ingenious villain whose next stroke of humour and of crime we pleasurably anticipate. Iago with Roderigo, or Edmund as he bids the gods stand up for bastards, though they are the most appalling of Shakespeare's Machiavels, still partake of this tradition, as in a different way does the engaging, ultimately dangerous rascal, Falstaff.[55] Shakespeare not only wrote Histories and Romantic Comedies as plays in two tones, but brought clowns in the shape of the Porter, the Gravedigger, and the Countryman with the asps further into the heart of tragedy than anyone else; earlier, Romeo has his Mercutio and Juliet her Nurse. Whether one early lesson in this direction came from *Tamburlaine* it is hard to say: but Marlowe, who seems to have cut some episodes of comedy when the play was published, and whose prologue banished irrelevant clownage, nevertheless made the comic scenes of Mycetes and Calyphas contribute to a lofty drama; and with Calyphas lead up to a tragical conclusion.

Although the advent of Marlowe has not always been seen in proper perspective against the tradition behind him, tradition without the individual talent cannot make an important artist. Marlowe had more: he had the genius which made him a great new force in the drama.

[54] *The Letters of W. B. Yeats*, ed. Allan Wade (1954), p. 722; T. S. Eliot, *Selected Essays* (1932), p. 123.

[55] See P. Happé's unpublished Ph.D. thesis in the University of London (1966): 'The Vice: 1350–1605', pp. 448–50 (Barabas), 454–526 (Richard III, Falstaff, Iago, Edmund).

Blank verse was not novel when by endowing it with 'sustained rhythmic splendour' he assured its triumph as the staple of Elizabethan dramatic poetry. Similarly, Tamburlaine is successor to Lucan's Caesar, Seneca's Hercules, the Senecan tyrant, and the native English gabbing potentate or champion; Barabas, to the native Vice and the Servus of Roman comedy, the rogues who work the plot: but they are raised to a power which makes of them something new, and their impact in consequence was beyond that of their prototypes. As protagonists, Tamburlaine, with Barabas and Faustus in their greatest scenes, have a magnitude and force unmatched on Elizabethan stages when they appeared. This comes above all from the verse and language they speak, and from what through their speech, decisions, and actions is so irresistibly conveyed— their motivation by inner drives, passionate and compelling. Up to a point, Hieronymo is comparable: his distress of mind, like that of Faustus, or of Tamburlaine at the death of Zenocrate, is made real to us, and he too is motivated by genuine passion. But his passion is merely human and commonplace beside that of Tamburlaine, Faustus, and, in certain passages, of Barabas, Mortimer, and the Guise, who aspire, by the ladder of some earthly ambition, to apotheosis. This, and other fresh qualities in Marlowe's characterisation, involve his gift (in which he surpasses all but a few playwrights) for realising states of intense feeling.

There are two main methods by which dramatists have expressed in the long set speech the mind of the speaker. One, highly conventional, puts into his mouth an intellectualised, formally organised report on his thoughts and emotions. In the hands of a Corneille, the convention is acceptable. The other method is Racine's and the mature Shakespeare's: the speaker appears to utter his mind directly, so that the speech mirrors the mental process as it develops.[56] Here Marlowe gave an important lead, as W. H. Clemen has shown; already in *Tamburlaine* the hero's speeches 'are actually growing while they are being spoken'.[57] We are all deeply in Clemen's debt for his whole study of Marlowe's place in the development of dramatic speech in this period. What he demonstrates above all are the ways in which Marlowe knits speech more

[56] Cf. U. M. Ellis-Fermor, *Shakespeare the Dramatist* (1961), pp. 111–23, 41–52, where she makes (pp. 121 n., 123) the distinction between Corneille and Racine she did not make in *The Frontiers of Drama* (1945), p. 108 and n. Because she is seeking to define the dramatic mode in its severest terms, she is less tolerant of Corneille's convention that I think it deserves. Dryden, at least in the rhymed heroic play, is Cornelian: cf. E. M. Waith, op. cit., p. 173.

[57] op. cit., p. 119; cf. pp. 150 (on *Faustus*), 161 (on *Edward II*).

closely into the fabric of the drama. Thus in Tamburlaine there is something new in the suiting of the style of expression to the personality. Marlowe's techniques point forward, too, when he uses description by other personages to help characterise his leading figures, and when he combines the set speech with spectacle, grouped characters, and stage-business to create a scene of strong and unified dramatic effect.[58] Even where at first sight Tamburlaine appears to share a weakness frequent in the plays of Marlowe's immediate predecessors, by 'speaking past' his interlocutors instead of to them, this is in keeping with a character whose egocentricity sets him so much apart.[59] Isolation of leading personages, by their character, situation, or both—an isolation which gives opportunity to display personality or suffering more fully, or to explore it in depth—is exemplified in Hieronymo as well as in Marlovian protagonists. Shakespeare adopts this method over and over again, from Titus in his madness and Henry VI at Towton, to Coriolanus and Timon; most notably of all in Richard III[60] and Hamlet. He was impressed also by Zabena's breaking down, as she goes out of her mind, from verse into prose. Ophelia, Othello in his fit, Lady Macbeth in her sleep-walking follow this precedent; Ophelia, with a reminiscence of Zabena's speech: 'Come, my coach';[61] Richard III's schizophrenic soliloquy after his ghost visions is not in prose; but it is distinguished from his normal style, though the convention used is an old-fashioned one.

A long list of phrases could be given to show Marlowe's contribution, especially from Tamburlaine, to the common stock of expressions drawn upon by the dramatists of the late 'eighties and 'nineties, Shakespeare among them. And one could examine more specific debts in Titus, Henry VI and Richard III; but a few instances must suffice. The action and stage-business of sieges in I Henry VI recall Tamburlaine and The Jew of Malta. At Orleans, as at Babylon 'they scale the walles'. In the Jew, the Governor's preparations:

> . . . you shall heare a Culuerin discharg'd
> By him that beares the Linstocke, kindled thus, (ll. 2273 f.)

evidently imply the presence and exit of one carrying a linstock, lighted; this suggested, no doubt, the boy crossing over the stage with his lighted

[58] op. cit., chs. 8, 10; especially pp. 114, 123, 125–9.
[59] op. cit., p. 121. Yeats awoke to the weakness (as ordinarily it is): 'I am at work on Shadowy Waters . . . making the people answer each other' (op. cit., p. 453).
[60] Who places himself outside humanity in three great soliloquies: 3 Henry VI, III.ii.124 ff., V.vi.68 ff.; Richard III, I.i.1 ff.
[61] U. M. Ellis-Fermor (ed.), Tamburlaine (1930) Part I, V.ii.255 n.

linstock, before the cannon is fired, off, in *1 Henry VI*, I.iv. Aaron in
Titus is related to Barabas not only when he launches into the catalogue
of his crimes, but in his character as a whole; the contrast no less than
the likeness between these two Machiavels as their authors present them
has been admirably studied by Nicholas Brooke.[62] Outdoing Barabas,
who is claimed as a reincarnation of Machiavelli, Richard III 'can set
the murderous Machiavel to school' (*3 Henry VI*, III.ii.193). Finally,
to illustrate Shakespeare's response to Marlowe's eloquence, one need
only set beside

> Blacke is the beauty of the brightest day
>
> (*2 Tamburlaine*, 2969)

(and what follows), the poetic openings of *1 Henry VI* and *Richard III*.

As some instances have indicated already, Marlowe's influence
continued on Shakespearean plays later than these. Since his drama is
often so lyrical the influence is naturally recurrent during Shakespeare's
lyrical phase (say from *Two Gentlemen of Verona* to *Richard II* and—in
virtue of Act V at least—*The Merchant of Venice*). For obvious reasons,
The Merchant has strong links with *The Jew of Malta*,[63] and *Richard II*
with *Edward II*.[64] But even later, some of the most famous passages in
Shakespeare have at least one root in Marlowe. As Tamburlaine strips
Bajazeth of his titles and dignities, so Hal strips Hotspur. Like Calyphas,
Falstaff scoffs at the military ideal (but is given a better, though not
conclusive case). Death, for Cosroe, arrests the organ of his voice; for
Hamlet, Death is strict in his arrest, and the rest is silence. Poppy and
cold mandrake juice cast Barabas into a catalepsy; but poppy and
mandragora can never bring sleep to Othello.[65] 'As it closes in,' Muriel
Bradbrook has finely said, 'Faustus' last hour shows him only where he
is.' Is it too fanciful to think that Shakespeare's imagination might be
responding, not only to Ovid's, but to this farthest reach of Marlowe's,

---

[62] op. cit., pp. 35–7.

[63] A. W. Ward, *History of English Dramatic Literature* (1875), I. 188–93;
H. Levin, op. cit., pp. 83, 92 f.; N. Brooke, op. cit., 41 f., who adds *Tamburlaine*
and *Massacre*.

[64] G. Bullough, *Narrative and Dramatic Sources of Shakespeare*, III (1960),
356–8; N. Brooke, op. cit., 39–41, who adds *Tamburlaine* and *Faustus*.

[65] *Tamburlaine*, 1523 f.; 3700–4, 3722–31; 859; *Jew of Malta*, 2083; *1 Henry
IV*, III.ii.145–50; V.iv.78 f.; V.i.127 f., iii (end); *Hamlet*, V.ii.328 f., 350;
Othello, III.iii.334. Cf. also *1 Tamburlaine*, 115, 1246, 1450 f., 1502, 1506 f.,
Jew of Malta, 1857, 2056 f.; *Edward II*, 762, with *Henry V*, II.i.75, I.i.195 (and
Two Gentlemen, III.i.88); *Lear*, III.iv.36 and V.iii.170; *Macbeth*, II.ii.42,
IV.i.79, V.i.86; *Tempest*, II.ii.1 f. and I.ii.301.

when he gave the like recognition to Edmund vanquished and dying, and had him express it in one of the most terrible of all simplicities: '*I* am *here*'?[66]

The longest-lived influence Marlowe had on seventeenth-century drama was, it seems, through his aspiring heroic characters, and the critique of such characters. On this topic, one must read E. M. Waith's book, *The Herculean Hero*, and Nicholas Brooke's introduction to *Bussy D'Ambois* as well as his article in *Shakespeare Survey*, cited already.[67] Briefly, Chapman continues from Marlowe in depicting heroes who act and speak as though they were self-sufficient, and their outlook self-authenticated, by right of their *virtù*. In Bussy, this claim is treated with mingled sympathy and censure; he is, to adopt Waith's term, a Herculean hero, whose nobility commands admiration despite repellent traits which are not glossed over, but accepted as part of the whole great man.[68] Byron, however, a classic type of the overmighty subject, has his claim refuted, both by the dramatic action and by what is said at certain places where the poet evidently speaks from strong conviction, though in unison with one of his characters.[69] For a man such as himself, Byron asserts, that 'to himself is a law rational', it is not lawful to 'stoop to any other law'. But Chapman makes it clear that when a man repudiates his roots in social obligation and in ethics human and divine, turning himself loose 'out of all the bounds of justice', his gifts will be 'cut from all their fruits'.[70] In *Coriolanus*, between which and Chapman's Byron plays there is obviously a relationship which ought to be explored, the tragic result is shown of a like attempt by the hero to 'stand As if a man were author of himself' (V.iii.35 f.). Indirectly, through Chapman and Shakespeare, this part of the Marlovian tradition reached Dryden. He found *Bussy D'Ambois* striking in the theatre, and compares his own extravagances in heroic drama with Chapman's.[71] Almanzor's famous

[66] M. C. Bradbrook, op. cit., p. 54; *Lear*, V.iii.174, cf. *Shakespeare's Ovid...
Golding's Translation of the Metamorphoses*, ed. W. H. D. Rouse (1961), iii. 298 f. Actaeon beset by his hounds:

And faine he would have beene away thence in some other stead,
But there he was.

[67] *Bussy D'Ambois* (Revels edn., 1964); and see n. 39, above.
[68] N. Brooke (ed.), *Bussy D'Ambois*, xxiv f.; E. M. Waith, op. cit., pp. 11–13, 62 f., 107.
[69] Cf. T. S. Eliot, *On Poetry and Poets* (1957), p. 100.
[70] *George Chapman*, ed. W. L. Phelps (Mermaid edn.), *The Conspiracy of Byron*, III.i. (p. 372), I.i. (p.337).
[71] *Essays of John Dryden*, ed. W. P. Ker (1926), I. 246.

> . . . know that I alone am King of me.
> I am as free as nature first made man,
> Ere the base laws of servitude began,
> When wild in woods the noble savage ran,

is founded on Bussy's

> Let me be King myself (as man was made) . . .
> Who to himself is law, no law doth need
> Offends no King, and is a King indeed.[72]

Plainly, too, Dryden in his heroic plays (prior to *All for Love*) had hoped to emulate Shakespeare's Coriolanus and Antony (besides Brutus and Cassius in their quarrel-scene). For retrospectively he confesses that when he hears Shakespeare's 'Godlike *Romans* rage'

> He, in a just despair, would quit the Stage.[73]

But the tradition also reached Dryden directly from Marlowe: as Nichol Smith pointed out, he knew *Tamburlaine*.[74] We are right, then, to number Marlowe as one of the several ancestors of the Restoration heroic play.

Among Dryden's characters in the line of descent from Marlowe, the cynical Morat is half-converted by love of Indamora, and dies to save her; Almanzor, the noble primitive, is reconciled with civil order through love of Almahide and by meeting at length in Ferdinand and Isabella an authority that is legitimate, so that he is content to become a subject. In thus 'placing' the claim of each to transcend the norms of humankind, Dryden is true to the whole tradition. For, as Nicholas Brooke has written, 'there is scarcely a criticism of the Tamburlaine figure which does not find strong utterance in Marlowe's later plays to say nothing of Part II of *Tamburlaine* itself'. But in Marlowe's work 'such criticism' (he continues) 'goes with a fundamental sympathy' which neither Shakespeare nor Chapman, nor (we may add) Dryden, shares in the same measure.[75]

In the vexed question whether the critique of Tamburlaine begins in Part II or Part I, a concept is concerned which is also of central importance in Shakespeare's *Henry VI* and *Richard III*. This is the concept

---

[72] *The Conquest of Granada*, Part I, I.i.207 ff.; *Bussy D'Ambois*, ed. cit., II.i.198, 203 f.; cf. Waith, op. cit., 170.

[73] Prologue to *Aureng Zebe*, ll. 15 f. (*The Poems of John Dryden*, ed. Kinsley (1958), I. 156).

[74] *John Dryden* (1950), pp. 34 f.   [75] *Shakespeare Survey*, 14, p. 36.

of the Scourge of God. It was available to Shakespeare outside *Tambur-laine*; but he certainly encountered it there, reiterated and powerfully expressed in Part II, so that Marlowe at the least must have marshalled him the way that he was going. The concept is founded on Isaiah X, 5–26; Roy W. Battenhouse has traced it also to Plutarch and Plotinus, and emphasised the high probability of Marlowe meeting it at Cambridge when preparing for the Anglican priesthood.[76] One can go further; there is good reason to suppose that Marlowe's audience, and Shakespeare's, shared it with them. For it probably belonged to the vernacular sermon-tradition. That is how R. W. Chambers explains the close parallel between the thirteenth-century version of it in the *Ancrene Riwle*, and Sir Thomas More's version in his *Apology*, written in 1533. Here, in a modern rendering, is the *Ancrene Riwle*:

> reflect, that whosoever harmeth thee . . . is God's rod: and that God beats thee with him, and chasteneth, as a father doth his dear child, with the rod . . . But, let him not think well of himself because he is God's rod. For, as the father, when he has sufficiently beaten his child, and hath well chastised him, casteth the rod into the fire, because he is naughty no longer, so, the Father of Heaven, when he, by means of a bad man or woman, hath beaten his dear child for his good, casteth the rod, that is, the bad man, into the fire of hell.[77]

And here, some three hundred years later, is More:

> . . . all the mischief shall be their own at length, though God for our sin suffer them for a scourge to prevail in some places here and there for a while; whom upon men's amendment he will not fail to serve at the last, as doth the tender mother, which, when she hath beaten her child for his wantonness, wipeth his eyen and kisseth him, and casteth the rod in the fire.

Both passages, Chambers infers, are examples of 'the life-like illustration of the commonplaces of the pulpit'.[78] Part of the doctrine is in Holinshed, as preached by a cleric who justified the cruelties of King John, a 'generall scourge' inflicted by a king who was 'but the rod of the

---

[76] 'Tamburlaine, The "Scourge of God" ', PMLA, LVI (1941), pp. 337–40; noting also that Philip Mornay, in *De la Verité de la Religion Chrestienne* (of which Sidney and Golding's translation was published 1586, close in date to *Tamburlaine*) expounds the term in applying it to Attila.
[77] J. Morton (tr.), *The Nun's Rule* (Mediaeval Library, 1926), pp. 138 f.
[78] Introduction to Nicholas Harpsfield's Life of More, ed. E. V. Hitchcock, E.E.T.S. o.s. 186 (1932), p. cliii, n. 2. I modernise the spelling of the *Apology*.

Lord's wrath'.[79] The concept was bound to be evoked in Marlowe's mind by the incident in some of his sources where Tamburlaine, rebuked for an atrocity, reported that he was the wrath of God and punishment of the world.[80] Its importance, and expected popularity, as a way of regarding Tamburlaine, is indicated by the prominence given to his cognomen, 'The Scourge of God', on the title-page of the two-part play in 1590.

For Battenhouse, this is Marlowe's governing conception of him in both parts, and includes from the beginning the prospect of his eventual condemnation and destruction. By the test of 'fervours and recurrences',[81] his identification as a Scourge of God is undoubtedly cardinal in Part II. It is invoked first with reference to the succession, which we cannot but surmise will furnish no heir to Tamburlaine's genius; and second, immediately upon what prove to be Zenocrate's last words. Next, in an extended passage, Tamburlaine expounds his title, vocation, and functions as the Scourge, asserting them as divine sanction for his ruthlessness. Before the end of the same scene he has glanced forward to the time when God will call a halt to his function. He reiterates it when, suiting the action to the title, he has entered scourging the kings who draw his chariot, and when he prepares to 'whip them on to Babylon', so that there, as his habit is, he may 'whip down' the city. He appeals to it again, as a divine sanction at his crucial defiance of Mahomet, after which he renounces him in favour of

> The God that sits in heauen, if any God.

Finally, he claims the title with his last breath:

> For *Tamburlaine*, the Scourge of God must die.[82]

There is comparatively little in Part I to correspond with this repeated insistence on the concept at the most emphatic points of the drama in Part II. Insofar as it is emphasised, it is by the promise of the Prologue that Tamburlaine shall be seen 'scourging kingdoms with his conquering sword'; and on two occasions, the second the more striking, by Tamburlaine himself: one in the build-up to the central crisis, the confrontation with Bajazeth; the other at the arrogant moment when he makes him his footstool (ll. 6, 1142 f., 1475 f.).

[79] op. cit., III.173 b.
[80] U. M. Ellis-Fermor (ed.), *Tamburlaine the Great* (1930), pp. 122 f. nn.; 295 f.
[81] Harry Levin, op. cit., p. 15, citing David Masson.
[82] ll. 2629 ff., 3046 ff., 3820–32, 3873–5, 4003, 4078 ff., 4294–6, 4311–3, 4641.

By his *hubris* here, and by his Titan-like threats to assault heaven, first upon the death of Zenocrate and then at the approach of his own, Tamburlaine, it seems safe to conclude, is provoking the Deity whose Scourge he is, as it was characteristic of a Scourge to do. But when he is stricken and dies, no condemnation is voiced; nothing suggests he is consigned to the fire.[83] We must acknowledge, I think, that Marlowe's nemesis for Tamburlaine is different: the Scourge is discarded not condemned. In his insatiable ambition, love, and aspiration beyond humanity, he is faced with man's limits, asserted by Death, God's Messenger; and the investiture of his son, a bid for vicarious fulfilment, is accompanied by ominous warnings of the fate of Hippolytus and Phaeton (ll. 4623–37).

The concept of the Scourge of God was not (as Battenhouse appears to assume) one and indivisible. The preacher in Holinshed, justifying John as a Scourge, did not conclude he would come to a bad end. The term can be applied to a virtuous hero, witness Shakespeare's Talbot, termed 'the scourge of France';[84] it is enough that he is the agent of God's chastisement. That Tamburlaine is presented as a Scourge of God does not, therefore, entitle us to assume, against the text, that he must be designed to end as a wicked tyrant at last repudiated and anathematised.

Except in Talbot, Shakespeare does appear to apply the fullest concept of the Scourge as one who incurs guilt in punishing the guilty, and so is subject to retribution. This is how Hamlet sees himself when he has killed Polonius:

> . . . Heav'n hath pleas'd it so
> To punish me with this and this with me,
> That I must be their scourge and minister. (III.iv.174 f.)

In the first tetralogy of history-plays, one essential line of continuity is established near the end of *1 Henry VI*, when in the same battle the English capture both Joan La Pucelle and Margaret of Anjou (V.iii).

---

[83] ll. 3070–5, 4438–42. Cf. Battenhouse, op. cit., pp. 345 f., and 'Marlowe Reconsidered', *JEGP*, Vol. 52 (1953), p. 537, where his point that the mortal sickness fulfils the prophecy at ll. 3814–19 (and, we may add, the curse at 3852–5) is an important one; I cannot however agree that Marlowe 'takes care to duplicate' the 'pattern-fate' of the 'Scourge-personage'. If one expects him to do this, surely what strikes one is that he does not. As we are led to expect, a nemesis does await the Scourge; but it is not like Joan's or Richard III's in Shakespeare, and leaves Tamburlaine, as Waith contends, a Herculean hero (op. cit., pp. 85–7).

[84] *1 Henry VI*, II.iii.14; cf. IV.ii.16, IV.vii.77 f.

This means that Joan, 'assigned to be the English scourge' in France, and now destined for the fire, will be succeeded by Margaret, who will shortly become 'England's bloody scourge' as termagant queen-consort of England itself.[85] And Shakespeare brings Margaret into *Richard III*, so that she may still embody in the final play the type of vengeance which is a crime itself to be avenged, and which throughout the tetralogy maintains the chain of wrong until Margaret's place is taken by Richmond. Preparatory to his coming, the whole accumulation of guilt has passed to Richard as sole surviving heir and arch-criminal; and upon Richard he executes a divine vengeance different in kind, which breaks the chain of crimes and punishments. In bringing retribution upon Clarence, and in fulfilling Margaret's curses upon other offenders (Hastings and Buckingham; and partially upon the queen and her kin), Richard is her successor as guilty avenger of guilt, but he is not actually called a Scourge. However, he is described in terms of a parallel concept, the hint of which Shakespeare had met in a comment upon him and his like in *The Mirror for Magistrates*. Richard, declares Margaret, is

> . . . hell's black intelligencer,
> Only reserved their factor, to buy souls
> And send them thither; but at hand, at hand
> Ensues his piteous and unpitied end:
> Earth gapes, hell burns, fiends roar . . . (IV.iv.71–5)

Dolman had written, in his contribution on Hastings:

> These may we well deeme fends, and dampned sprytes,
> And whyle on earth they walke, disguysed devyls,
> Sworne foes of vertue, factours for all evylls.
> (ll. 243–5; ed. cit., p. 277)

Since the idea of the Scourge is traditional, Shakespeare is not bound to have derived it solely from *Tamburlaine*. Frequently, as I have been at pains to indicate, Marlowe's influence must have interwoven itself with traditions having many strands. Among these we do not now hesitate to include lines of development in dramatic structure and sense of theatre, having regard to the different stages for which plays were designed. Tucker Brooke's verdict was once orthodox: that Marlowe never learnt to integrate poetry and drama; that in *Edward II* he was dramatic at the expense of poetry, and elsewhere poetic at the expense of drama

[85] *2 Henry VI*, V.i.118; *1 Henry VI*, I.ii.129.

(pp. 233, 308 f.). I have had to disabuse myself of the notion that he was a poet first, and a dramatist a long way second. His dramatic construction is not that of Shakespeare or *The Spanish Tragedy*, with everything closely calculated to further a total complex pattern as it grows;[86] but it has its own coherence, and shows particular skill in its juxtapositions. The more recent critics have demonstrated his practical sense of the theatre, illustrated for example in his ability to fit a star-actor with a succession of immensely effective parts; his use of costume and the physical features of his stages; his command of spectacle, his 'economical yet expressive and symbolic use of properties'.[87] But in these respects his influence upon his fellow as a young dramatist, Shakespeare, was (again) one among many. If I am asked 'where was it unique?' I reply with Nicholas Brooke's statement of the simple truth: 'What makes Marlowe's influence different' (at that time) 'from anyone else's is that he alone was a poetic dramatist of genius'.[88]

[86] Cf. my study of *The Comedy of Errors* in *Early Shakespeare*, ed. J. R. Brown and Bernard Harris (1961).

[87] Clemen, op. cit., p. 127; cf. pp. 122, 129; Harry Levin, op. cit., pp. 48, 66 f., 69, 79, 97 f., 141–3.

[88] *Shakespeare Survey*, 14, p. 34.

Marlowe and Brecht

MICHAEL HATTAWAY

Marlowe and Brecht

THE BASIC POINT of this paper, that Marlowe's plays work in large
part by irony, by alienation as much as identification, must have been
considered by everyone here although doubtless you will disagree as
to its importance and effect. Indeed to call in to a discussion of Marlowe
the works of a dramatist separated from him by over three centuries
may seem to be a procedure as suspect as Kott's invocation of Beckett
in his discussion of *King Lear*. Yet for critical as well as historical
reasons it does seem to me that the dangers of anachronism and super-
ficiality might be avoided.[1] Marlowe, for all his concentration on supermen, never fails to represent (albeit sparingly) the societies that had to
tolerate them, and the best that has been written about him recently
has stressed his intelligence, control, and enquiring scepticism, rather
than the recklessness and transcendental emotionalism of his thought.
If in his tragedies there is wonder and admiration, responses which,
as Eugene Waith has shown,[2] could figure large in Renaissance
theories of tragedy, these are balanced sometimes by explicit moral
comment, often by a show of violence that jerks the audience out of
complacency. I am suggesting in other words that Marlowe is one of
the most intellectual of the Elizabethans in that he offers his audience
a number of clearly defined choices.

This technique of evoking alternative or ambiguous responses was
firmly formulated by Brecht, and although his theories, as most of us
feel, are over-rigid and sometimes invalidated by their *a priori* assump-
tions, they do provide, as I shall attempt to show, some explicit and
useful approaches to the earlier playwright. I believe moreover that it
is no accident that a number of notable productions of Marlowe have
occurred at the time when Brecht has been coming into his own on the
English stage.

In fact of course there is some historical evidence to link the two

---

[1] I have been anticipated by R. B. Parker—see his 'Dramaturgy in Shakespeare and Brecht', *University of Toronto Quarterly*, XXXII (1963), pp. 229–46.
[2] *The Herculean Hero* (London, 1962).

dramatists. For although Brecht made only a couple of cursory references to Marlowe in his *Schriften zum Theater*, he did, at a significant
stage in his career, find that Marlowe provided useful material for the
theatre. In 1924, in conjunction with Lion Feuchtwanger, he staged his
Leben Eduards des Zweiten von England. This is a free adaptation of
Marlowe's *Edward II*, a kind of Marxist commentary on it, which
nevertheless retains a skeleton that is recognisably Marlovian. So too,
even though it was written before its author had begun to schematise
his ideas, there is a lot in it that is typically Brechtian. As we should
expect, Brecht's play is even more of a political pageant than the
original, a chronicle of the clash between royal absolutism and the
people, a display of the results of bad government. It is a play less about
regicide than revolution; the emphasis has been moved from the king
to the kingdom. Edward is stripped of his decadent glamour (no
wanton poets or pleasant wits here) and is placed, along with the
intriguing politicians, against a stark background laid waste by the wars
he had caused but refused to interest himself in. Mortimer is a modern
dictator quick to seize the main chance but over-confident in the power
of his cunning, and we are repeatedly reminded that Gaveston has hoist
himself from butcher's son to king's whore. Following the hint given by
Marlowe's song (ll. 992 ff., all references are to Tucker Brooke's
edition, Oxford, 1910) there is a ballad seller and *Moritaten* which take
up the specific attacks on the king made in the stage directions. The
representations of actual historical events are given an air of accuracy
if not illusion by the exact dates in the subtitles Brecht sandwiched
between the scenes. The political struggle is drawn into the scenes
Marlowe gives to the passion of the king, for just before Edward's
death Mortimer visits him in an attempt to get him to abdicate publicly
before the commons. Finally the emphasis of the verse has been radically
changed; the classical and cosmological references have been almost
stripped away, and concrete images, references to animals (including
buffaloes and eels) and to food are prominent.[3] The high astounding
terms have been transmuted into a Lutherian earthiness.

What was it that Brecht found in Marlowe, and do his practice and
writings help us to see elements of Marlowe's technique more clearly?
First he found a play about politics and war, presented as a chronicle or
as Brecht called it an 'epic' on an uncluttered, unnaturalistic stage. A
whole society is represented there and the audience is given some understanding of the social limitations of heroics and the dangers of luxurious

[3] I was helped with the language by Miss Hedwig Thimig.

sensualism. In this play and in the whole of Marlowe's work Brecht doubtless found a show of violence and cruelty that matched the violence he had written in to his own early plays. Moreover, like Baal, the hero of Brecht's first play, Edward II as well as Tamburlaine and Barabas are social outcasts and inverted idealists.[4] Even Marlowe's grotesque throwaway lines might have appealed to the student of gangsterdom and cabaret. Most important however he found a hero with whom it is tempting but dangerous to sympathise. The murder of Edward and his particular relationship with his wife (named Anna in Brecht) are more or less as they are in Marlowe and would normally invoke our compassion for the hero. But after the brutalities, the misery of the people, and the wretched and monotonous intriguings that have occurred earlier in the play, such feelings are bound to be at least partially smothered. So too with Mortimer, for although as in Marlowe he claims to be the fool of fortune we see that he is responsible for his own actions, simply another kind of politician living off the fat of the land. Our intellects not our emotions are engaged, we are alienated, and to put it more generally, irony is basic to Marlowe's as to Brecht's technique.

Two accounts of the two versions of the play help to show up the similarities between them. I have taken the first from John Willett's useful study *The Theatre of Bertold Brecht* (London, 1959):

> The few photographs and accounts that have survived suggest that in this production Brecht was anticipating his later work, just as his language was anticipating his unrhymed verse of the 1930s. 'Sawing gently at the nerves,' said Marieluise Fleisser, and Herbert Ihering (writing in 1926):
>
> > He did not analyse the characters; he set them at a distance. . . . He called for a report on the events. He insisted on simple gestures. He compelled a clear and cool manner of speaking. No emotional tricks were allowed. That ensured the objective, 'epic' style.
>
> It seemed truly to be a turning point in German classical production, and Ihering sees it as leading to Erich Engel's *Coriolanus*, and even to the Stravinsky-Cocteau *Oedipus Rex*, whose premiere in 1928 was in Berlin (pp. 144–5).

The second is briefer: Clifford Leech's description of a Marlowe

[4] See John Willett, *The Theatre of Bertold Brecht* (London, 1959), p. 66.

Society production of *Edward II* in *The Critical Quarterly*.[5] Although
he notes that all the characters demand a share of the audience's
sympathy, he writes that 'above all, this production was characterised by
neutrality'. The play itself was 'hospitable to all sorts of feelings and
ideas', with the result that 'there is no theory here which Marlowe
illustrates, no warning or programme for reform, no affirmation even
of a faith in man. The playwright merely focuses attention on certain
aspects of the human scene.'

Each author therefore, to use Jonson's words, spoke 'to the capacity of
his hearers'.[6] In fact Marlowe in his prologues flings down an intellectual challenge:

> *View but his picture in this tragicke glasse,*
> *And then applaud his fortunes as you please.*
> (*Tamburlaine*, 7–8)

and Machiavel introduces the Jew thus:

> I craue but this, Grace him as he deserues,
> And let him not be entertain'd the worse
> Because he fauours me. (*The Jew of Malta*, 33–5)

We are not invited to accept experience passively, but to inspect the
'picture of the world' before us.[7] For from Marlowe springs a line of
dramatists that possibly bypasses Shakespeare, but which includes
Jonson, the Webster of *The White Devil*, Tourneur, Marston, and which
continues even in Wycherley. His ideal world is presented not as
Shakespeare presents it, at the end of the play, but it is evoked by
allusion or even by inversion. (Tamburlaine's *virtù*, for example, is the
exact opposite of the virtues of the beatitudes,[8] and although no one
would want to measure the play against such a simple standard it is
difficult not to admit it as one controlling factor in our total reaction.)
As in Brecht moreover the actual shape of the plot is less important
than our changing reactions to the characters as the narrative progresses.
This seems to have been too little remarked in recent criticism for if we
concentrate on plot we are inevitably confronted with an irreconcilable
conflict between romantic and homiletic versions of the plays. The
pleasure we get from Marlowe stems from a conscious process as scene

[5] Vol. I (1959), pp. 181–96.
[6] *Works*, ed. Herford and Simpson, VIII, p. 587.
[7] *Brecht on Theatre*, tr. John Willett (London, 1964), p. 37.
[8] Matthew v.1 ff.

is weighed against scene, language against action and spectacle, speech against idea, character against emblem or icon. To quote Jonson again, Marlowe wants

> attentiue auditors,
> Such as will ioyne their profit with their pleasure,
> And come to feed their vnderstanding parts,
> *(Works,* III, p. 435)

He is far from being a subjective dramatist; his characters are projected from many points of view, they gain in complexity as an actor in crossed lighting gains solidity, and to enter into a merely 'empathetic' relationship with them is to deny Marlowe's artistry.

It is possible in fact to create an argument about Tamburlaine that would be very like the dialectic Brecht conducts about Galileo in *A Short Organum* §63. Galileo in the opening scenes has been shown wolfing his food:

> Isn't the pleasure of drinking and washing one with the pleasure which he takes in the new ideas? Don't forget: he thinks out of self-indulgence. . . . Is that good or bad? I would advise you to represent it as good, since on this point you will find nothing in the whole play to harm society, and more especially because you yourself are, I hope, a gallant child of the scientific age. But take careful note: many horrible things will happen in this connection. The fact that the man who here acclaims the new age will be forced at the end to beg this age to disown him as contemptible, even to dispossess him; all this will be relevant. *(Brecht on Theatre,* pp. 198–9)

Of Tamburlaine we could say:

> Here is Tamburlaine treating the witless Mycetes as he deserves. Don't forget: Tamburlaine is boldly rebelling against a consecrated magistrate as Marlowe, if the Baines note is to be believed, seemed to think was a justifiable course of action . . . Is that good or bad? Renaissance states needed strong kings and lawgivers and so long as there is nothing in the play to suggest that Mycetes' subjects suffered from Tamburlaine's rule, I would advise you to represent it as good, especially since you yourself are, I hope, capable of being moved by a man whose ambition is matched by his eloquence. But take careful note: many horrible things will be done by this man. The man who will treacherously and methodically betray Cosroe, whose appetite for bloody spectacle will not be glutted, the man who dies after he

has defied every opponent and even God himself is this same man, and all this will be relevant.

How does Marlowe distance his spectators sufficiently for them to be able to put together a character as complex as this? First and most obviously by his control over language, by his Jonsonian ability to create a style artificial enough to be readily manipulated by the author. (We remember that Eliot called Jonson 'superficial' without being derogatory.[9]) The catalogues of kingdoms in *Tamburlaine* are both artefact and instrument and with them the playwright can hew out his personalities. The chorus's travelogues in *Doctor Faustus* place the hero's never-satiated appetite for diversions. Certainly there is bombast, but often it is delivered before an eloquent tableau or it is ridiculous in its extravagance. Marlowe's hyperboles pass 'beyond the limites of credit' as Puttenham wrote of this figure,[10] and it is strange that Jonson did not recognise the extension of his own technique in Marlowe when he wrote:

> And though his language differ from the vulgar somewhat; it shall not fly from all humanity, with the *Tamberlanes*, and *Tamer-Chams* of the late Age.[11]

Frequently in *Tamburlaine* we find that extravagance is an index of the hero's self-dramatisation, a mark of immaturity, as Leavis interpreted this quality in *Othello*:

> For he shall weare the crowne of *Persea*,
> Whose head hath deepest scarres, whose breast most woundes,
> Which being wroth, send lightning from his eies,
> And in the furrowes of his frowning browes,
> Harbors reuenge, war, death and cruelty:
> For in a field whose superficies
> Is couered with a liquid purple veile,
> And sprinkled with the braines of slaughtered men,
> My royal chaire of state shall be aduanc'd:
> And he that meanes to place himselfe therein
> Must armed wade vp to the chin in blood. (2643–53)[12]

[9] *The Sacred Wood* (London, 1920), p. 115.
[10] *The Arte of English Poesie*, ed. Willcock and Walker (Cambridge, 1936), p. 191.
[11] *Discoveries*, in *Works*, VIII, p. 587.
[12] Similar passages are quoted by L. C. Knights, 'The Strange Case of Christopher Marlowe', *Further Explorations* (London, 1965).

Here the figure of the colossus is belittled by the childishness of the scene so literally imagined, and the aesthetic attractiveness of the spectacle is undercut by the ugliness and cruelty of the sentiments. Any number of authorities could be invoked to castigate Tamburlaine's actions—some relevant *sententiae* from St Paul, Seneca, and Boethius are conveniently listed by Cesare Ripa in his article on 'Ambitione' in the *Iconologia*—but the language alone has proved to us that pride is the inevitable concomitant of ambition.

In one place Marlowe shows up the emptiness of this kind of rhetoric by a device that has become a stock music-hall joke. Callapine, son of Bajazeth, is trying to persuade Almeda his keeper to allow him to escape to the waiting galleys of his allies:

> The Grecian virgins shall attend on thee,
> Skilful in musicke and in amorous laies:
> As faire as was *Pigmalions* Iuory gyrle,
> Or louely *Io* metamorphosed.
> With naked Negroes shall thy coach be drawen,
> And as thou rid'st in triumph through the streets,
> The pauement vnderneath thy chariot wheels
> With Turkey Carpets shall be couered:
> And cloath of Arras hung about the walles . . . (2531–45)

To which Almeda: 'How far hence lies the Galley, say you?' 'How much did you say you'd offer?'—the scene shows that anyone, no matter what his motives, can compose a *suasio*, a speech of this form. This extravagance, I would suggest moreover, makes the setting Tamburlaine describes for Zenocrate ('Now, bright *Zenocrate*, the worlds faire eie') in the next scene ring a little hollow. The device of a grand style in an incongruous setting is used again when Ithamore uses a version of 'Come liue with mee, and be my loue' to woo the courtesan Bellamira.[13]

Sometimes Marlowe achieves his distancing effect by balancing one argument squarely against another as was the procedure of formal Pyrrhonian scepticism, or as in the manner of an academic debate. The example is Ramus' disquisition with the Guise in *The Massacre at Paris* or, more subtle, the paradoxically orthodox sentiments which Mephostophilis uses to reason with Faustus. Most economically perhaps, has Marlowe demolished pretentiousness in the opening scenes of *The Massacre*, a play that often seems to me to contain the essence of Marlowe's technique. I disagree with those critics who see it as biased

[13] *The Jew of Malta*, ll. 1806–16.

reportage—it seems to me that it is good journalism and that it derives its vigour from its crude dramatisation of opinions rather than ideas. The actors play characters at one remove and these are as ridiculous as conceptions as they are as people. The comic and melodramatic posturings of the French court are fully established in 57 lines (if we forget for the moment our doubts about the authority of the text) and, passing into the verse of the next scene, simply do not allow the Guise to soar aloft:

> The Mother Queene workes wonders for my sake,
> And in my loue entombes the hope of Fraunce:
> Rifling the bowels of her treasurie,
> To supply my wants and necessitie.
> Paris hath full fiue hundred Colledges,
> As Monestaries, Priories, Abbyes and halles,
> Wherein are thirtie thousand able men,
> Besides a thousand sturdy student Catholicks,
> And more, of my knowledge in one cloyster keeps
> Fiue hundred fatte Franciscan Fryers and priestes . . .
>
> (133–42)

His moral cynicism has been demolished by Marlowe's own cynical stance. The mannered façade falls away to reveal just another puny mortal trying to be heroic in a reduced Machiavellian world—it is impossible to distinguish Marlowe's contempt here from his despair. The characters so often called supermen are merely a special kind of humour. They are embodiments of phantasies that can be allowed the fullest reign, but which the author never allows to be taken as natural.[14]

Marlowe's second ironic device, a device common to all Elizabethan dramatists, is his habit of playing scene off against scene. Although, unlike Shakespeare, his plays generally have an extensive rather than an intensive structure (that is his subplots are little developed), the comic scenes of *Doctor Faustus* provide an important exception to this generalisation. There is no doubt in my mind that these scenes are an integral part of at least the plan of the play, and that they dramatise the lengths to which Faustus is drawn by his insatiable appetite for pleasure and experience. If Brecht had written the play they would have been there to show the hero stepping off his pedestal to have some rumbustious

---

[14] I cannot agree with Wilbur Sanders, *The Dramatist and the Received Idea* (Cambridge, 1968), who calls his chapter on *The Jew of Malta*, 'Dramatist as Realist'.

fun (*Spass*), but Marlowe had a more serious intention. For Faustus' antics simply do not measure up to the knowledge and power sought by a serious magician and they show up Faustus' lack of self-knowledge as well as his obtuse refusal to heed Mephostophilis' suggestion that the highest wisdom and cosmic power will never come to him from the devil. Faustus is suffering from what Ripa summarised as 'Cecità della Mente',[15] blindness of the mind, the blindness of those who put all their trust in their outward senses. In his difficult poem 'Hymnus in Cynthiam' Chapman allegorises this scepticism by describing a thicket in which are imprisoned those who, like Doctor Faustus, smother the faculties of what the Neo-Platonists termed the *anima prima*:

> such cursed sights,
> Such Ætnas filled with strange tormented sprites,
> That now the vaprous obiect of the eye
> Out-pierst the intellect in facultie.
> Basenesse was Nobler then Nobilitie . . .
> Eyes should guide bodies, and our soules our eyes,
> But now the world consistes on contraries:
> So sense brought terror; where the mindes presight
> Had saft that feare, and done but pittie right.[16]

Faustus' terror at the sight of the gaping hell mouth drives his knowledge of Christ from his mind.

I have in fact argued elsewhere[17] that these scenes dramatise Marlowe's commitment to a Protestant ethos. By their anti-papal satire Marlowe is able in a subtle way to evoke the audience's indulgence for this buffoonery, and thereby to suggest that along with his other works, the pact with the devil, even his demoniality, these actions contribute in no way to Faustus' damnation. Faustus' faith alone could save him, and his damnation is the direct result of his despair, his inability to trust in Christ that is 'the power of God and the wisdom of God' (I Cor. i.24), the power and the wisdom he had set his eyes on at the beginning of the play. It is significant that Tamburlaine too dies with his eyes feasting on his 'latest benefit'.

As a second example of obvious choric scenes we can look to the Olympia scenes of *2 Tamburlaine*.[18] For once the word 'pity' appears

---

[15] *Iconologia* (Padova, 1611), p. 76.
[16] *The Poems of George Chapman*, ed. P. B. Bartlett (New York, 1941), pp. 37–8, ll. 309–23.
[17] In an article to appear in *Renaissance Drama*.
[18] See also the three poor men at the beginning of *Edward II*.

explicitly here (3430–31) and although emotion is somewhat lost in the onrush of the action, these scenes seem to me to fulfil the choric function of the scenes in *Henry VI* that show the Kentish gentleman Alexander Iden[19] or the son that has killed his father and the father that has killed his son.[20] The Olympia episode derives from Ariosto, and the chivalric ideals of the family, and death before dishonour, show up the harsh politics and theology of the scourge of God. On other occasions the commentary is less obvious, and comes from the audience's balancing one scene against another, scenes that are linked by verbal or visual similarities. The prayer of Orcanes the unbeliever[21] shows up the 'impatient words'[22] of Tamburlaine's last defiance. Like his lament for Zenocrate this speech has a petulance that destroys the pathos. More complex are the scenes in *Edward II* that contain references to Fortune. From his superior viewpoint the spectator of this play, I would suggest, sees merely a fallen world, a struggle for power among squabbling factions.[23] It is far from the ordered providential world of Shakespeare's histories that reinforce St Paul's dictum that all power is from God, for each scene is the direct result of human actions. As in Jonson's *Sejanus*, Marlowe's idea of history comes from classical rather than Christian Renaissance sources, if it does not come from Machiavelli himself. The pattern and purpose of history has become contingent upon human actions—as Brecht shows in the deposition of the Governor in *The Caucasian Chalk Circle* where he is at pains to strip away any necessary pattern from the events.

Not only does Marlowe's irony work within the play, for he commonly alludes specifically to an orthodox or 'received' idea and measures his characters' actions against it. To an audience keenly aware of the dependence of a still feudal monarchy on the good will and economic support of the nobility the attempt of Edward II to govern as an absolute monarch would seem political lunacy. Again no sixteenth-century audience would ever imagine that Faustus' inverted Pascalian wager would come off, for their ultimate belief in God's omnipotence (even to blaspheme as Faustus and Marlowe did, one must be worried by one's faith), as well as the aesthetic expectations aroused by the tragic form, would demand his overthrow. As L. C. Knights wrote of Jonson, 'in [his] audience, we may postulate a lively sense of human limitations'.[24]

[19] *2 Henry VI*, IV.x.   [20] *3 Henry VI*, II.v.
[21] *2 Tamburlaine*, ll. 2896 ff.   [22] Ibid., l. 4446.
[23] As in *Edward II* the notion of fortune is reduced, so in *Dido* the Gods themselves are reduced to being slaves of very human passions.
[24] *Drama and Society* (London, 1937), p. 166.

If we approach the plays more closely we often find Marlowe invoking in very specific terms the first part of a theme the conclusion of which would be well known to the audience. It is not necessary to remind this audience that Faustus employed what Luther regarded as the devil's syllogism to prove the necessity of damnation[25] (the *impasse* of rational deduction shows man that he must trust in his faith), or how the *consummatum est* proclaimed the salvation of man, the salvation still open to Faustus. Again when Tamburlaine proclaimed himself the scourge of God, the agent sent to chastise the wicked or presumptuous, he forgot that the scourge himself was scourged. Here is Calvin on the subject:

> And this is to be holden in minde, that when God performeth by ye wicked that thing which he decreed by his secret judgement, they are not to be excused, as though they did obey his commandement, which in deede of their owne euil lust they do purposely breake.[26]

(Incidentally it is possible that in *The Tempest* we have Shakespeare's commentary on this idea that points out the brutality of tyrants like Tamburlaine by showing how Man, like God, can forgive. For Prospero, another scourge of God, after bringing down two tyrants finds it possible to end with an act of mercy.) *The Jew of Malta* is studded with religious references in startling contexts and there is the famous example in *Tamburlaine*.

When Tamburlaine is stirred with the *ardor divinarum rerum*[27] and tells of how in ecstasy the soul climbs after knowledge infinite, the consummation of his speech, 'the sweet fruition of an earthly crowne', would make the audience immediately aware that he had confused his desire for God with his desire for fame. In Greene's *Selimus* (1594), a patent imitation of *Tamburlaine*, the author uses this device more openly when he makes the hero argue similarly that man's possession of an unfettered intellect gives him absolute moral freedom:

> But we, whose minde in heauenly thoughts is clad,
> Whose bodie doth a glorious spirit beare,
> That hath no bounds, but flieth euery where;

[25] Susan Snyder, 'The Left Hand of God', *Studies in the Renaissance*, XII (1965), pp. 18–59.

[26] *The Institution of Christian Religion*, tr. T. Norton (London, 1587), I. xviii, pp. 69–70.

[27] See Erwin Panofsky, *Studies in Iconology* (New York, 1939), p. 138 n.

> Why should we seeke to make that soule a slaue,
> To which dame Nature so large freedome gaue.[28]

Even Machiavel's lines in *The Jew of Malta*:

> I count Religion but a childish Toy,
> And hold there is no sinne but Ignorance (ll. 14–15)

set off an easily plotted argument in the hearers' minds. The presence of the words 'religion' and 'sin' suggests that 'ignorance' is an oblique reference to lack of faith. Whose is the ignorance they ask, to which the answer is their own. To combat Machiavel and Barabas a wisdom is necessary that is at once more worldly than that of Christian apologists like Hooker and more rooted in belief than that of the Christians in the play. As T. W. Craik has pointed out, 'the unorthodox view that religious truth is relative'[29] is expressed in this play.

This form of irony is the irony of allusion, the irony of the poet who leaves it to his hearers to supply the verbal context. Marlowe however was a dramatist and added a visual dimension to his verbal emblems. His characters in other words, as Professor Bradbrook has notably pointed out,[30] are icons derived perhaps from the great figures carried in shows, pageants, and processions. Erwin Panofsky has described the difference between formal and iconological analysis: a formal analysis is concerned with objects and expressions, and he groups these two subdivisions under the heading of *motifs*. An iconological analysis on the other hand is concerned with the subject matter, with the identification of images, stories, and allegories which are intelligible as opposed to being sensible. Now I would submit that Brecht's work presupposes an iconological analysis on the audience's part. The spectator recognises Mother Courage and her cart, Galileo, Macheath, the significance of the judgement sequence in *The Caucasian Chalk Circle*; he sees the objects and their expressions, the motifs, but he also supplies information from what he knows about the refugee, 'the gallant child of the scientific age', the king of the beggars, the judgement of Solomon respectively. Brecht evokes these stock reactions and then proceeds with sardonic twists to force the audience to rethink their attitudes. He wants his actors not merely to show feelings, but to convey attitudes, and it could be that the

[28] Greene, *Works*, ed. Grosart (n.p., 1881–6), XIV, ll. 281–5.
[29] Introduction to New Mermaid, *The Jew of Malta* (London, 1966).
[30] 'The Inheritance of Christopher Marlowe', *Theology*, LXVII (1964), pp. 298–305 and 347–53.

notion of the icon might help our conception of that key word 'Gestus' which Willett says 'means both gist and gesture; an attitude or a single aspect of an attitude, expressible in words or actions'.[31] The 'Gestus' like the icon embodies society's visual conception of an idea. Brecht himself expands his theory rather cryptically:

> Each single incident has its basic gest: *Richard Gloster courts his victim's widow. The child's true mother is found by means of a chalk circle. God has a bet with the devil for Dr Faustus's soul. Woyzeck buys a cheap knife in order to do his wife in*, etc. The grouping of the characters on the stage and the movements of the groups must be such that necessary beauty is attained above all by the elegance with which the material conveying that gest is set out and laid bare to the understanding of the audience.
>
> (*A Short Organum*, § 66)

By this he means, I think, that these actions are the meaningful centre of each scene and that they contain in summary form, in themselves, a great deal of human experience.

Now Marlowe often employs what Brecht would call *gestisch* scenes, what I would call icons. A good example is the coronation of Zenocrate at the end of Part I of *Tamburlaine* which Professor Bradbrook has likened to representations of the Coronation of the Virgin. The question we must ask ourselves is whether Marlowe is questioning the validity of the icons themselves or the parodies of them. Is he in other words an iconoclast or a venerator? The answer would be I think that he tends towards confirmation of the icon's validity, if not wholly to veneration. For whereas Brecht's comparisons are with purely human stories, Marlowe refers his characters to the immutable worlds of myth or religion. The ends of Barabas, Edward, Doctor Faustus remind us of medieval representations of the torments of the damned and the punishments are not so much cruel as fitting for their particular crimes. G. K. Hunter has shown how *The Jew of Malta* works by inverting the story of Job,[32] and Doctor Faustus in his study reminds us of paintings of St Jerome. Marlowe, however, reverses the story of the saint's turning from profane to sacred learning. More generally it reminds us of the story of Solomon who, endowed with divine wisdom, was also held to be the author of Ecclesiastes, the man most aware of the vanity

[31] *Brecht on Theatre*, p. 42.
[32] 'The Theology of Marlowe's *The Jew of Malta*', *Journal of the Warburg and Courtauld Institutes*, XXVII (1964), pp. 211–40.

of human learning. Tamburlaine's chariot gives rise to a host of associations about which Dr Cockcroft informs me he has written an article that is to appear shortly. Even if we do not think that Tamburlaine is aping the triumphs of the Gods, described by Petrarch and Boccaccio and depicted in innumerable paintings, we notice the absence of the slave to whisper *memento mori* to the emperor. So too there is a possible reference to Plato's chariot metaphor, with the implication that Tamburlaine's will has run away with his reason, or an echo of the moralisation of the chariot motif found in the first dumb show of Gascoigne and Kinwelmersh's *Jocasta* (1566).[33]

This was the method; how was it executed? Although acting is the most elusive of the arts, and the one most dangerous to make generalisations about, it does seem that the acting styles of the troupes Marlowe and Brecht worked with may have had something in common. This can be described as a certain formalism, a histrionic performance in which no attempt was made to create an illusion of reality for the audience. Certainly there are choruses, soliloquies, and songs in both Elizabethan and Brechtian plays. In these theatres actors worked against sets that were emblematic rather than illusionistic, and it seems that in Marlowe's time they made little attempt to enter into a close relationship with the spectators. As Professor Armstrong has conjectured, Marlowe through Alleyn initiated a new style of acting that made the actor far more remote than had been customary in conceits of clownage with actors like Richard Tarleton.[34] And Dr A. J. Gurr has contrasted Alleyn's style with the more modulated technique of Shakespeare's Burbage and writes: 'there is reason to believe that Alleyn's violence of voice and gesture in his most famous parts established a tradition of exaggeration'.[35] With this we can compare a couple of remarks of Brecht. He was asked what acting ought to be like and he replied:

Witty. Ceremonious. Ritual. Spectator and actor ought not to approach one another but to move apart. Each ought to move away from himself. Otherwise the element of terror necessary to all recognition is lacking.

And again when asked 'Oughtn't the actor then to try to make the man he is representing understandable?':

[33] See J. W. Cunliffe ed., *Early English Classical Tragedies* (Oxford, 1912), p. 69.
[34] 'Shakespeare and the Acting of Edward Alleyn', *Shakespeare Survey*, 7 (1954), pp. 82–9.
[35] 'Who strutted and bellowed?', *Shakespeare Survey*, 16 (1963), pp. 95–101.

Not so much the man as what takes place. What I mean is: if I choose to see Richard III I don't want to feel myself to be Richard III, but to glimpse this phenomenon in all its strangeness and incomprehensibility.[36]

Moreover it is possible that some of Alleyn's effect stemmed from the fact that being the master of his trade he could make his personality part of his character, just as Brecht claimed that the actor 'appears on the stage in a double role':[37] as himself and as the character he is playing.

Strongly stylised unnaturalistic acting in fact is demanded by the nature of the plays these two dramatists wrote, plays that gain their overall effect from tableaux in which grouping and visual symbolism are all important. The virgins of Damascus are matched by the beggars of *The Threepenny Opera*, Tamburlaine's tents by the drabness of the sets Brecht used where appropriate. John Russell Brown has surveyed recent productions and pointed to how the best have drowned the most mighty lines in a bath of blood and has further noted the moments when the audience was aware of the monotony of roles played on the peaks of ambition.[38] Certainly formality was used in the best production of Marlowe I have seen, the Royal Shakespeare Company's *Jew of Malta* of a few years ago. This was necessary to preserve the balance between the two alternatives given to the producer—to present Barabas either as scapegoat or as a vice treated as an ass. One remembers the statuesque prologue who spoke with tight-lipped resonance, the scenes of serpentine intrigue, the nuns with huge white headpieces, and a truly Brechtian climax when Barabas cried with choked-off passion 'liue with me' (2192). The nihilism of his earlier aside 'Deuils doe your worst, I liue in spite of you' (2043) had gone like a spear to his own heart.

I have said that both these dramatists rely on icons and thereby implied that their plays are fairly openly didactic. Yet because the image is actually presented in a living way, because of the presence of an actor who is a fellow human being, it makes it much more difficult to come to a simple decision as to these plays' meaning. Tamburlaine may be proud and presumptuous, but he has a presence, a grandeur that it would be churlish to deny, and Barabas, although cruel and vindictive, was sorely put upon—as was Job himself. Edward too does win our sympathy at the end of the play, however much Brecht in his version

---

[36] *Brecht on Theatre*, pp. 26–7.   [37] *A Short Organum*, § 49.
[38] 'Marlowe and the Actors', *Tulane Drama Review*, 8 (1964), pp. 155–73.

suppressed his agony. Marlowe did not go so far as to portray him as a martyr, as he had been portrayed in for example the roof bosses of Bristol cathedral,[39] but having established the event of his abdication and imprisonment in social terms, he could measure this against its effects on the people most closely involved. He could therefore draw in his audience at the end of the play, having held them at a distance for the majority of the action. Thereby he gained an intelligent, and carefully controlled, complex response from his audience. Like Brecht he explored the relationship of man to his world, and like Brecht made the best and fullest use of the existing maps of human experience. Neither dramatist, however, failed to record the unknown and incongruous things he found on his journeys.

[39] See Bradbrook's article, cited in note 30.

Comic Method in Marlowe's Hero and Leander

BRIAN MORRIS

Comic Method in Marlowe's
Hero and Leander

MARLOWE'S *Hero and Leander* is a great comic fragment. Professor Leech has analysed some parts of it and claimed it as a 'major comic poem'.[1] 'Fragment' seems to me more appropriate than 'poem', but I agree with Leech's verdict, and welcome its implications. It supposes a comprehensive comic vision on Marlowe's part, which he did not (perhaps could not) impose on the whole story; it suggests an attitude to human love which is neither the celebration of rarified passion nor the simple enjoyment of the flesh; it asks us to believe that Marlowe deliberately denied the lovers what his exemplars, Ovid and Musaeus,[2] had considered their true decorum. All three implications can be vindicated from the poem itself.

The comic vision is comprehensive because it obeys its own perverse logic throughout the two Sestiads. The comedy works by the deliberate inversion of all orthodox attitudes towards human dignity and human love, by the frustration of normal expectations. A Renaissance reader, familiar with Ovid, if not with Musaeus, would have expected the story of Hero and Leander to be told richly, certainly with pathos, perhaps even tragically, and the first five lines of the poem would offer him no affront.[3] But the description of Hero (5–50) gradually asserts abnormality. She is introduced with the first of Marlowe's 'invented myths':

> . . . Hero the fair,
> Whom young Apollo courted for her hair,[4]

[1] Clifford Leech, 'Marlowe's Humor' in *Essays . . . in honour of Hardin Craig*, ed. Hosley (1963), pp. 69–81. See also M. C. Bradbrook, 'Hero and Leander', *Scrutiny*, II, and Russell A. Fraser, 'The Art of *Hero and Leander*', *JEGP* (October 1958), pp. 743–54.

[2] Musaeus is the primary source. Marlowe probably used a Greek–Latin edition, since there was no contemporary English translation except one that Abraham Fleming said he had published in 1577. See Douglas Bush, *Mythology and the Renaissance Tradition in English Poetry* (New York, 1932), p. 126.

[3] These lines are a close translation of the opening of Musaeus' poem.

[4] All quotations from *Hero and Leander* are taken from *Marlowe's Poems*,

the description proceeds with a detailed survey of Hero's garments, in which the main point is the triumph of Art over Nature:

> Her veil was artificial flowers and leaves,
> Whose workmanship both man and beast deceives.
> Many would praise the sweet smell as she past,
> When 'twas the odour which her breath forth cast;
> And there for honey, bees have sought in vain,
> And beat from thence, have lighted there again.

A brief, cool reference to the whiteness of her hands is followed by a prolonged account of her buskins,

> Where sparrows perch'd, of hollow pearl and gold,
> Such as the world would wonder to behold:
> Those with sweet water oft her handmaid fills,
> Which as she went would cherup through the bills.

The only reference to Hero's body in the remaining fourteen lines is to her 'naked neck' which Cupid is said to have embraced, mistaking her for his mother. In the whole passage the byzantine ingenuity of her dress contrasts steeply with her almost unremarked flesh.

The description of Leander is quite opposite. He is pictured naked, and the narrator dwells sensuously on his body:

> Even as delicious meat is to the taste,
> So was his neck in touching, and surpast
> The white of Pelops' shoulder: I could tell ye,
> How smooth his breast was, and how white his belly . . .
>
>   . . . let it suffice
> That my slack muse sings of Leander's eyes,
> Those orient cheeks and lips, exceeding his
> That leapt into the water for a kiss
> Of his own shadow . . .

The gorgeous outside, the panoply, the pageant of Art is Hero's; the beautiful body belongs to Leander.[5] The first description is detached

---

ed. L. C. Martin (1931). Quotations from the plays are taken from *The Works of Christopher Marlowe*, ed. C. F. Tucker Brooke (Oxford, 1910).

[5] This conclusion is supported by the classical parallels Marlowe draws in his description of Leander. His body is 'as straight as Circe's wand', which would suggest sinister pleasure to any alert Renaissance reader (cf. 'Others [were] converted into beasts by Circe . . . For as Circe's rod, waved over their heads

and sharply observant of detail; the second an exotic indulgence. The inverted pattern is completed by the public verdict on Leander's beauty:

> Some swore he was a maid in man's attire,
> For in his looks were all that men desire.

Yet this grave inversion of the traditional techniques of physical description does not create comic characters. Both Hero and Leander are so far neutral, statuesque figures, and the comedy resides in the narrator's odd manipulation of his story. Moreover, the inversion of attributes is only the first part of a larger strategy; its ironies are proleptic.

The inverted roles are developed when the lovers meet in the Temple of Venus. Both Sestiads are concerned with the coming-together of people (a rare theme in Marlowe's plays), and in the First Sestiad the engagement is conventionally spiritual, almost theoretic. They love by the book. Hero, worshipping in the Temple, appears at first the modest, chaste innocent we expect:

> There Hero sacrificing turtles' blood,
> Vail'd to the ground, vailing her eyelids close,
> And modestly they opened as she rose:

but when Leander kneels to pray to her,

> Chaste Hero to herself thus softly said:
> 'Were I the saint he worships, I would hear him';
> And as she spake those words, came somewhat near him.

The detached, amused tone of the narrator in the gravely casual phrase 'came somewhat near him' points up the solemn innocence of this wooing, and the detachment is further enforced by such gnomic comments as 'True love is mute, and oft amazed stands'. When Leander goes on to 'display Love's holy fire' the narrator takes the opportunity to assert Hero's artfulness in a crisp couplet:

---

from the right side to the left: presents those false and sinister perswasions of pleasure, which so much deformes them: so the reversion thereof, by discipline, and a view of their owne deformity, restores them to their former beauties'. Sandys, *Ovids Metamorphosis Englished* . . . , 1632, sig. Mmm). He is then compared with Ganymede and Pelops, both beautiful boys beloved by gods (see Apollodorus, *Epitome*, II.3, and Pindar, *Olympian Odes*, I.37), and finally with Narcissus and Hippolytus, who both rejected the love of women (Ovid, *Metamorphoses*, III. 341 ff., Euripides, *Hippolytus*, and Pausanias, II.xxxii). Both in description and allusion Leander's sexuality is, to say the least, peculiar.

> . . . sighs and tears,
> Which like sweet music enter'd Hero's ears;
> And yet at every word she turn'd aside,
> And always cut him off as he replied.

And this display of feminine reluctance elicits a firmly comic response from both Leander and narrator:

> At last, like to a bold sharp sophister,
> With cheerful hope thus he accosted her.

The trisyllabic rhyme and the cocky comic tone mask the new presentation of Leander as sophistical seducer, presenting the time-honoured arguments against virginity almost exactly as Milton's Comus does nearly half a century later. But whereas Milton's seducer is unambiguously identified as evil, and his sentiments as sin, Leander's 'simplicity and naked truth' contrast absurdly with the sophisticated and intemperate fecundities he is made to express. In a practically uninterrupted speech he piles up analogical arguments for some one hundred and thirty lines, a persuasive piece of pleading. Yet, at his climax, the narrator clips Hero's response into a couplet:

> These arguments he us'd, and many more,
> Wherewith she yielded, that was won before;

The hyperboles are exploded, the pretensions pricked, and Hero, the artful dissembler, emerges in firm control:

> Hero's looks yielded, but her words made war . . .
>
> Yet evilly feigning anger, strove she still,
> And would be thought to grant against her will.

Throughout the encounter the Ovidian arts of Love are displayed by Hero. The innocent Leander becomes absurd because, with all his eloquence, he has no idea what he is talking about.

The inversion of attributes, and the frustration of expected responses, is only one of the techniques at work in this comedy; its function is to focus the reader's attention sharply upon the theme of the poem—the absurdity of young love. This theme is exemplified in a more complex way, and at a deeper level, by the pattern of five attempted seductions. In each of the five (Leander's wooing in the Temple, the myth of Mercury, the first meeting of Hero and Leander at Sestos, the encounter between Neptune and Leander, and the final union of the lovers)

Marlowe exhibits a concern which was one of his most constant preoccu-
pations in the plays: the power of speech to sway and order the minds
and wills of men—the Eloquence of Persuasions. In the development
of this pattern Marlowe shows the diminishing power of words, and the
increasing efficacy of action as the means to achieve the right true end of
love. Yet this development is not allowed to assert its point undisturbed.
The attempted seductions continue to expose the inverted sexual
attributes with which Marlowe began, and each episode is tonally
controlled by the omniscient, and increasingly tyrannical, narrator.
The effect is to place complex but crippling inhibitions on the romantic
narrative, to educe from the reader the realisation that young love may
be tender, but is certainly absurdly comic.

In the Temple of Venus, and under the influence of love at first sight,
Leander mounts his vast, wholly verbal attack on Hero's virginity. The
immediate impact on the reader is ironic: Hero's 'gentle heart' is
already 'strook', their hands have already touched, their 'yielding hearts
entangled', Leander's words have already entered Hero's ears 'like
sweet music'. Prolonged argument is superfluous; yet Leander orates
for some one hundred and thirty lines. The points he makes are few:
my love may act as a foil to set off your surpassing beauty; the most
beautiful things perish if they are not used; virginity must be compared
with marriage to be appreciated; virginity is an insubstantial idol;
chastity invites calumny; virginity is sacrilege in one who is 'Venus'
nun'. These arguments are, as Douglas Bush has pointed out, the
ultimate in stock persuasions.[6] The eloquence resides in Leander's
rhetoric. Each several point is exemplified by a string of analogies from
the central, traditional fund of commonplaces. Lines 231–40, for
example, are only a slight expansion of Ovid, *Amores*, I.viii.51–2,[7] and
the effect of this recognition must have been to confirm, in an Elizabethan reader's mind, his sense of almost contemptuous familiarity with
this traditional exercise in seduction. The key-word had already been
planted in line 197, where Leander approaches his speech like a bold
sharp 'sophister'. A 'sophister' was essentially 'a specious reasoner', and
Leander's case is meant to sound prolonged, eloquent, and hollow.
The most apt comparison is with Tamburlaine's great speech to
Theridimas, in which he says:

---

[6] He gives a dozen examples, ranging from Seneca to Sidney. See *Mythology
and the Renaissance Tradition in English Poetry*, p. 135.
[7] Translated by Marlowe in *All Ovids Elegies*, probably while he was still at
Cambridge. See Martin, ed. cit., pp. 15 and 40.

> Forsake thy king and do but ioine with me
> And we will triumph ouer all the world.
> I hold the Fates bound fast in yron chaines,
> And with my hand turne Fortunes wheel about,
> And sooner shall the Sun fall from his Spheare,
> Than Tamburlaine be slaine or ouercome.[8]

This is Marlowe's true Eloquence of Persuasions, in which character and tone uniquely command the traditional allusions. Theridimas makes the inevitable response:

> Not Hermes Prolocutor to the Gods,
> Could vse perswasions more patheticall . . .
>
> Won with thy words, & conquered with thy looks,
> I yeeld my selfe, my men & horse to thee;

Hero's reply to Leander cannot be framed in these serious, heroic terms, since she was 'won before', and the heroic ground has been cut from beneath her feet. His unrelieved verbal persuasion is prolonged, sophistical, and, above all, utterly unnecessary. It is a comic exercise imposed upon the narrative, a burlesque version of the serious Eloquence of Persuasions which had formed so vital a part of the dramaturgy of *Tamburlaine*.

Complementing Leander's sophistry, in the First Sestiad, is the invented myth of Mercury. The function of the myth is complex; it is deliberate digression, and it introduces extraneous elements which seem to bear no relation to the theme. Paul W. Miller argues that it is intended to show Marlowe's 'final acceptance of divine justice', and that it is an interpretative parallel to the Hero–Leander story.[9] Perhaps it is. But on a simpler level it provides a second attempted seduction, and illustrates again Marlowe's concern with the persuasive powers of rhetoric. Mercury uses his 'heaven-born' powers to attract the country maid's attention:

> On her this god
> Enamoured was, and with his snaky rod
> Did charm her nimble feet, and made her stay,

[8] Tucker Brooke, pp. 18–19.
[9] 'A Function of Myth in Marlowe's *Hero and Leander*', *Studies in Philology* (April 1953), pp. 158–67.

Yet to accomplish his particular persuasion he relies on wholly human methods:

> And sweetly on his pipe began to play,
> And with smooth speech her fancy to assay,

Smooth speech gives way to less smooth activity, and, frightened by his boldness, she makes off at high speed with Mercury in pursuit. His second attempt is a matter of purely verbal persuasion, and his more tactful deployment wins from her precisely the response which Hero gave to Leander:

> After went Mercury, who us'd such cunning,
> As she, to hear his tale, left off her running;
> Maids are not won by brutish force and might,
> But speeches full of pleasure and delight;
> And, knowing Hermes courted her, was glad
> That she such loveliness and beauty had
> As could provoke his liking, yet was mute,
> And neither would deny, nor grant his suit.

Mercury, 'prolocutor to the gods' and patron of all orators, achieves what success he does with the country maid precisely because he has seductive powers of speech. His actions are repulsed when they are tumbling in the grass, and when actions are unsuccessful he resorts to the magic of words. By comparison with Leander's wooing of Hero—a stylised statuesque performance—Mercury's rough-and-tumble rhetoric (mentioned but not quoted by Marlowe) is only partially successful. He does not enjoy her; she imposes on him an impossible task which diverts him from the object of his exercise. Marlowe is showing, as he had shown before in the two parts of *Tamburlaine*, the diminishing power of the Eloquence of Persuasions. Just as Tamburlaine's rhetoric is first turned against him by Callapine, and finally shown to be powerless against the death of Zenocrate, so Leander's 'winning words' are diminished in the account of Mercury's speech.

The abyss between innocence and action widens in the Second Sestiad, in which the spiritual coming-together of the lovers is re-enacted in physical terms. Both Ovid and Musaeus make this a natural consummation; Leander asserts his masculinity by swimming the Hellespont, and is rewarded with Hero's body—'Oscula, di magni! trans mare digna peti', in Ovid's words.[10] Their love is efficiently

---

[10] *Heroides*, xviii, 102.

consummated at the first available opportunity. Marlowe, on the other hand, invents a meeting before the famous swim, a meeting in which things do not go according to the romantic paradigm. This scene, the third of the attempted seductions, translates into action Leander's attempted seduction by eloquence in the First Sestiad. Significantly, the activity is distanced; it is described by the narrator, whose ironic reticence plays traitor to any romantic assertion. Leander gets 'by stealth' to Hero's tower:

> O who can tell the greeting
> These greedy lovers had at their first meeting?
> He ask'd, she gave, and nothing was denied;

But this last line (we learn later) does not mean what it appears to mean. Hero continues her coquetry:

> Ay, and she wish'd, albeit not from her heart,
> That he would leave her turret and depart.

Leander's innocence is put to the test—and not found wanting:

> Like Aesop's cock, this jewel he enjoyed,[11]
> And as a brother with his sister toyed,
> Supposing nothing else was to be done . . .
> Albeit Leander, rude in love, and raw,
> Long dallying with Hero, nothing saw
> That might delight him more, yet he suspected
> Some amorous rites or other were neglected.

The innocence, already absurd, is made even more comic by the narrator's bland understatement. At last, Hero's struggles arouse him to some sense of what is required, but once again her artfulness saves her:

> She, with a kind of granting, put him by it,
> And ever, as he thought himself most nigh it,
> Like to the tree of Tantalus she fled,
> And seeming lavish, sav'd her maidenhead.

Finally, the morning intervenes and Leander departs 'fearing to be

---

[11] Not understanding the value of the thing before him. Martin's note (p. 54) is corrected by T. W. Baldwin, 'Marlowe's Musaeus', *JEGP* (October 1955), pp. 478–85. Marlowe introduces this passage by comparing Hero with Salmacis, the nymph who wooed Hermaphroditus (Ovid, *Metamorphoses*, IV. 285 ff.)—a comparison which yet further enforces the ambivalent sexuality of Leander.

miss'd', leaving Hero intact to fight another day. This episode shows the total failure of Leander's enterprise when his seductive words give place to actions which are ineloquent because they are uninformed. Leander has yet to learn the techniques of physical persuasion. What emerges about Marlowe's art from these three attempted seductions is the way in which the reader's response is conditioned by the hedging comments of the narrator, which inhibit the full celebration of any passion by a powerful irony and simple scepticism:

> His secret flame apparently was seen,
> Leander's father knew where he had been,

He relates the growth of Leander's love with the same brisk cheerfulness as he describes everything else.

The tone shifts, becomes more complex, in the fourth attempt at seduction, the encounter between Leander and Neptune during Leander's second swim to Sestos. Critics usually achieve a deep reticence about the nature of this episode. Even Erich Segal, to my mind one of the most perceptive, calls it 'one of the several touches of homosexuality in the poem'.[12] It is, in fact, a frank, overt homosexual flirtation, described in luxuriant detail and observed with a fine comic detachment. Neptune is a lusty old paederast who feels no need of words to manifest his intentions. He mistakes Leander for Ganymede, and his actions speak for him:

> . . . therefore on him he seiz'd.
> Leander striv'd, the waves about him wound,
> And pull'd him to the bottom . . .

> The lusty god embrac'd him, call'd him 'love',
> And swore he never should return to Jove.

The description is prolonged, and the verse becomes sinuously physical:

> He clapp'd his plump cheeks, with his tresses play'd,
> And smiling wantonly, his love bewray'd.
> He watch'd his arms, and as they open'd wide,
> At every stroke, betwixt them would he slide,

---

[12] 'Hero and Leander: Góngora and Marlowe', *Comparative Literature*, pp. 338–56. Segal compares the versions of Góngora and Marlowe and finds that both 'stand diametrically opposed to all previous treatments of the legend'. He says 'Both Marlowe and Góngora have chosen this theme as a vehicle for cynical views of conventional love'. My judgement of Marlowe's poem is the same as his, though we differ in most details of interpretation.

> And steal a kiss, and then run out and dance,
> And as he turn'd, cast many a lustful glance,
> And throw him gaudy toys to please his eye,
> And dive into the water, and there pry
> Upon his breast, his thighs, and every limb,
> And up again, and close beside him swim,
> And talk of love.

But Leander's innocence remains intact, wickedly contrasted with Neptune's paederastics by the all-knowing narrator:

> . . . Leander made reply,
> 'You are deceiv'd, I am no woman, I.'
> Thereat smil'd Neptune . . .

All Neptune's frenzied activity is made futile by Leander's complete inability to grasp what is going on, and Neptune, far from attempting a seduction by eloquence, is reduced to words to try to make his purpose clear. What follows is a development of both the comic techniques Marlowe has employed; it is an attempted seduction of a peculiar kind, and a presentation of inverted sexual attributes through the medium of speech. Neptune begins the story of a shepherd sitting in a vale and playing with a lovely boy,

> That of the cooling river durst not drink,
> Lest water-nymphs should pull him from the brink.
> And when he sported in the fragrant lawns,
> Goat-footed Satyrs and upstarting Fauns
> Would steal him thence.

The relationship of this passage to *Edward II* could hardly be clearer. Gaveston, who might 'have swum from France, And like Leander gaspt vpon the sande', proposes to sway the pliant king by exactly the same means:

> Like Syluan Nimphes my pages shall be clad,
> My men like Satyres grazing on the lawnes,
> Shall with their Goate feete daunce an antick hay.
> Sometime a louelie boye in Dians shape,
> With haire that gilds the water as it glides . . .
> Shall bathe him in a spring . . .[13]

Yet Leander's virtue remains intact. He interrupts the tale after only

[13] Tucker Brooke, p. 315.

eight lines with a cry 'Aye me', and a periphrastic announcement to the effect that 'time's getting on'. The whole episode ends in failure for Neptune. His activity is powerless to arouse; his eloquence, however rich in rhythm and association, is unable to convince. He is reduced to searching the Ocean for gifts, in a last attempt to change Leander's mind:

> 'Tis wisdom to give much, a gift prevails,
> When deep persuading Oratory fails.

This last stratagem is prevented by Leander's safe arrival on shore at Sestos.[14] In the development of the seduction pattern through the poem the fulsome eloquence of Leander's plea in the First Sestiad has shrivelled to Neptune's half-told tale, but the range and plenitude of physical action has steadily increased. The activity of passion has not yet achieved its desired end, but it has become a more powerful persuasive instrument than speech.

The final scene, when Leander and Hero come together, is completely silent. Leander has one short, simple speech when he reaches the tower, in which the arts of persuasion are firmly renounced; they are no longer necessary:

> At least vouchsafe these arms some little room,
> Who hoping to embrace thee, cheerly swum.
> This head was beat with many a churlish billow,
> And therefore let it rest upon thy pillow.

The histrionics are gone, the appeal is a simple plea for pity, and Leander does not speak another word in the poem. His actions speak for him, and the comic tone is taken up by the gravely detached narrator, who comments crisply on the activity, re-emphasising the coquetry and artfulness of Hero. The lovers' union is accomplished through metaphors of battle and strategy, presented not with a direct and simple sensuousness but with an oblique, and thoroughly 'metaphysical' wit. Hero plays at eluding her pursuer,

> And every limb did as a soldier stout
> Defend the fort, and keep the foeman out.
> For though the rising ivory mount he scal'd,

---

[14] The whole episode is generally regarded as Marlowe's invention. But see Martin T. Williams, 'The Temptations in Marlowe's *Hero and Leander*', *Modern Language Quarterly* (September 1955), pp. 226–31, who tries (unsuccessfully, in my view) to link it with the Caenis-Caeneus story in Ovid, *Metamorphoses*, XII.

> Which is with azure circling lines empal'd,
> Much like a globe (a globe may I term this,
> By which Love sails to regions full of bliss),
> Yet there with Sisyphus he toil'd in vain,
> Till gentle parley did the truce obtain.

The breast becomes a globe, the assault becomes a journey, the image is further complicated by the marvellously apt but completely casual allusion to Sisyphus, and the whole passage directs attention not to the quality of the love but to the comic triumph of Marlowe's art. Hero's constant 'awareness', her strategic handling of the varying situations, her art in retaining social modesty while sacrificing no pleasure, are exposed and exploited in contrast with Leander's invincible innocence, which is itself the constant mark of the narrator's mockery. The actual union of the lovers is introduced with a hyperbolic epic simile—'Even as a bird, which in our hands we wring . . .'—and the victorious Leander is made the subject of a fully heroic comparison:

> Leander now, like Theban Hercules,
> Enter'd the orchard of th' Hesperides;

At this, the climax of the narrative, it is evident that Marlowe does not present his lovers as serious, orthodox protagonists of a Petrarchan love-affair, still less as the tragic victims of a remorseless fate. It is a paradox of his art that he makes them larger than life, by exaggerated description, and at the same time absurdly human and vulnerable, by the sharp detachment of his narration. Hyperbole loses its dignity and enforces the embracing comic purpose. In this last episode the simple, human actions are crystallised in a suave, brilliant, and ruthlessly mannered narrative, so that both the simplicity and the humanity are burlesqued and made vulnerable. The inversion of sexual attributes denies seriousness to the narrative; the attempted seductions are foiled by loquacity or punctured by wit; the Eloquence of Persuasions progressively recedes from the story, and, as the fragment ends, it is played upon the reader.

Throughout the Second Sestiad Marlowe is deliberately playing off one kind of love against another. The most serious and richly descriptive imagery is deployed in the account of Neptune's flirtation with Leander; observation is close and detailed, and the poet dwells lovingly, daringly on this sensuous picture of unnatural passion. The heterosexual love, on the other hand, is described objectively, with a mature cynicism and a cryptic wit. It seems that Marlowe is concerned to contrast two ideas of love, and to give the persuasive poetry to the peripheral attitude. This preoccupation with unnatural love has its analogues in the plays. Although it has no part in the ambience of either Tamburlaine or Faustus it is significantly present in what was probably Marlowe's first play, *Dido Queen of Carthage*. *Dido* opens with a fifty line dialogue between Jupiter and Ganymede, in which Jupiter begins with a request 'Come gentle *Ganimed* and play with me'. Ganymede complains that Juno has struck him without cause, and, when Jupiter threatens to punish her, asks to be a witness to the punishment. Jupiter is sensuously indulgent to the whim:

> What ist sweet wagge I should deny thy youth?
> Whose face reflects such pleasure to mine eyes,
> As I exhal'd with thy fire darting beames,
> Haue oft driuen backe the horses of the night,
> When as they would haue hal'd thee from my sight:[15]

The dialogue proceeds, in a slow, richly evocative way, with similar trivialities which Ganymede is begging from Jupiter, and ends:

> *Gan.* I would haue a iewell for mine eare,
> And a fine brouch to put in my hat,
> And then Ile hugge with you an hundred times.
> *Iup.* And shall haue *Ganimed*, if thou wilt be my loue.

Marlowe's engagement with his source-material in *Dido* is, for the most part, close and literal, but this first scene arises from what is the barest hint in Virgil.[16] The prevailing tone at the opening of *Aeneid IV* is of heroic human assertion, set against a background of the enmity of heaven (one which should have attracted the Marlowe who was so shortly to write *Tamburlaine*); yet *Dido* begins not on earth, but among the gods; it begins not with the heroic and human voice, but with the luxuriously beautiful, enervated, unnatural relationship between the god and the boy. The love of Dido and Aeneas is by comparison cold and unevocative. In the cave scene Dido's pleas are solemn and unsexual, and they end in a bribe:

> Hold, take these Iewels at thy Louers hand,
> These golden bracelets, and this wedding ring,

[15] Tucker Brooke, p. 393.
[16] *Aeneid*, I.28.

> Wherewith my husband woo'd me yet a maide,
> And be thou king of *Libia*, by my guift.[17]

Heterosexual love is hard, jewelled, and cold, and it is on the Jupiter–Ganymede scene, and the scene in which Cupid is disguised as Ascanius and flirts cunningly, precociously with Dido that Marlowe lavishes a specially sensuous care.

Edward II is centrally concerned with the effects of homosexual love upon a king, and the unnatural passion is presented as beautiful, sensational, powerful, and, in this special case, fatal. Edward finds his kingdom well lost,

> So I may haue some nooke or corner left,
> To frolicke with my deerest *Gaueston*.[18]

It is a sacrificial love on both sides; Edward loves his minion 'Because he loues me more then all the world', and Jupiter and Ganymede, Hercules and Hylas are called up to image and to sanctify this unnatural, beautiful, and mortal passion. In his concern with the morally unorthodox Marlowe anticipates a great deal of later Jacobean drama. His allegiances are with Ford, and the sensational 'brooding over the swamp' in *'Tis Pity She's a Whore*. The piercing exploration of homosexual love which is the dynamic of *Edward II* is, however, only part of the complex pattern of human love in *Hero and Leander*. The poem works by contrast and ironic antithesis, but within this pattern the Leander–Neptune episode stands out as a passage in which the physical and overtly erotic description enforces the peculiar power of homosexual love, and suspends orthodox moral judgements.

Marlowe's use of classical mythology in the poem has received considerable attention, and the most serious conclusions have been drawn. Yet it seems to me essentially a part of his comic manner. Gods and goddesses are introduced familiarly into the story, classical allusions range from the most familiar to the most recondite, and where the available myths are not sufficient Marlowe, like so many of his contemporaries, does not scruple to invent his own. There is, so far as I know, no classical authority for the statement that Apollo courted Hero for her hair and offered her his throne (I.5–7). This is a simple fancy, establishing an appropriate status for Hero, but Marlowe more commonly invents explanations for current mythological situations. He explains Cupid's blindness, for example:

---

[17] Tucker Brooke, p. 420.   [18] Tucker Brooke, p. 323.

> Some say, for her the fairest Cupid pin'd,
> And looking in her face, was strooken blind.
> But this is true, so like was one the other,
> As he imagin'd Hero was his mother . . .

Both explanations belong wholly to Marlowe's imagination, yet he is prepared to debate the matter for four lines, as if it mattered. He accounts for a natural phenomenon in terms of his story:

> So lovely fair was Hero, Venus' nun,
> As Nature wept, thinking she was undone . . .
> Therefore, in sign her treasure suffer'd wrack,
> Since Hero's time hath half the world been black.

Similarly, in the description of Leander, it is his beauty which makes the moon pale:

> Fair Cynthia wish'd his arms might be her sphere;
> Grief makes her pale, because she moves not there.

The game of 'myth-making' is common enough in Elizabethan poetry, but in this poem it functions specifically as an instrument of humour. The myth is pressed into service to explain the story, or the story to explain the myth, in such a way that our response is to adroitness rather than aptness; our admiration for inventive ingenuity overwhelms any feeling for heroic status of character or situation, so that the classical analogy, by the terms of its presentation, burlesques its subject instead of energising it. In the larger instances, notably the Mercury myth, the effect is on a larger scale. Marlowe's invention takes off, so most commentators agree, from one, or at most two, passages in the *Metamorphoses*.[19] These hints are expanded into a glowing narrative, which, for all its energy, has little connection with the events of the poem. All the ingenuity is expended in the service of a fairly trite moral:

> Yet as a punishment they added this,
> That he and Poverty should always kiss.
> And to this day is every scholar poor,

Is it come to this? Clearly, the Mercury myth is justified only by the quality and height of its invention; as narrative it is finally irrelevant.

In the establishment of the burlesque tone the key passage is the description of the Temple of Venus in Sestiad I. Marlowe is indebted to

[19] *Metamorphoses*, II.708 ff., seems the most likely.

no source here, beyond the traditional descriptions of temples in terms
of the classical myths appropriate to them. His technique is similar to
Spenser's in the description of the House of Busirane. Spenser establishes the ambience of luxury and excess by his account of the tapestries,
the works of art, with which the walls were decorated:

> And in those Tapets weren fashioned
> Many faire pourtraicts, and many a faire feate,
> And all of loue, and all of lusty-hed,
> As seemed by their semblaunt did entreat;
> And eke all *Cupids* warres they did repeate,[20]

The examples follow, stanza upon stanza, detailing the amours of Jove
and the escapades of Cupid, building up an ethos, in terms of visual art
and myth, into which Busirane himself has no need to enter. The myths
make his character for him. Similarly, Marlowe creates a peculiar
shrine for the goddess of love. The catalogue opens with Proteus,
carved 'in discoloured jasper stone',[21] and proceeds to a fantastic
Bacchus:

> . . . and o'erhead
> A lively vine of green sea-agate spread;
> Where by one hand, light-headed Bacchus hung,
> And with the other, wine from grapes outwrung.[22]

The conjunction of Venus with this Bacchus imposes a certain limited
view of the goddess, which is enforced by the description of the pave-
ment in the temple. Marlowe's tone is robust and confident:

> There might you see the gods in sundry shapes,
> Committing heady riots, incest, rapes:

And these are itemised: Danae, Jove and his sister, Ganymede,
Europa, Mars and Vulcan (a delicate subject in Venus' temple), Silvanus
and Cypressus. It is indeed a pageant of 'loue and lusty-hed', and forms
an absurd contrast to the innocent, young lovers who come to worship
there. Marlowe's point, and it could hardly be made more strongly, is

[20] *The Faerie Queene*, III.xi.29.
[21] The presence of Proteus probably indicates the Protean shapes of love,
especially the many disguises adopted by Zeus.
[22] I can find no classical or Renaissance source for this figure. The nearest is
an illustration in Cartari, *Le Imagini dei Dei de gli Antichi* (Lyons, 1581), p. 362,
which relates to the story of Bacchus festooning (his) ship with vines and ivy
(Philostratus, *Imagines*, I.19). In the picture several people are swinging from
the vines, but not Bacchus.

that the divine exemplars of love behave in this manner, and that only the innocent, inexperienced frail humans cherish illusions about tenderness, and modesty and the gentle heart. Marlowe's Venus would hardly have approved of his Neptune, but she would have understood his point of view.

Young love is absurd. It may seem that Marlowe's theme represents a rather cheap discovery about the human condition by one who was accustomed to explore humanity and its sufferings more deeply. The absurdity is exposed, mercilessly, right through the poem, in different ways and at varying levels. But it is not exploited. A trenchant enquiry would direct the poem inexorably towards tragedy, and, as I have tried to show, the dominant tone is comic. The central figure is the suave, detached narrator, who asserts an unshakeable comic control over narrative, allusion, and language alike. Marlowe's bias is increasingly towards the full burlesque, and away from the impending tragic end of the story. Perhaps that is why he never finished it.

Snakes Leape by Verse

ROMA GILL

Snakes Leape by Verse

THE SPELL-BINDING SONGS of the *Amores* have lost none of their power in the *Metamorphoses* when Medea claims that 'By charmes' she can 'burst the Viper's jaw'.[1] But for Marlowe the *carmina* have an even greater magic:

> Snakes leape by verse from caues of broken mountaines.
>
> (II.i.25[2])

This rendering of Ovid's '*carmine dissiliunt abruptis faucibus angues*' shows Marlowe's translation at its worst. In excuse one might plead that his Latin text read *desiliunt* for *dissiliunt*; that *fauces* could mean 'a mountain pass'. The errors are those that a schoolboy could make—especially a schoolboy who was going to end his next line with 'fountaines' and badly needed the rhyme. In the *Elegies* Marlowe's Latin, and his English, are often those of the schoolboy, careless or ignorant of idiom and too lazy to check his guesses with a dictionary.

In 'marking' the poems as translations—Ovid in one hand, Marlowe in the other—one is first of all struck by thoughtlessness of the 'leaping snakes' kind. Seeing the line

> *flere genis electra tuas, Auriga, sorores*

Marlowe connected '*electra*' with the sister of Orestes and wrote

> Heau'n starre *Electra* that bewaild her sisters. (III.xi.37)

Again, he could be partly excused by laying, as L. C. Martin does,[3] some of the blame on his Latin text; but this, together with credit for

---

[1] *Ouid's Metamorphoses*, tr. Arthur Golding (1567), vii.271.

[2] Quotations from Marlowe's *Ouids Elegies* are taken from Tucker Brooke's edition of the *Works* (1910, reprinted 1966). Since Marlowe usually translates line-for-line, the Latin quotations which accompany his versions are not separately numbered. The text used for the *Amores* is that of the Loeb series edited by Grant Showerman (1914, reprinted 1963). This text includes one poem (III.v) which was not in the edition that Marlowe used (and which is probably not Ovid's work).

[3] Cf. the note to the poem in his edition, *Marlowe's Poems* (1931), p. 251.

identifying Electra as one of the Pleiades (hence 'Heau'n starre') must
be counterbalanced by censure for a grammatical error in making a
supposed nominative (*'electra'*) subject of an infinitive (*'flere'*) and for a
gap in general knowledge where he should have realised that

> The brotherless *Heliades*
> Melt in such Amber Tears as these.[4]

Three Latin usages in particular escaped Marlowe. Where Ovid gazes
contemptuously at the piddling little stream, *'nescio quem hunc spectans
... amnem'*, Marlowe, not recognising, or more likely not understanding, the *nescio quis* form flounders with 'I know not what expecting
...' (III.v.103). The same form is mistaken in another poem, when
Ovid scorns the rival who has supplanted him:

> ... *nescio cui, quem tu conplexa tenebas.*

Marlowe translates

> I know not whom thou lewdly didst imbrace, (III.x.11)

a line which can be read to suggest that the mistress was entertaining
not one but several lovers. At times the misconstruing makes for a total
reversal of meaning. Whereas Ovid's Corinna aborted herself without
the poet's knowledge (*'clam me'*), Marlowe has it that the operation
was performed 'secretly with me' (II.xiii.3). Ceremonial processions
are, for Ovid, greeted with respectful silence: the spectators at the
chariot-races are commanded *'linguis animisque favete'* and the wor-
shippers at the festival of Juno *'ore favent'*. But Marlowe likes noise:
'let all men cheere', he orders at the races (III.ii.43), and when the
procession honouring Juno approaches 'lowd the people hollow'
(III.xii.29). These make sense—even if it is not Ovid's sense. But when
Marlowe writes

> What day was that, which all sad haps to bring,
> White birdes to louers did not alwayes sing (III.xi.1–2)

we have to turn to the Latin to begin to understand the English:

> *Quis fuit ille dies, quo tristia semper amanti
> omina non albae concinuistis aves?*

Yet even with this assistance, and granting that Marlowe read *omnia*

---

[4] Andrew Marvell, 'The Nymph complaining for the death of her Faun',
ll. 99–100.

for *omina* (whether or not it was printed so in his text), the English has little meaning because this time it is Ovid's sentence structure that has eluded him and not just a word or phrase. Much the same sort of meaninglessness is found in II.xiv.8 where the *ut* clause is not recognised as an adverbial clause of purpose:

> *ut careat rugarum crimine venter*

becomes

> Because thy belly should rough wrinckles lacke,

and once again the Latin has to be called to aid. It is perhaps unlikely that Marlowe possessed a dictionary. Certainly he did not use it if he thought he was safe with a guess, choosing the English word nearest in sound to the Latin. The method works reasonably well when he translates

> *Iuppiter, admonitus nihil esse potentius auro*

as

> *Ioue* being admonisht gold had soueraigne power, (III.vii.29)

and at III.v.50 the sense is still clear enough, although the Latin '*loca sola*' is visible beneath the English 'sole places'. But Marlowe should have given more thought to II.ix.20. The line

> His sword layed by, safe, though rude places yeelds

cannot be understood until the Latin is consulted and the error becomes apparent. Ovid, in his line

> *tutaque deposito poscitur ense rudis,*

alludes to the custom of presenting the retiring gladiator with a harmless wooden foil—*rudis*. One begins to question the efficacy of the Elizabethan education system when an Archbishop Parker Scholar can make such elementary mistakes.

Schoolboy howlers, however, enliven the marker's task; the wholly accurate translation may make rather dull reading. Marlowe sticks closest to his text when he is least interested in its subject. The theme of II.xi, for instance, a cautious argument against the dangers of seafaring with concern for the voyaging mistress, was not likely to recommend itself to an adventurous egotist. Marlowe plods through the translation, dutiful but uninspired. Boredom is evident in the adjectives: 'crooked Barque' ('*panda carina*'); 'carefull ship-man' ('*navita sollicitus*'); 'prosperous winde' ('*vento . . . secundo*'); 'knowne ship' ('*notam . . .*

puppim'). What is lost in this translation is not the sense but the feeling. While Ovid promises a wild rapture of delight to greet his mistress on her return, a rapture that overflows the hexameter and emphasises the kisses—

> *excipiamque umeris et multa sine ordine carpam*
> *oscula; pro reditu victima vota cadet*

—Marlowe is restrained, and his eye is not on the returning mistress but on the rhyme he needs for the following line:

> Ile clip and kisse thee with all contentation,
> For thy returne shall fall the vowd oblation. (II.xi.45–6)

At his most accurate and least involved Marlowe writes pure 'translationese', a language that bears a close resemblance to the one from which he is translating but little or none to idiomatic English. With the line

> Wish in his hands graspt did *Hippomenes*, (III.ii.30)

although he has substituted '*Hippomenes*' for Ovid's '*Milanion*' (in line 29) to secure a rhyme for the preceding 'these', the order is that of the Latin:

> *optavit manibus sustinuisse suis*

There is the same uncomfortable metaphrasis in

> What? not *Alpheus* in strange lands to runne (III.v.29)

where Marlowe scribbles down his word-for-word version of

> *quid, non Alpheon diversis currere terris.*

He makes sure there is a rhyme for 'wunne' in the following line, but otherwise he seems to care little for either the poetry or the sense, proving the justice of Dryden's comment that ' 'Tis almost impossible to Translate verbally, and well, at the same time'.[5] Metaphrasis is Marlowe's usual resort when he is bored with the *Amores*. Ovid remonstrates with Corinna for dyeing her hair (I.xiv) and for attempting an abortion (II.xiii and xiv), but Marlowe is unable to imagine himself in such an intimate situation and unable to simulate the necessary mixture of anger and anxiety. His is a narrower range of feeling where emotions are deeper and more personal. Not until the writing of *Hero*

[5] 'Preface Concerning Ovid's Epistles' (1683).

and Leander did he begin to achieve that cool objectivity that charac-
terises the *Amores*.

Although a slighter work than the *Metamorphoses*, the *Amores*
presents the translator with greater problems. The fifteen books of
transformation stories were a massive work for Arthur Golding, but
at all times he had the narrative line to guide him. Marlowe had no
such support. The three books of the *Amores* form a slender collection
of highly polished poems where urbanity and technical virtuosity are
all-important. Ovid's poems, as L. P. Wilkinson stresses, are not
personal; 'It is beside the point to seek for autobiography in Ovid's
erotic elegies'.[6] Instead of being cries—of pain or pleasure—from the
heart of the individual lover they utter sentiments to which every
amorous bosom can return on echo, and were written in order

> That some youth hurt as I am with loues bowe
> His owne flames best aquainted signes may knowe,
> And long admiring say, by what meanes learnd
> Hath this same Poet my sad chaunce discernd? (II.i.7–10)

The real Ovid speaks, if at all, as the poetic theorist and commentator
who at the outset declares 'I haue no mistresse, nor no fauorit' (I.i.23)
to provoke and inspire the verse; who promises to abandon this triviality
shortly because '*a tergo grandius urguet opus*';[7] and who takes his leave
at the end of the third book when '*pulsanda est magnis area maior equis*'.[8]
The Naso who speaks for the rest of the time in the *Amores* is a persona
only. He experiences every mood of every lover, whether he is triumphant in his mistress's arms, jealous at a banquet, servile at her
locked door, or even impotent in her bed. It is irrelevant to question the
sincerity: one can only admire the elegance.

In the *Amores* the elegiac couplet reaches perfection: Wilkinson
indeed calls Ovid the Pope of the Latin elegy, as Tibullus was its
Waller.[9] The feelings of Naso may for the most part have been oft
thought—and intentionally so—but the style of Ovid raises them above
the commonplace. They were ne'er so well expressed. His Latin,
according to Dryden 'a most Severe and Compendious Language',[10]

---

[6] *Ovid Recalled* (1955), p. 46.

[7] Marlowe is less confident of vocation in his mistranslation: 'Some greater
worke will vrge me on at last' (III.i.70).

[8] Ovid's mighty steeds are carthorses to Marlowe: 'A greater ground with
great horse is to till' (III.xiv.18).

[9] op. cit., p. 31.

[10] op. cit.

lent itself to the gymnastics of rhetorical devices, above all to symmetry and to repetition with variation. These two need to be singled out. Not only are they most delightful in Ovid's poems: they are also the most likely to suffer or be lost in translation. The Ovidian balance of

multa supercilio vidi vibrante loquentes

where the pivotal verb separates nouns from adjectival participles can hardly be reproduced in an uninflected language. Marlowe does his best, but the result is clumsy and unidiomatic:

I sawe your nodding eye-browes much to speake. (II.v.15)

With the chiastic symmetry of

candida me capiet, capiet me flava puella

he is more successful, translating

A white wench thralles me, so doth golden yellowe (II.iv.39)

Where Ovid gives a formal beauty to his poem about the locked-out lover (I.vi) with the repeated

tempora noctis eunt; excute poste seram

Marlowe, because of the exigencies of rhyme, has to resort to what Fowler would have called 'elegant variation':

Night goes away: the dores barre backeward strike. (line 24)
Strike backe the barre, night fast away doth goe (line 32)
Night runnes away; with open entrance greete them (line 40)
Night goes away: I pray thee ope the dore (line 48)

nights deawie hoast
March fast away: the barre strike from the poast. (lines 55–6)

In the inflected language one word can be repeated, the same and not the same:

carmina sanguineae deducunt cornua lunae,
et revocant niveos solis euntis equos;
carmine dissiliunt abruptis faucibus angues,
inque suos fontes versa recurrit aqua.
carminibus cessere fores, insertaque posti,
quamvis robur est, carmina victa sera est.

Marlowe, despite his gross mistranslation of line 25, makes a great effort, but the language compels him to add particles and, although quite powerful, the lines lack Ovid's grace:

> Verses reduce the horned bloudy moone
> And call the sunnes white horses backe at noone.
> Snakes leape by verse from caues of broken mountaines
> And turned streames run back-ward to their fountaines.
> Verses ope dores, and lockes put in the poast,
> Although of oake, to yeeld to verses boast. (II.i.23–8)

The very first poem in the collection should alert a translator to the difficulties inherent in Ovid's verse form. The Latin poet can demonstrate the meaning of his

> *Sex mihi surgat opus numeris, in quinque residat*

while the English writer must rely on a footnote, or on informed readers, to explain

> Let my first verse be sixe, my last fiue feete. (I.i.31)

There is no direct equivalent in English for the elegiac couplet with its soaring hexameter and receding pentameter. The heroic couplet is the closest parallel, but here Marlowe and Ovid are at different ends of their respective traditions. Whereas many before Ovid had written in his form, Marlowe could look to few precedents in the use of the couplet and not the line as the basic unit and the couplet, in turn, as a part of the greater unit which is the poem. Marlowe himself still thinks in terms of the line, giving a heavy pause on the rhyme-word and a consequent awkwardness in the reading. Ovid, for instance, gives us a couplet with an easy enjambement in

> *Esse quid hoc dicam, quod tam mihi dura videntur*
> *strata, neque in lecto pallia nostra sedent.*

Marlowe, in its place, offers two separate lines hooked together by the rhyme:

> What makes my bed seeme hard seeing it is soft?
> Or why slips downe the couerlet so oft? (I.ii.1–2)

The couplets are often detachable; the poem would not suffer greatly if one of them were removed. The dialectical influence of the Metaphysical poets was necessary before, in Pope's hands, the couplet could become an organic part of the poem.

Abraham Fleming spoke in scorn when he rejected, as a possible medium for his translations of the *Georgics* and the *Bucolics*

> foolish rhyme, the nice obseruance whereof many times darkeneth, corrupteth, peruerteth and falsifieth both the sense and the signification.[11]

Marlowe's translations often invite such scorn, for the self-imposed discipline of rhyme compelled the poet to some strange shifts. In III.iii.39–40, where he is referring to Jupiter's affaire with Semele, he writes

> But when her louer came, had she drawne backe,
> The fathers thigh should vnborne *Bacchus* lacke.

This looks like metaphrasis, but when we turn to the Latin we find that Ovid's line is less specific but far more graceful:

> *non pater in Baccho matris haberet opus.*

The need to find a rhyme for 'backe' here, for 'black' in II.vi.49–50, and for 'back' again in III.xii.17–18 has forced Marlowe to the clumsy distortion of 'lacke'. In the last of these more than mere clumsiness is involved. Marlowe, translating

> *invisa est dominae sola capella deae*

crams most of Ovid's sense into the first part of the line then adds his own 'did lack' to make up the rhyme:

> And Rams with hornes their hard heads wreathed back.
> Onely the Goddesse hated Goate did lack.

He solves one problem and creates another. Ovid continues with an account of the hunting, at any time, of the she-goat; Marlowe, trying to catch up with the Latin, brings the beast—most improperly—into the procession:

> Now is the goat brought through the boyes with darts,
> And giue to him that the first wound imparts. (III.xii.21–2)

Where Ovid writes '*dubius Mars est*' Marlowe translates '*Mars* in great doubt doth trample' (II.ix.49) for no reason other than that 'example' in the following line needs a mate. The parrot's grave is apparently strewn with pebbles instead of bearing the one small inscribed tombstone that Ovid desired:

[11] *The Bucolics of Virgil together with his Georgics* (1589), 'The Argument'.

> A graue her bones hides, on her corps great graue
> The little stones these little verses haue. (II.vi.59–60)

Ovid's *'lapis exiguus'* has been shattered. If the rhyme dictates, a word can be coined:

> When bad fates take good men, I am forbod
> By secreat thoughts to thinke there is a god; (III.viii.35–6)

and the English language twisted into strange shapes:

> What? not *Alpheus* in strange lands to runne
> Th' *Arcadian* Virgins constant loue hath wunne?
> (III.v.29–30)

The translation here, as I said before, is metaphrastic: word-for-word in the Latin order. Marlowe is too careful of his rhyme and too careless of the sense:

> *quid? non Alpheon diversis currere terris*
> *virginis Arcadiae certus adegit amor.*

Most of these are to be found in poems which have other flaws, poems in which Marlowe's attention is not fully engaged. Where he is really interested the rhymes are less forced, although even here they may distract him from Ovid's total meaning. In I.viii Ovid makes play with the name 'Dipsas' ('thirsty'), saying that it is most apt for the old bawd who has never been sober enough to see the sun rise:

> *nigri non illa parentem*
> *Memnonis in roseis sobria vidit equis.*

Marlowe, mistaking the meaning and emphasis of *'sobria'* and planning 'rise' for the end of the second line, misses the point of Ovid's couplet entirely:

> she being wise
> Sees not the morne on rosie horses rise. (I.viii.3–4)

In the same poem the mistress is told by Dipsas to extort gifts from her lover upon any and every occasion, and when all other pretexts fail to pretend it is her birthday by having a birthday-cake on view. Marlowe, having correctly translated *'munera'* (but making it singular) as 'gift', is at a loss for the rhyme and consequently is forced to omit the amusing detail of the birthday-cake:

When causes fale thee to require a gift,
By keeping of thy birth make but a shift. (I.viii.93–4)

It is not until the Latin and English versions are compared that the mistranslation in I.v is apparent. The poem *'Corinnae concubitus'* is one of the very best of Marlowe's translations, successful not only as a rendering of the Latin but as a poem in its own right. With evident enjoyment Marlowe shares in Ovid's description of the scene—the flickering shadows of a darkened room on a hot afternoon. Corinna enters, wearing what Ovid describes as a *'tunica . . . recincta'* but what Marlowe, visualising her as an English woman, calls 'a long loose gowne' (l. 9); both poets relish the sight of her naked body then, after gazing in wonder and touching with tenderness, Ovid embraces Corinna. A silence follows; and then a sleep:

> *Cetera quis nescit? lassi requievimus ambo.*
> *proveniant medii sic mihi saepe dies.*

Marlowe follows Ovid as far as the embrace, but his attention now is on the poem's last line. Having translated it to end with 'this' he finds his rhyme in 'kisse':

> Iudge you the rest: being tirde she bad me kisse,
> *Ioue* send me more such after-noones as this. (I.v.25–6)

The search for a rhyme has prevented consummation.

Usually the translation is best when Marlowe stands a little way back from the Latin and concentrates on transmitting sense and feeling rather than translating the exact words; this is Dryden's 'second way' of translation:

> The second way is that of Paraphrase, or Translation with Latitude, where the Author is kept in view by the Translator, so as never to be lost, but his words are not so strictly follow'd as his sense; and that too is admitted to be amplified, but not alter'd.[12]

'Paraphrase' is seldom Marlowe's method throughout a whole poem, but on occasion it produces some of his best rhymes. In I.x, for instance, where Ovid refers to the prostitute who sells her body—

> *et miseras iusso corpore quaerit opes*

—Marlowe selects the Elizabethan slang 'Cony' and reinforces its meaning by the rhyme:

[12] op. cit.

> The whore stands to be bought for each mans mony
> And seekes vilde wealth by selling of her Cony. (I.x.21–2)

The rhymes of I.iv often have an anglo-saxon vigour, as in the strong
verb endings of lines 5 and 6:

> Wilt lying vnder him his bosome clippe?
> About thy necke shall he at pleasure skippe?

Ovid cannot communicate the degree of disgust that these monosyllables
express. Near the end of the poem a free translation of '*sitque maligna
Venus*' has given 'vnpleasant' for the rhyme-word; and in the preceding
line Marlowe has added 'pezant':

> Constrain'd against thy will giue it the pezant,
> Forbeare sweet wordes and be your sport vnpleasant.
>
> (I.iv.65–6)

The slam of a double rhyme ends the poem:

> But though this night thy fortune be to trie it,
> To me to morrow constantly deny it. (I.iv.69–70)

In these accomplished rhymes, foreshadowing those of *Hero and
Leander*, is the sense that Marlowe understood his job and recognised
the power of rhyme to enforce or contradict the statements of a poem.

A major feature of Roman elegy, certainly of Ovid's poems, is the
parallel from Greek legend—the comparison, say, of the beloved with
Venus for beauty or Minerva for wit. Even L. P. Wilkinson admits that

> To us it is apt to seem a tiresome substitute for thinking of something
> to say: we may find it hard to recapture the romantic aura, to feel the
> thrill that a Roman elegist may have felt in comparing his present
> situation with that of fabled heroes half-divine.[13]

The difficulty increases with unfamiliarity. For the Romans it was
enough that Ovid should allude to '*vitis . . . repertor*'; the decoding
they could do for themselves. Marlowe solves the problem for his
readers by writing firmly—if less poetically—'*Bacchus*' (I.iii.11). With
tact and, for the most part, with accuracy he reduces the patronymics
and coded descriptions to the most well-known names. Thus '*Schoe-
neida*' in I.vii.13 is identified for us as '*Atalanta*', '*Phoceus*' in II.vi.15
becomes '*Pylades*' and in the same poem '*scelus Ismarii . . . tyranni*'
(line 7) is deciphered as '*Tereus* leudnesse'. Marlowe is sufficiently at

[13] op. cit., p. 18.

ease with this mythology to be able to substitute one version or part of a story for another. In III.xi, where Ovid writes

concinit Odrysium Cecropis ales Ityn

Marlowe, who had ended the preceding line with 'Beare', found a rhyme in 'teare' and changed to a different part of the same myth:

Bird-changed *Progne* doth her *Itys* teare. (III.xi.32)

Martin suggests that Marlowe's Latin text read *concidit* for *concinit*, but admits that he has been unable to find this reading.[14] I think it more likely that the change was occasioned by the rhyme, especially since *concidit* could not metrically take the place of the dactyl *concinit*. In the first elegy one can follow Marlowe's train of thought when he exchanges Ovid's Minerva for Diana. Ovid wrote

> *quid, si praeripiat flavae Venus arma Minervae,*
> *ventilet accensas flava Minerva faces?*
> *quis probet in silvis Cererem regnare iugosis,*
> *lege pharetratae Virginis arva coli?*

The opposite to Venus, for English readers at any rate, is Diana the virgin goddess; and the thought of Diana fanning the flames of love is more incongruous than if Minerva were to be named. But the substitution of Diana for Minerva in the first two lines leads to an awkward repetition in the second couplet:

> What if thy mother take *Dianas* bowe?
> Shall *Dian* fanne, when loue begins to glowe?
> In wooddie groues ist meete that *Ceres* raigne,
> And quiuer-bearing *Dian* till the plaine? (I.i.11-14)

These parallels may seem tiresome, as Wilkinson suggests. Often, used by Marlowe, they seem a debased coinage, mere poetic counters. But the technique he learned in the *Elegies* was to be repeated in the plays. A parallel with the Trojan hero emphasises the romantic, sensuous nature of Faustus' love for Helen, symbol of all that was great and gracious in Greek culture:

> I will be Paris, and for love of thee,
> Instead of Troy shall Wittenberg be sacked;
> And I will combat with weak Menelaus,

[14] op. cit., p. 251.

> And wear thy colours on my plumed crest;
> Yea I will wound Achilles in the heel,
> And then return to Helen for a kiss. (V.i.103–8)

The undertones of destruction in this speech are brought out and most clearly shown by the same technique of paralleling when the praise of Helen finally establishes her as a force of evil and, for Faustus, damnation:

> Brighter art thou than flaming Jupiter,
> When he appeared to hapless Semele. (V.i.111–12)

Ovid may have delighted in presenting himself as the poet of naughtiness—

> *ille ego nequitiae Naso poeta meae* (II.i.1)

—but he is always polite in his naughtiness. His themes include seduction, abortion, and impotence; but the language is always delicate. One of his admirers has observed that

> Part of the pleasure of reading him is to appreciate the tact with which he can say wicked things in words as pure as sunlight.[15]

This could never be said of Marlowe. At times he even seems impatient with the Latin poet's delicacy. Those poems which he translates most freely express not Ovid's neat, amusing circumlocutions but an Elizabethan directness and Marlowe's own delight in shocking. The behaviour which Ovid prescribes for Corinna at the banquet in I.iv keeps within the bounds of good manners: the joke depends on how much she can communicate with her lover and still appear superficially demure. This is altered in Marlowe's version: the mistress is no longer a lady. I have already remarked that the coarseness of the sentiments is echoed in and emphasised by the 'clippe' / 'skippe', 'pezant' / 'vnpleasant' rhymes. Its presence makes for a textual crux in line 34:

> Euen in his face his offered Goblets cast.

The Latin, '*reice libatos illius ore cibos*', has given authority to most editors since Dyce (but not to Tucker Brooke) to emend 'Goblets' to 'gobbets', a word which adds remarkably to the nastiness of the line and of the whole poem. In the address to the ring (II.xv) divergences between the Latin and the English versions might be explained as mistranslations—but some seem too deliberate. The poet wishes to be metamorphosed into the ring so that, like Ovid's flea, he may have free

---

[15] Gilbert Highet, *Poets in a Landscape* (1957), p. 181.

access to all parts of the mistress's body. Ovid's ring refuses to be shut in the jewel box:

> *si dabor ut condar loculis, exire negabo.*

It might be argued that Marlowe was too lazy to look up *'loculis'* in a dictionary, just as he failed to check *'rudis'* in another poem (II.ix.20). Certainly his ring has no thought of a casket:

> I would not out, might I in one place hit. (II.xv.19)

Demands of rhyme might be offered as an explanation for the slight but meaningful variation in the next couplet:

> My life, that I will shame thee neuer feare,
> Or be a loade thou shouldst refuse to beare. (II.xv.21–2)

Yet 'wear' would be just as good a rhyme, and would convey Ovid's sense more accurately. Marlowe, in fact, is less completely changed into the ring than Ovid was. Towards the end of the poem Ovid changes back into a man, feeling that even as a ring the sight of his naked mistress would be too exciting and *'mea membra libidine surgent'*. Marlowe is perhaps rather more precise when he makes the *'membra'* singular:

> But seeing thee, I thinke my thing will swell. (II.xv.25)

III.xiii is another lively poem where Marlowe allows his translation to spell out Ovid's meaning. The unspoken is spoken when he renders *'quae nocte latent'* as 'nights pranckes' (l. 7); and when Ovid observes that there is a place that calls for wantonness (*'Est qui nequitiam locus exigat'*) Marlowe makes it clear just what that place is:

> The bed is for lasciuious toyings meete. (III.xiii.17)

Ovid is more specific in this poem than in most—so specific, in fact, that Grant Showerman, the Loeb translator, needs to resort at times to the dots of modesty. But when Ovid tells Corinna that he will believe in her protestations of innocence even though he has seen her sins with his own eyes—

> *fuerint oculis probra videnda meis*

—Marlowe is definite about the nature of the *'probra'*:

> I see when you ope the two leau'd booke. (III.xiii.44)

I must admit to being puzzled by this metaphor; I do not question the appropriateness of 'two leau'd booke', but Marlowe's right in it. Nowhere else does he show this kind of inventiveness. Elegy III.vi is not to be put into Mr Showerman's English at all; and yet Ovid pursues the delicate subject of temporary impotence with his usual good-mannered wit. Marlowe has none of the modern translator's embarrassment, and he attacks the subject with relish. Where Ovid is oblique, Marlowe is direct:

> *tacta tamen veluti gelida mea membra cicuta*
> *segnia propositum destituere meum.*

Obliqueness makes Ovid's *'propositum . . . meum'* fit—just—for the drawing-room. Marlowe has no polite hesitation:

> Yet like as if cold Hemlock I had drunke,
> It mocked me, hung downe the head, and sunke.
>
> (III.vi.13–14)

The movement of the lines, the slow descent to the bitterly rhyming 'sunke', enforces the meaning. The poem, at least, has great energy. Marlowe accepts the situation and imagines himself in it, translating not only the words from Latin into English but also the thoughts and feelings from Ovid's polite world to his own more boisterous one.

The conventions through which Ovid moves with such ease and grace are shackles to Marlowe. The difference between the two poets is well brought out by an apparent mistranslation of II.iv.48. Ovid writes of his *'ambitiosus amor'*, the love which canvasses the different wenches of the city and finds something pleasing in all of them. Marlowe, having dutifully followed the Latin through a catalogue of female attractions, departs from the path for one moment in his translation of Ovid's phrase as 'my ambitious ranging minde'. Although he is affirming contentedness with all women, the phrase seems to indicate a sense of dissatisfaction, an awareness of triviality. The 'ranging minde' is too powerful for this subject. Marlowe seems most in tune with Ovid when he is writing about poetry, and especially in I.xv, the poem which in all early editions of the *Elegies* is accompanied by Ben Jonson's version. The two translations have been compared by J. B. Steane who, while noting the neatness and greater accuracy of Jonson's work, applauds the vigour of Marlowe's.[16] The two poets reveal their different natures when they come to translate *'vilia miretur vulgus'*: Jonson writes 'Kneele hindes to trash', a more compact rendering than Marlowe's expanded

---

[16] *Marlowe: a critical study* (1964), pp. 281–2.

Let base conceipted witts admire vilde things. (I.xv.35)

Jonson's is a crude disgust, Marlowe's an intellectual disdain. With the last line of the poem Jonson is the more accurate:

> *ergo etiam cum me supremus adederit ignis*
> *vivam, parsque mei multa superstes erit.*

Jonson makes it plain that the '*vivam*' is metaphorical:

My name shall liue, and my best part aspire.

In contrast to this prosaic rendering Marlowe has the triumphant

Ile liue, and as he puls me downe mount higher. (I.xv.42)

The second part of the line is perhaps less accurate as a translation, but in its antithesis and in its spirited assertion it is one of the most truly Marlovian lines in the whole volume.

Marlowe's Naturalism

D. J. PALMER

Marlowe's Naturalism

THE PRESENT REACTION against romantic interpretations of Marlowe as an atheist rebel was inevitable; and now it is, or should be, more difficult to argue that scandal about Marlowe's personal life has any serious bearing on the plays, or that Marlowe identified himself with the attitudes of his dramatic heroes. Nevertheless it is equally difficult to recognise Marlowe's likeness in the picture of an orthodox Elizabethan Christian offered to us by some of the recent studies of his work.[1] Marlowe brought to the stage an intellectual as well as a poetic brilliance, and his work shows an interest in currents of thought somewhat out of line with the generally received ideas of his time. The unconventional complexion of his art is seen most distinctively in his conception of the natural order. Since Elizabethan drama is primarily concerned with man's experience of this world, the natural order is, virtually by definition, Marlowe's frame of reference as a playwright. His treatment of Nature, however, is informed by an unusual emphasis upon the self-sufficiency of purely material cause and effect, in an order of being apparently subject only to the immediate imperatives of morally neutral forces. This essay will examine the plays in the light of Marlowe's naturalism, which has much in common with the libertine empiricism so deeply repugnant to the traditional moralists of the age. But I shall argue that Marlowe's unconventional ideas do not represent a flat contradiction of the orthodox patterns of tragic justice, any more than the destruction of his libertine heroes implies an appeal to a moral order they do not acknowledge. Instead we can see his work as an endeavour to rationalise the older tragic schemes, in terms of a new realism and critical temper.

There is scant reference in Marlowe's plays to the traditional conception of Nature as a divinely-appointed Chain of Being, the conception

[1] R. W. Battenhouse (*Marlowe's Tamburlaine*, 1941) and Douglas Cole (*Suffering and Evil in the Plays of Christopher Marlowe*, 1962) are among the critics who place Marlowe in a Christian context. See the discussion by Irving Ribner, 'Marlowe and the Critics', *Tulane Drama Review*, 8, No. 4 (Summer 1964), 211–24.

expounded in Hooker's eloquent prose,[2] and celebrated in many passages of Shakespeare, most notably in Ulysses' famous speech on degree in *Troilus and Cressida*.[3] Marlowe, it seems, had little use for the whole structure of values based on Nature's law of order and degree, the structure that we tend to regard as so characteristically Elizabethan.[4] His heroes, whose egotism recognises no law except their own boundless appetites, move in a world like that conceived by the naturalists, for whom there was no absolute moral order based on natural law. To many conventional minds in Marlowe's day such thinking was dangerously subversive and little better than outright atheism, as Machiavelli's popular reputation illustrates. But it was not only confirmed profligates and opportunists who might claim that to follow Nature was not to be virtuous. The doctrine of natural law as the normative basis of moral ideas was questioned by serious thinkers, including those moral empiricists who found such diversity and inconsistency of behaviour among men that it seemed virtue and justice were dependent merely upon custom and opinion, and certain Christian philosophers who believed that the corruption and depravity of fallen man was inevitably attended by a general collapse of the system of natural order from its original perfection.

The sixteenth-century debate concerning natural law[5] had its precedents in ancient philosophy, and while Cicero's Stoic doctrine of Nature as the Law of Reason supported the orthodox position of Hooker, underlying the attacks on natural law made by Cornelius Agrippa, Machiavelli, Montaigne, and others, were the arguments of the Sceptics and the Epicurism of Lucretius. The attack therefore came from several quarters, and it would be an oversimplification to divide Renaissance thought on the subject into two mutually exclusive camps. Seneca himself, for instance, had occupied an ambiguous position that played its own part in complicating Elizabethan conceptions of the natural state of man. He held that in the Golden Age man was happy and innocent through natural goodness, but not virtuous, since virtue is

[2] *Of the Laws of Ecclesiastical Polity*, Book 1 (Everyman's Library edn., 2 vols., 1958, i, 147–232).   [3] Act I, Sc. iii.
[4] See E. M. W. Tillyard, *The Elizabethan World Picture* (1943), and the remarks by Helen Gardner in *The Business of Criticism* (1959), pp. 34–5.
[5] The following paragraphs are indebted to Louis Bredvold, 'The Naturalism of Donne in Relation to some Renaissance Traditions', *JEGP*, XXII (October 1923), 471–502, and Robert Ornstein, 'Donne, Montaigne, and Natural Law', *JEGP*, LV (April 1956), 213–20. See also H. Haydn, *The Counter-Renaissance* (1950), though the general thesis of this book needs to be qualified, as Ornstein points out in *The Moral Vision of Jacobean Tragedy* (1960), pp. 10–46.

exercised only through effort and discipline. According to Seneca, as
Nature had deteriorated, man had become dependent on the laws of
civilisation to regulate and order his life. Thus civilisation and its
institutions are paradoxically both inferior to the perfection of the
natural state, and also symptomatic of natural imperfection. In addition
to the dual conception of Nature implied by this mythological view of
human development, there was also the traditional Aristotelian distinction between *natura naturans* and *natura naturata*, for an explanation of
which we may turn to that popular Elizabethan moral treatise, *The
French Academie*:

> When they speak generallie of nature, they make two principall
> kindes: the one spirituall, intelligible and the unchangeable beginning
> of motion and rest, or rather the vertue, efficient, and preserving
> cause of all things; the other, sensible, mutable, and subject to
> generation and corruption, respecting all things that have life, and
> shall have end.[6]

In this fundamental distinction are reflected some of the differences
between the philosophers of natural law and their opponents. While the
Nature of which Hooker wrote is 'the preserving cause of all things',
that divinely-appointed order to which Shakespeare so often refers but
of which there is little mention in Marlowe's work, the libertine
naturalists take as their frame of reference the corrupt and mutable
natural condition, the apparently lawless and anarchic state inhabited
by Marlowe's heroes and embodied in their unfettered self-assertion and
in their eventual eclipse.

On whichever plane of understanding the argument rested, the self-
regulating autonomy of Nature was universally acknowledged, and it
was thought of as an order of being entirely intelligible to the unaided
powers of reason and the senses. The learning of the ancients, their
achievements in every sphere of knowledge concerning the natural
order, from the physical sciences to ethics and politics and the arts,
proved that an understanding of Nature did not depend upon divine
revelation but on man's own natural capacities. It was by following the
spirit of the ancients themselves that their discoveries were incremented
and their errors corrected by students of the natural sciences during the
Renaissance. Nevertheless too exclusive a concern with natural causes,
the shift of attention from ultimate causes to secondary agents, and

[6] Pierre de la Primaudaye, *The French Academie*, trans. T. B. (1586). 1602
edn., p. 162.

from efficient to material causes, was admonished by conservative thinkers who felt that in the very self-sufficiency of natural or rational explanations lay the possible danger of making the Creator seem superfluous to his creation. On this point, as on so many others, *The French Academie* reflects conventional opinion, in condemning those 'who have been such curious Inquisitors of the causes of all naturall things, that through frivolous and unprofitable questions they have fallen into that impietie, as to seeke for another beginning of all things, than God'.[7] The Law of Nature was the instrument of divine will; to abandon this concept of the immutable and eternal natural law as the efficient cause of all things, in order to base oneself upon an empirical reality divorced from moral imperatives, was clearly to invite the hostility of orthodox moralists, as Machiavelli's ill-fame once more illustrates.

But it is within the compass of such an empirical conception of natural causes that Marlowe constructed his tragic plots. Not only do his heroes refuse to obey any higher law than that of their own wills, but the course of their fortunes, even in death itself, insists only on a naturalistic plane of being upon which man subjectively imposes his own moral order. How unconventional and original Marlowe's method of presentation is can be gauged from the conventional Elizabethan idea of tragedy as the demonstration of divine justice mediated through the natural order.[8] Although tragedy before Marlowe is secular in orientation, the tragic patterns into which his predecessors shaped their material were strongly influenced by the traditional belief in a providentially-ordained moral order. The justice that overtakes Marlowe's protagonists does not set them in a wider moral context or appeal to a higher order of reality, but rather reaffirms the insurmountable limits of the natural state. The naturalism of Marlowe's heroes liberates them from moral law, but it also confines them within the world of natural causes; they are men, not gods, and the same realistic appraisal of the natural condition that inspires their unbounded opportunism also ironically circumscribes it. Thus, although Marlowe's naturalism does not assume a moral order, his tragic irony produces a sense of justice in the downfall of his libertine heroes, a rational version of that 'unknown fear' of which the old courtier Lafeu speaks in *All's Well That Ends Well*, in words that describe very well the naturalistic spirit of Marlovian tragedy:

[7] Ibid., p. 152.
[8] See Willard Farnham, *The Medieval Heritage of Elizabethan Tragedy* (1936), pp. 340–67.

They say miracles are past, and we have our philosophical persons, to make modern and familiar things supernatural and causeless. Hence is it, that we make trifles of terrors, ensconcing our selves into seeming knowledge, when we should submit our selves to an unknown fear.[9]

II

Two figures whose names might be taken to represent complementary aspects of Marlowe's naturalism are Ovid and Machiavelli. How much first-hand knowledge Marlowe had of Machiavelli's work is uncertain; but Ovid he evidently knew well, and in addition to translating the *Amores*, and imitating his manner in *Hero and Leander*, he frequently alludes to Ovid throughout the plays. However I am less interested in the direct textual influence of Ovid and Machiavelli than in lending their names to related elements in Marlowe's subject matter. The spirit of Ovidian naturalism is reflected in the libertine indulgence of sensual appetite, while the lawless, anarchic conflict which Marlowe presents as the natural state of society could be described as Machiavellian, though Marlowe may have met such a conception in Lucretius.

The love poetry of the *Elegies* celebrates the sensual pleasures of physical passion, but it is essentially an unromantic, unidealised eroticism. Contrasted with courtly Petrarchan poetry, the *Elegies* are really much less sensuous. They are less concerned with feminine beauty than with masculine satisfaction, and the verse is often as bare of ornament as its subject:

> Starke naked as she stood before mine eye,
> Not one wen in her body could I spie.
>
> (Bk. I, Elegia 5, ll. 17–18)[10]

The dramatic realism of the *Elegies* reflects the arrogant egotism of an Ovidian lover, who, unlike his courtly counterpart, does not worship from afar, but wittily and boldly forces his attentions on his mistress. Since love of this kind has nothing to do with virtue, it is assumed that the lady's modesty is only a pretence, or a challenge to the lover's skill in seduction.

The decorative exuberance of *Hero and Leander* is Elizabethan rather than classical, but the Ovidian spirit of this poem is felt nevertheless in

the narrator's sophisticated wit, and in the sharply-observed naturalistic
imagery that prevents the sensuous richness from cloying:

> His hands he cast upon her like a snare,
> She overcome with shame and sallow feare,
> Like chast *Diana*, when *Acteon* spyde her,
> Being sodainly betraide, dyv'd downe to hide her.
> And as her silver body downeward went,
> With both her hands she made the bed a tent,
> And in her owne mind thought her selfe secure,
> O'recast with dim and darksome coverture.
>
> (Second Sestyad, ll. 259–66)

Some of the rhymes anticipate the manner of Byron's *Don Juan*, that
later masterpiece of libertine naturalism, and indeed there is an interesting parallel in the role of the narrator in both poems, though Marlowe
has none of Byron's vulgarity.

Leander's seduction of Hero employs the classic arguments of
Renaissance naturalism. His attitude is materialist and empirical, and
denies the existence of anything unknown to the senses:

> This idoll which you terme *Virginitie*,
> Is neither essence subiect to the eie,
> No, nor to any one exterior sence,
> Nor hath it any place of residence,
> Nor is't of earth or mold celestiall,
> Or capable of any forme at all.
> Of that which hath no being doe not boast,
> Things that are not at all are never lost.
>
> (First Sestyad, ll. 269–76)

Only someone as naive as Hero would take Leander's sophistry at its
face value. The reader is expected to enjoy its ingenuity and witty
audacity, to observe the false analogies and the manipulation of logic.
Yet in themselves these arguments do openly declare the philosophical
basis of Leander's naturalism. He is less interested in logical proof than
in getting into Hero's bed, but our critical detachment from the situation falls short of an implicit refutation of the philosophy. The ideas
and the way in which they are used are indivisible: the libertine mode
of argument is essentially casuistical, and Leander's unsentimental
realism is shared by the narrator of the poem:

> Love is not ful of pittie (as men say)
> But deaffe and cruell, where he meanes to pray.
>
> (Second Sestyad, ll. 287–8)

Such is also the pitiless cruelty of love in *Dido Queen of Carthage*, where Ovid is strangely blended with Virgil to make a tragedy that in several respects is the counterpart of Lyly's Ovidian comedies. The introductory episode in Olympus, where Jupiter is discovered lasciviously dandling Ganymede on his lap, or the later scene in which the Old Nurse becomes infatuated with Cupid in his disguise as Ascanius, expose in parody the wanton fires that consume the Queen herself.

In *Edward II*, Gaveston knows how to seduce the king with 'wanton Poets, pleasant wits', to exploit Edward's sensuality for his own ends, and there is in Gaveston's speech more emphasis on lascivious pleasure than on the unspoilt beauty of the Golden Age:

> My men like Satyres grazing on the lawnes,
> Shall with their Goate feete daunce an antick hay.
> Sometime a lovelie boye in *Dians* shape,
> With haire that gilds the water as it glides,
> Crownets of pearle about his naked armes,
> And in his sportfull hands an Olive tree,
> To hide those parts which men delight to see,
> Shall bathe him in a spring, and there hard by,
> One like *Actaeon* peeping through the grove,
> Shall by the angrie goddesse be transformde,
> And running in the likenes of an Hart,
> By yelping hounds puld downe, and seeme to die. (ll. 59–70)

The Ovidian myth of Actaeon's metamorphosis, commonly glossed as figuring the untamed fury of the passions, is used here ironically to foreshadow Gaveston's own fate, pulled down by Mortimer's yelping hounds. That typically Marlovian use of the word 'yelping' itself adds a harsh realistic dissonance to the lyricism of the preceding lines. Gaveston's pastoral pageant does not represent a Nature chaste and innocent, but rather a natural state of lawless abandon, where men become beasts in their lusts, and where the sexual ambivalence, far from being accounted unnatural, is an assertion of natural licence.

The play which makes the greatest use of Ovidian naturalism is *Doctor Faustus*. Faustus sells his soul to 'live in al voluptuousnesse' (l. 328); he is seduced first by his own sophistry in the play's opening soliloquy, and then by visions of sensual delight. In a moment when the fear of damnation reasserts itself, he recognises that 'the god thou servest is thine owne appetite' (l. 443). Thwarted in the intellectual satisfactions he sought from communion with spirits, he is readily distracted by the rather different kind of intercourse procured for him by Mephostophilis. The eroticism of the great speech to Helen is shot through with irony, not least in the allusions to the tales of 'haplesse *Semele*' and 'wanton *Arethusa*' (ironically inappropriate epithets) in Ovid's *Metamorphoses*, both victims of the lawless passions that inspire men and gods alike in the Ovidian world.

Based on a similar conception of the natural state, as a condition swayed by wild and anarchic forces, are the values of Machiavellian naturalism. The ruthless opportunism of political ambition corresponds to the libertine pursuit of sensual pleasure; neither admits any prohibition to the achievement of its desires, for neither recognises any ultimate authority greater than the arbitrary imperatives of its own drives. The wilful arrogance of Marlowe's Ovidian sensualists is paralleled by the aggressive motivation of those whose energies are directed towards society. Leander's empirical casuistry is akin to the Machiavellian strategy for overthrowing an enemy, and in either case physical force must complete what craft began. Edward and Mortimer, though contrasted in personality and aims, are complementary in the unscrupulous pursuit of their own egocentric wills: sensuality and brutality are two sides of the same coin in a natural state where men are little more than savage beasts. The contrast between the cowardly Calyphas and his brothers in *Tamburlaine* makes a similar point.

Machiavellian or Lucretian naturalism represents an atomised society in which, to adopt Lord Palmerston's words, there are no permanent allegiances, only permanent self-interest; it is an image of chaos, of the conflict of individual wills, or it would be if the strong man did not impose his own will by conquering and subjugating the weaker. This in substance is the teaching of the historical Machiavelli, and if Marlowe was not acquainted with his work, he nevertheless managed to produce in his tragedies some fairly accurate reflections of the doctrines associated with Machiavelli. The figure who speaks the Prologue to *The Jew of Malta* is the Machiavelli of popular tradition, the incarnation of Italianate villainy for a Protestant audience, and a stage-character readily moulded into the form and functions of the old morality Vice. Nevertheless, the speech is not simply a description of the unscrupulous cunning of Machiavellian methods; on the contrary, there is an ironic contrast between the hypocrisy of the Machiavellians and the honesty of Machiavelli himself. This anatomy of his enemies, who are also his best pupils, is not altogether unworthy of the real Machiavelli, whose claim to originality was his thoroughgoing empiricism, his boast that he wrote of men as they really are, not as they should be or pretend to be.[11]

If Guise and Barabas are versions of the conventional Machiavellian villain, Mortimer and especially Tamburlaine are more complex creations closer to the true spirit of Machiavelli's naturalism. But it is not only in Marlowe's heroes that this naturalism is expressed. Almost all the characters in these plays share the same individualistic attitudes, and though they may sometimes appeal to rule of law or religious sanction, they are motivated by those basic appetites for power, revenge, or wealth, that also inspire their enemies. The central difference between Bajazeth and Tamburlaine, Friar Lodowick and Barabas, or even Gaveston and Mortimer, is that the major figures are naturally stronger, more able, and therefore more successful. The worlds they inhabit correspond to the Machiavellian or Lucretian image of man in the natural state, in which each man is the enemy of his neighbour.

However much or little Marlowe drew directly upon Machiavelli, his translation of the First Book of Lucan's *Pharsalia* reflects his interest in the struggle for power in an anarchic society, and in the rise of the opportunist who recognises no rule of law but his own will. The subject of Lucan's epic poem is the civil wars of Caesar and Pompey. Machiavelli had illustrated many of his own doctrines from Roman history, but whether Marlowe's interest in the *Pharsalia* anticipated *Tamburlaine* or *Edward II* or *The Massacre at Paris* we do not know. Clearly, however, the interest which his version of Lucan's First Book holds for a student of the plays is more than stylistic. The theme is civil war, which Lucan describes as a return to primeval Chaos. Such a theme might well appeal to the most orthodox Elizabethan, providing a conventional lesson in the unnatural evils of civil war, overturning order and degree. But we do not hear much about order and degree in Marlowe's poem. Instead he follows Lucan in anatomising the condition of society that 'made madding people shake off peace', and it is the political realist who describes the degeneracy and corruption which bred civil war:

> When fortune made us lords of all, wealth flowed,
> And then we grew licencious and rude,

[11] *The Prince*, Chap. 15. Trans. L. Ricci (Modern Library edn., 1950, p. 56).

The soldiours pray, and rapine brought in ryot,
Men tooke delight in Iewels, houses, plate,
And scorn'd old sparing diet, and ware robes
Too light for women; Poverty (who hatcht
Roomes greatest wittes) was loath'd, and al the world
Ransackt for golde, which breeds the world decay;
And then large limits had their butting lands,
The ground which *Curius* and *Camillus* till'd,
Was stretcht unto the fields of hinds unknowne;
Againe, this people could not brooke calme peace,
Them freedome without war might not suffice,
Quarrels were rife, greedy desire stil poore
Did vild deeds, then t'was worth the price of bloud
And deem'd renowne to spoile their native towne,
Force mastered right, the strongest govern'd all. (ll. 161–77)

Although Lucan's Rome is a republic, we also find in *Tamburlaine*, *Edward the Second*, and *The Massacre at Paris* a weak and corrupted regime as the prelude to the outbreak of strife; Cosroe, Edward, and Charles are the feeble monarchs who are eclipsed by the rise of powerful opportunists like Lucan's Caesar. The astrologer who is introduced in the closing lines of the First Book of the *Pharsalia* describes the universe of Marlovian tragedy:

The worlds swift course is lawlesse
And casuall; all the starres at randome radge. (ll. 641–2)

III

Perhaps the most definitive appeal to Nature in Marlowe's work is that made by Tamburlaine at the outset of his irresistible career; it is the antithesis of Ulysses' speech in Shakespeare's *Troilus and Cressida*:

The thirst of raigne and sweetnes of a crown,
That causde the eldest sonne of heavenly *Ops*
To thrust his doting father from his chaire,
And place himselfe in the Emperiall heaven,
Moov'd me to manage armes against thy state.
What better president than mightie *Ioue*?
Nature that fram'd us of foure Elements,
Warring within our breasts for regiment,
Doth teach us all to have aspyring minds;

Our soules, whose faculties can comprehend
The wondrous Architecture of the world:
And measure every wandring plannets course,
Still climing after knowledge infinite,
And alwaies mooving as the restles Spheares,
Wils us to weare our selves, and never rest,
Untill we reach the ripest fruit of all,
That perfect blisse and sole felicitie,
The sweet fruition of an earthly crowne. (ll. 863–80)

By 1587, ambition was a well-established tragic theme, but as a justi-
fication of ambition arguments like Tamburlaine's had never been heard
before on the stage. Their philosophical and scientific premises, placing
ambition outside the usual sphere of moral judgement, are radically
different from the conventional dramatic treatment of 'thirst of reign',
but perfectly characteristic of Marlowe's naturalism.

The speech has, of course, attracted much attention from commentators, some of whom have been puzzled by the provenance of this
conception of Nature as a state of perpetual conflict between the
elements. Paul Kocher, for example, discusses the possibility that
Marlowe was using an Empedoclean or Heraclitan doctrine of elemental
strife, only to reject the notion, and he turns instead to compare the
passage with the familiar conception of the opposing elements as
treated by Du Bartas. To Kocher, the puzzling feature of Tamburlaine's
speech is his omission of the usual idea of balance or harmony between
the elements which governs the stability of the world, and Kocher
concludes that 'instead of being borrowed from any thinker ancient or
modern, it was a new interpretation of phenomena selected from the
common knowledge of the time. No one before Marlowe, we may say,
had arranged the evidence in quite that way or drawn so drastic a
conclusion from it.'[12] Kocher is surely right about the unconventional
application of these ideas, but he probably overcomplicates the terms of
reference by which Tamburlaine is justifying himself.

It was a basic doctrine of Aristotelian physics that according to the
law of Nature each of the four elements seeks its own place, fire rising
to the highest sphere, earth sinking to the centre of the universe, and
air and water finding their places in between, with air above water; but
Aristotle also observed that in nature the four elements are not finally

[12] *Christopher Marlowe: A Study of his Thought, Learning, and Character*
(1946), p. 76.

able to realise this potentiality, but are continually striving to do so.[13]
In the opening chapter of *The Boke Named The Governour* (1531), Sir
Thomas Elyot uses the same analogy between the elements and the
human condition to uphold the orthodox doctrine of an established
order and degree according to natural law:

> But to treate of that whiche by naturall understandyng may be
> comprehended. Beholde the foure elementes wherof the body of
> man is compacte, howe they be set in their places called spheris,
> higher or lower, accordynge to the soveraintie of theyr natures, that
> is to saye, the fyer as the most pure element, havyng in it nothing
> that is corruptible, in his place is higheste and above other elementes.
> The ayer, whiche next to the fyre is most pure in substance, is in
> the seconde sphere or place. The water, which is somewhat con-
> solidate, and approcheth to corruption, is next unto the erthe. The
> erthe, which is of substance grosse and ponderous, is set of all
> elementes most lowest.
>
> Beholde also the ordre that god hath put generally in al his
> creatures, begynning at the moste inferiour or base, and assendynge
> upwarde . . . Now to retourne to the astate of man kynde . . . hit
> appereth that god gyveth not to every man like gyftes of grace, or
> of nature, but to some more, some lesse, as it liketh his divine
> maiestie . . . And like as the angels which be most fervent in con-
> templation be highest exalted in glorie, (after the opinion of holy
> doctours), and also the fire which is the most pure of elements, and
> also doth clarifie the other inferiour elementes, is deputed to the
> highest sphere or place; so in this worlde, they whiche excelle other
> in this influence of understandynge, and do imploye it to the detayn-
> ing of other within the boundes of reason, and shewe them howe
> to provyde for theyr necessarye lyvynge; suche ought to be set in a
> more highe place than the residue where they may se and also be
> sene; that by the beames of theyr excellent witte, shewed through
> the glasse of auctorite, other of inferiour understandynge may be
> directed to the way of vertue and commodious livynge.[14]

The thought of Tamburlaine's speech runs exactly parallel to this
passage, the crucial point of difference being simply that while Elyot
appeals to the immutable principle of natural law, *natura naturans*,

---

[13] See e.g. *De Caelo*, 311 a (Loeb Classical Library edn., trans. W. K. C.
Guthrie, 1939, Bk. IV, chap. iii).
[14] *The Boke Named The Governour* (Everyman's Library edn., 1907), pp. 3–4.

Marlowe is concerned with the natural world of generation and corruption, *natura naturata*, in which the four elements are continually striving to fulfil their potential, and in which Elyot's argument for established authority is not always empirically justified. Tamburlaine's identification of himself with Jove at the beginning of his speech is significant in this respect, too, for the overthrow of Ops, or Saturn, brought to an end the Golden Age, and under Jupiter's reign Nature has fallen from her original perfection, her stability no longer guaranteed. Cicero offered a different but not a contradictory interpretation of the myth in terms of the Stoic theology:

> ... now these immoral fables enshrined a decidedly clever scientific theory. Their meaning was that the highest element of celestial ether or fire, which by itself generates all things, is devoid of that bodily part which requires union with another for the work of procreation.[15]

In Tamburlaine, himself the microcosm of this cosmic strife, fire and earth, the soul and the body, are also united but in opposition, as the continuation of his speech declares.

It has often been pointed out that the speech concludes with an ironic and startling anticlimax, and certainly, both rhythmically and in terms of their sense, the final lines bring us down from the 'restles Spheares' with a resounding thump on 'earthly crowne'. I would agree with Kocher and others who find a deliberate moral provocation in the assertion that man's greatest good rests in worldly things. Once more, the conventional attitude of the author of *The French Academie* provides an appropriate comment on Marlowe's unconventional naturalism:

> The Philosophers teach us by their writings, and experience doth better shew it unto us, that to covet and desire is proper to the Soule, and that from thence al the affections and desires of men proceed, which draw them hither and thither diverslie, that they may attain to that thing, which they think is able to lead them to the enjoying of some good, whereby they may live a contented and happie life. Which felicitie, the most part of men, through a false opinion, or ignorance rather of that which is good, and by following the inclination of their corrupt nature, doe seeke and labour to finde in humane and earthly things, as in riches, glorie, honor, and pleasure. But for as much as

[15] *De Natura Deorum*, II, xxiv (Loeb Classical Library edn., trans. H. Rackham, 1933, p. 185).

the enjoying of these things doth not bring with it sufficient cause of contentation, they perceive themselves always deprived of the end of their desires, and are constrained to wander all their life time beyond all bounds and measure, according to the rashness and inconstancie of their lusts.[16]

But Marlowe does not compel us to judge Tamburlaine's ambition in this way. If his spirit or 'aspyring mind' is analogous to the element of fire, soaring to the eternal motion of the spheres, the element of earth, of which he is also compounded, renders him mortal: he will eventually come to rest. This is the real nature of the irony in the speech: Tamburlaine will be deprived of the end of his desires, not because the play invites us to regard his values as false and basely material, but simply because he must die.

This speech of self-definition therefore contains in itself the philosophical frame of the whole tragedy. If this implies that Marlowe conceived both parts of the play as a whole, I do not resist the implication, since Marlowe must have known from the inception of his work that one of the most remarkable features of Tamburlaine's history, from the point of view of conventional tragedy, was its end. Fortescue, in *The Forest*, which was one of Marlowe's sources, wrote that, despite Tamburlaine's invincible career, 'yet as a man in the ende, he paieth, the debte due unto nature', and Whetstone's choice of words is equally significant: 'by the course of nature [he] died.' The Nature that charters his ambition also circumscribes it.

In its insistence upon the primacy of Nature, *Tamburlaine* is a kind of heroic pastoral. The hero is 'a Scythian Shepherd, so embellished / With Natures pride, and richest furniture' (ll. 350–1), whose rise to power is based solely on his own inborn qualities. He tells his followers as he makes them kings,

> Your byrthes shall be no blemish to your fame,
> For vertue is the fount whence honor springs,
> And they are worthy she investeth kings. (ll. 1768–70)

Such 'vertue' closely resembles the 'virtù' of Machiavelli's gospel, and the word is reasserted in Tamburlaine's confession of his love for Zenocrate:

> I thus conceiving and subduing both
> That which hath stoopt the tempest of the Gods,

[16] 'The Author to the Reader.'

> Even from the fiery spangled vaile of heaven,
> To feele the lovely warmth of shepheards flames,
> And martch in cottages of strowed weeds,
> Shal give the world to note for all my byrth,
> That Vertue solely is the sum of glorie,
> And fashions men with true nobility. (ll. 1964-71)

So concludes this soliloquy on beauty, a speech that in celebrating the grace and wonder 'which into words no virtue can digest', plays another variation on the pastoral theme of Nature's supremacy over Art.

Tamburlaine's dazzling progress of conquest through the kingdoms of the earth in Part I of the play is dramatised as that of a prodigy in Nature. He is identified with natural forces; his wrath is like a storm at sea, his army like the stars in heaven; but most commonly he is compared to the meteors and comets that blaze across the sky, phenomena that keep no regular course like the perfect motions of the planets, or to the thunder and lightning, the force of Jove himself. Such violent images recall Lucan's description of Caesar, as Marlowe renders it, 'urging his fortune, trusting in the gods':

> So thunder which the wind teares from the cloudes,
> With cracke of riven ayre and hideous sound
> Filling the world, leapes out and throwes forth fire,
> Affrights poore fearefull men, and blasts their eyes
> With overthwarting flames, and raging shoots
> Alongst the ayre and nought resisting it
> Falls, and returnes, and shivers where it lights. (ll. 152-8)

In Part II, however, this identification of Tamburlaine with natural forces is inverted. With Zenocrate's death, Nature for the first time is at odds with the hero's will, and Tamburlaine can no longer see himself as fulfilling Nature's purposes. Instead he turns upon Nature itself, and whereas previously his earthly triumph was described in the imagery of the heavens, now by a significant rhetorical inversion, the imagery of battle and slaughter is transferred to the heavens themselves:

> I will persist a terrour to the world,
> Making the Meteors, that like armed men
> Are seene to march upon the towers of heaven,
> Run tilting round about the firmament,
> And breake their burning Lances in the aire,
> For honor of my woondrous victories. (ll. 3875-80)

These lines conclude the scene in which Tamburlaine has killed Calyphas, his cowardly son; an ironic episode, since the father shows himself no less unnatural than the son whose 'shame of nature' he has purged.

The play, of course, does not ask us to approve Tamburlaine's savage cruelty at any stage in his career. His ruthless and inexorable slaughter, his rough sadistic jests, are of a piece with those qualities we do admire, such as his inspired leadership, his tenderness towards Zenocrate, his undaunted spirit in the face of overwhelming odds. What is consistently presented is an heroic image of man in his natural state, a barbarian, a heathen, an uncivilised but magnificent animal, yet so much more than an animal in his possession of an aspiring soul, capable of loving beauty as well as honour. This figure of natural man is not complete, however, without his conception of the gods. That man is by nature aware of the existence of a godhead is a commonplace of Elizabethan thought which Marlowe turned to his own purposes in *Tamburlaine*. And since Marlowe's treatment of religion has been a matter for considerable controversy, it may help to clarify the issue by fixing a bearing from the unimpeachable orthodoxy of Philip de Mornay's treatise *Of the Trewnes of Christian Religion*, as translated by Sir Philip Sidney:

> Now like as all men may reade in this booke [i.e. of Nature] as well of the world as of themselves; so was there never yet any Nation under heaven, which hath not thereby learned and perceived a certeine Godhead, notwithstanding that they have conceived it diversly, according to the diversitie of their own imaginations . . . it is not so natural a thing in man to love company, and to clad himselfe against hurts of the wether, (which things wee esteeme to be verie kindly:) as it is naturall unto him to knowe the author of his life, that is to say, God.[17]

Marlowe's play, being set in a pagan world, is not concerned with the reality of the gods or their purposes, but with man's understanding of a divine principle in the light of natural theology alone. The play does not present Tamburlaine as 'the Scourge of God', it dramatises the belief shared by the hero and some of his enemies that he enjoys divine protection, and is an instrument of their will. Other enemies naturally take a rather different view, and see him as a blasphemous upstart.

[17] *The Complete Works of Sir Philip Sidney*, ed. A. Feuillerat, Vol. III (1923), pp. 272–3.

Marlowe's use of natural theology creates a sense of dramatic irony in the relativity of different attitudes to the gods, but nowhere, not even in Orcanes' prayer to the Christian God, and his subsequent victory over the faithless Christians, does the play endorse the religious awareness of its characters or show any event as the result of divine will. It has been argued that Tamburlaine's death, following hard upon his railing against Mahomet, is a visitation of heavenly justice upon the blasphemer; but, apart from the fact that Mahomet was a prophet and not a god, Tamburlaine's horrendous curses and impious defiance are themselves symptoms of his mortal fever. It is precisely because he knows death awaits him that he dares God out of Heaven. The play shows us the conditions under which men variously interpret the will of their gods, and how they attribute a divine authority to their own desires and fears. There is nothing cynical or atheistic in this. As far as the heathens are concerned, Marlowe's naturalism in this respect is quite in keeping with the orthodox Christian position of his time, which regarded the deities of classical mythology as personifications of natural forces. The Stoic theology in Cicero's *De Natura Deorum* commended itself to Christian humanism, and it is echoed by Hooker when he writes of the pagans, 'even so many guides of nature they dreamed of, as they saw there were kinds of things natural in the world'.[18] Marlowe's learning, here and elsewhere, is more orthodox in origin than conventional in its applications.

Classical mythology in *Tamburlaine*, however, also serves to identify the hero with superhuman powers, to suggest, both in his confident self-comparisons with Jove and in his later titanic defiance of the gods, that Tamburlaine is godlike. Eugene Waith has written one of the most illuminating studies of the play, in which he discusses the influence of the Senecan figure of Hercules upon Marlowe's conception of his hero. As Professor Waith says, 'Tamburlaine is not the son of a god, but his facile references to the gods, sometimes friendly, sometimes hostile, may be interpreted as part of the heroic character of which Hercules is the prototype. He has the assurance of a demigod rather than the piety of a good man.'[19] This classical association, as Waith points out, is one means by which the play puts Tamburlaine beyond the scope of orthodox moral approval or disapproval. But the significance of Tamburlaine's godlike stature is related to the naturalism of the play as a whole. As a man, he is godlike in his aspiration to bring all nature beneath

[18] ed. cit., p. 160.
[19] *The Herculean Hero* (1962), p. 84.

his sway, he is the natural lord of creation. He is, in the words of Hamlet, 'in apprehension, how like a god', and yet he is 'quintessence of dust', and mortal. The same tragic perception embraces Faustus' desire to control Nature ('a sound Magician is a Demi-god'), and his eventual recognition of failure, 'What art thou Faustus but a man condemnd to die?' (l. 1143).

IV

The Senecan influence in *Tamburlaine*, which Professor Waith has described, is as different from the conventional Seneca of other Elizabethan tragedies as the use of morality devices in *Doctor Faustus* is from their original functions in the old morality plays. Marlowe's naturalism is reflected in his dramatic methods as well as in the attitudes and fortunes of his heroes, since their careers imply a transformation of the traditional patterns of Elizabethan tragedy. Thus Tamburlaine's death is preceded by a very scientific account of his symptoms, as physiological in detail as Seneca's treatment of the death of Hercules, but with a radically different effect, for Marlowe is insisting on the natural causes that bring Tamburlaine's career to an end, where a conventional homiletic tragedy would have presented the end of insatiable ambition as a rather more demonstrable proof of providential justice, or at least of the existence of a moral order. Yet, as I have suggested, Tamburlaine's death is an appropriately ironic conclusion in terms of the conception of Nature that originally inspired his ambition. In *Doctor Faustus* the allegorical apparatus of the morality drama and even the theme of magic are used, not to dramatise man's subjection to the supernatural, but paradoxically to insist upon the primacy and autonomy of the natural order. Douglas Cole has observed that 'the morality conflict between spiritual good and evil lies at the heart of *Doctor Faustus* while the more particular devices associated with this dramatic form are often reversed in the play to focus attention on the moral energies, choices, and blindness within Faustus himself'.[20]

It might at first seem strange to argue that a play whose central theme is eternal damnation, the ultimate reality of a world beyond Nature, is nevertheless firmly rooted in the terrestrial order. But it is Marlowe's achievement in this play to translate into natural terms, into terms of human experience in this world, the other-worldly concepts with which his Christian theology is concerned. It is a very theological play:

[20] *Suffering and Evil in the Plays of Christopher Marlowe* (1962), p. 247.

Faustus' sins begin with pride and end in despair; he chooses evil of
his own free will, but enslaves his body as well as his soul to temptation.
Ironically, he deprives himself of his freedom by using it wrongfully,
and so fearing he is no longer free to sue for grace, he surrenders to the
devil. The course of his tragedy is plotted in close accordance with
orthodox Christian doctrine and belief. But the play maintains the
autonomy of Nature through Faustus' free will, even his freedom to
resist the saving grace of God.

Faustus' own naturalism is expressed in his commitment to libertine
voluptuousness, in his refusal to acknowledge natural limit in seeking
magical powers, and in his denial of any moral or spiritual reality. The
traditional allegory of the Seven Deadly Sins, for instance, dwindles to
a mere spectacle, an entertainment in which pleasure is not mingled
with instruction. But to expose his desires as illusory and his dreams
as unreal, the play has its own naturalistic realism. Magic, first of all, is
emptied of any supernatural properties: Mephostophilis informs
Faustus that his spells and incantations have no special virtue to compel
spirits to attend him. Faustus soon discovers the limits of the magical
powers offered to him by the devil; they do not extend beyond the
natural order. He may learn some of Nature's secrets (and Mephostophilis is evidently a sceptical empiricist himself on the subject of
astronomy),[21] and he may learn some simple conjuring tricks; but the
devil's magic, as Sir Walter Raleigh wrote (himself the victim of
rumours about necromancy), is confined to these two modes of operation, 'by knowing the uttermost of nature and by illusion; for there is
no incomprehensible or unsearchable power, but of God only'.[22]

Mephostophilis' description of hell is a famous piece of naturalism,
translating the theological idea in terms of the realities of this world:

> Hell hath no limits, nor is circumscrib'd
> In one selfe place; for where we are is hell,
> And where hell is, there must we ever be. (ll. 553–5)

The traditional symbolic Hell is 'a fable' at which Faustus scoffs, but
Mephostophilis' rejoinder is itself an appeal to empirical reality: 'Ay,
think so still, till experience change thy mind.' Faustus' final soliloquy
is the discovery of this naturalised hell, the dramatic reality of the

[21] See F. R. Johnson, 'Marlowe's Astronomy and Renaissance Skepticism',
ELH, XIII (1946), 241–54.
[22] Quoted by E. A. Strathmann, in *Sir Walter Ralegh: A Study in Elizabethan
Skepticism* (1951), p. 178.

spiritual concepts of damnation and despair. Marlowe's characterisation of Mephostophilis himself, particularly in the opening scenes of the play in which he displays such tragic suffering and dignity, is an extraordinary humanising of the devil compared with the conventional fiends of medieval tradition, and of course it anticipates in this respect Milton's presentation of the Satan of *Paradise Lost*.

Despite its subject matter, then, the world of *Doctor Faustus* consistently excludes the miraculous. Faustus' conjuring has no more inherent force than the papal malediction, and the apparition of Helen of Troy is as much make-believe as the pageant of the Seven Deadly Sins, since in both cases the actors are insubstantial spirits. Ritual becomes parody, and spiritual and physical realities are inverted. The scene in which Faustus confirms his bargain with the devil is particularly rich in these ironies. This supernatural league is solemnised in an elaborate pantomime imitating the drawing up of a legal deed of gift— 'a pretty case of paltry legacies' indeed, since of course the contract in itself has no binding power, even though written in Faustus' blood: the only blood that has power over human souls is that of Christ. Faustus' 'bill' is therefore a blasphemous parody of the invisible bond sealed by Christ on the Cross, as we realise in his misappropriation of the Saviour's dying words, 'consummatum est'. The congealing of Faustus' blood is another instance of the way in which the spiritual has become physical, the metaphor taken literally, and when Mephostophilis fetches a chafer of coals to induce the wound to flow, hell-fire has been virtually domesticated. Faustus' pleasures and his suffering are alike contained within the natural order; it is his body alone that the devil can satisfy, or, when he is about to repent, menace with tortures. But the realities of the physical universe, which are all that Faustus acknowledges, are never more dramatically asserted than in his final soliloquy, when the heavenly spheres, the mountains, the earth, and the ocean, are all too inexorably the confines of his last hour of mortal existence. It is Nature that will not be swayed from her course in this last scene.

The transference from spiritual to physical values in this play, and Marlowe's naturalising of the sacred, have been studied in an essay by C. L. Barber.[23] He focuses attention in particular on the prevalent imagery of eating and drinking, which throughout the tragedy represents Faustus' gluttonous appetite as a blasphemous inversion of the

[23] 'The form of Faustus' fortunes good or bad', *Tulane Drama Review*, 8, No. 4 (Summer 1964), 92–119.

soul's thirst for salvation through Christ's blood. Barber similarly shows how Marlowe treats the emblematic idea of Faustus' soaring pride and his 'hellish fate' in literal terms of physical movement upwards and downwards. There is indeed in all the plays a characteristic technique of giving literal significance to metaphor, either by converting poetic images into dramatic actuality, or by depriving conventional symbols of their traditional emblematic frame of reference. This notable aspect of Marlowe's dramatic method is no less an expression of his naturalism than his unconventional treatment of moral and philosophical themes.

To take a single example from *Tamburlaine*, for instance, there is the notorious scene in Part II, in which Tamburlaine appears in his chariot drawn by two captive kings. Here Tamburlaine, whip in hand according to the stage direction, gives tangible proof of his claim to be the 'Scourge of God'. It is of course a part of Tamburlaine's character that he should physically enact his own poetic hyperboles and metaphors. But Marlowe may also have known that the dumb-show at the beginning of Gascoigne's Inns of Court tragedy *Jocasta* (1566) represented Sesostres, another oriental conqueror, drawn in his chariot by captive kings to signify Ambition.[24] In *Tamburlaine* Gascoigne's emblem has come to life, and lost its homiletic meaning.

In *The Jew of Malta*, Barabas' opening soliloquy gives a literal meaning to the image of 'infinite riches in a little roome', which, as G. K. Hunter has shown,[25] was a conceit traditionally applied to the Virgin Mary, who bore the Son of God in her womb. Barabas' naturalism, his devotion to earthly treasure, is a parody of the sacred emblems:

> Beauteous *Rubyes*, sparkling *Diamonds*,
> And seildsene costly stones of so great price,
> As one of them indifferently rated,
> And of a Carrect of this quantity,
> May serve in perill of calamity
> To ransome great Kings from captivity. (ll. 62–7)

But the naturalism of the Jew is matched by the dramatic naturalism which makes him the architect of his own destruction. There is justice in the way Barabas meets his death by falling into his own trap, but it

---

[24] The play is to be found in *Early English Classical Tragedies*, ed. J. W. Cunliffe (1912).

[25] 'The Theology of Marlowe's *The Jew of Malta*', *Journal of the Warburg and Courtauld Institutes*, Vol. 27 (1964), 210–40.

does not imply a moral universe; it only creates a parallel effect by the use of dramatic irony. The world of the play remains entirely self-consistent; Barabas' fatal mistake is that he fails to allow to his enemies the same degree of suspicious mistrust towards him as he holds towards them. He does not come to grief because he is a Machiavel, but because he is not Machiavellian enough. Professor Hunter points out that the cauldron into which Barabas falls corresponds to a traditional icono-graphical representation of Hell; yet this does not make Barabas Antichrist. Instead, it illustrates again Marlowe's naturalising of the traditional emblematic schemes; his art is in the strictest sense icono-clastic.

My final illustrations of this aspect of Marlowe's dramatic method concern *Edward II*. Here Edward's appeals to the traditional emblems of royalty are significantly hollow and contradicted by the grim realities of the power struggle. Marlowe's insistence on the literal, and his presentation of the action in terms of natural causes, create dramatic tensions that could not be achieved by any direct use of a symbolic dimension. The spy who betrays the fugitive king to his enemies, 'a gloomy fellow in the mead below', is a mower, a figure who only appears very briefly at this point in the play, but for long enough to cast the shadow of his scythe over the inevitability of Edward's death. Lightborne similarly is no symbolic figure; he exists like the mower entirely in his own right as a man, but his name and his function are all the more dreadful for that. In this double tragedy of Edward and Mortimer, each re-enacts on the literal, naturalistic plane the traditional emblematic schemes of medieval and Elizabethan tragedy. Mortimer's allusion to Fortune's wheel in his final speech describes in this figure the lawless opportunist world through which he has made his way; while Edward's humiliation in prison represents, with typical Marlovian stress upon the brute physical fact, a morally neutral and thoroughly naturalistic realisation of the conventional platitudes about the falls of princes:

> And there in mire and puddle have I stood,
> This ten dayes space, and least that I should sleepe,
> One plaies continually upon a Drum,
> They give me bread and water being a king,
> So that for want of sleepe and sustenance,
> My mindes distempered, and my bodies numde,
> And whether I have limmes or no, I know not.

O would my bloud dropt out from every vaine,
As doth this water from my tattered robes:
Tell *Isabell* the Queene, I lookt not thus,
When for her sake I ran at tilt in Fraunce,
And there unhorste the duke of *Cleremont*. (ll. 2507–18)

But nowhere is Marlowe's conversion of metaphor into literal dramatic reality, the reductive irony of his naturalism, seen to greater effect than in the manner of Edward's death, his anus pierced by a red-hot poker.

V

While Marlowe's naturalism reflects his sophisticated and unusual approach to the drama, his insistence on the autonomy of natural causes and his development of the ironic method of plot-construction represent an important contribution to the development of Elizabethan drama. So few plays from the period immediately before Marlowe's own short career have survived, that it is impossible accurately to piece together the history of that development. But there is a discernible difference between the tragedies of the earlier period and those of the 1590s in at least one respect, and that is in the diminishing authority of overt moral statements made in the drama. If later playwrights make fewer direct appeals to the hand of providential justice to explain cause and effect in their actions, it was not because they were less pious, but because they had greater and more sophisticated artistic resources for presenting their plots in terms of the operation of natural causes, than their homiletic predecessors had possessed. In this respect, Marlowe's unconventional naturalism greatly extended the range of dramatic techniques, so that eventually even Shakespeare's Ulysses, that arch-Machiavel, speaks of 'degree', not as the author's mouthpiece, but in his own ironic dimension.

Marlowe the Orthodox

W. MOELWYN MERCHANT

Marlowe the Orthodox

IT IS IMPORTANT not to confuse immaturity with unorthodoxy. Rash and violent speech—this scarcely needs saying today—may be accompanied by an impeccable conformity and can signify two distinct but often related intentions: to try out one's own thinking and to test the other man's. The aim of this exploration of Marlowe's orthodoxy, both religious and political, is to try to clear away some of the clumsier irrelevances about his personal beliefs in relation to those of his contemporaries and to arrive at some modest reappraisal of one or two aspects of his plays. It is of course difficult to escape his 'atheism' and there is no need to traverse again the ground so fully explored by Paul Kocher. I may perhaps simply repeat what I have said elsewhere:

> [His] union of rash speculation and a desire to flaunt opinions in the face of puritan zeal was dangerous to Marlowe and his associates; at the same time it masked a true gravity in Marlowe's thinking . . . This was a lively, precocious and recalcitrant intelligence, skirmishing in and out of religious, social and political orthodoxy.[1]

It is in fact important to relate Marlowe's religious orthodoxy, over which critical debate has most seriously ranged, to his social and political orthodoxy, which has been less frequently considered. When our more responsible critics examine Marlowe's essential seriousness of tone they rarely confine this gravity to the theological sphere. When Clifford Leech analyses the variety of the comic element in Marlowe, he relates it to the dramatist's 'recognition of the puniness of human ambition, the ludicrous gap between aspiration and any possible fulfilment, the basic one-ness between the grandest, most self-absorbed figure and the slightest of crushable pygmies'. Harry Levin places with equal seriousness this temper of Marlowe's excess:

> If Marlowe learned the lyric mode from Ovid and the epic mode from Lucan, it may well have been Lucretius, who schooled him in tragic discernment of the nature of things. For Lucretius, too, life

---

[1] Introduction to the New Mermaid *Edward the Second* (1967) p. 11.

was grand and grave and harsh, and death was premature. Neither poet took the middle way; poetry takes the way of fine excess.[2]

This is the quality to which we most warmly respond even in our most critical moments, a mixed reaction which answers to a real dislocation in Marlowe's thought and attitudes. Before we explore this fact in the plays, it may be as well to define our terms more closely and especially the force and the limitations with which I shall here use the term 'orthodoxy'. The sense in which the term applies in his political thought will best emerge in considering *Tamburlaine* and there will probably be little dissent from my premisses. But theological orthodoxy arouses more passionate feelings and our present use had better be clarified. Orthodoxy in the religious sense involves intellectual assent to a creed which should issue in (and may be preceded by) a desire for liturgical worship and its individual expression in meditation. In turn these intellectual assents and devotional practices should issue in the good life. I have twice used the tacit qualification 'should': intellectual orthodoxy in any creed is relatively easy to determine, as is its counterpart, intellectual heresy; the sincerity of its 'fruits', in worship or in works, is a matter no man can presume to determine.

But even considered at the intellectual level, orthodoxy is not, at its most mature, monolithic or conservative. It is on the contrary ambiguous, ironic and sceptical of the competence of the human intellect to formulate absolutes. Among the tenets of Christian orthodoxy —to consider the area with which we are immediately concerned—there is the recognition of the necessity for witty incongruity in the formulation of doctrine: creation *ex nihilo*; the incarnation with its union of infinity with finitude ('immensity cloistered in thy dear womb'); the death of the 'Lord of Life'. Yet credal orthodoxy demands that we compass these incongruities to the point of assent, while, to make the situation still more intellectually complex, the degrees of assent required differ sharply among the clauses of our creeds themselves. Consider the variety of response demanded by the following phrases:

'... Jesus Christ His only Son ... born of the Virgin Mary ...
... Suffered under Pontius Pilate ...
... Sitteth at the right hand of God the Father'

Few Christians—yet all of them orthodox—would assent in identical manner to each of these phrases, the first 'doctrinal', the second 'historical' and the third 'metaphorical', to make a crude but momen-

---

[2] Harry Levin, *Christopher Marlowe the Overreacher* (1954) p. 190.

tarily useful distinction. It is perhaps worth asking in an aside, if we test Marlowe's 'atheist lecture' by these standards—setting aside the absurd elements in the reportage and his own wilful attempts to shock the bourgeois—whether we are not left with the defensive mockery of a man who had by upbringing and training been committed to examining these confounding incomprehensibles.

There is a still further problem of assessment, in an extension of the familiar Elizabethan commonplace of the distinction between status and person: no king matches his regal office, no priest his orders, no believer his profession. That Marlowe 'died swearing' is no necessary invalidation of his orthodoxy, for if it is a necessary doctrine of the Church, in order that regular and valid sacraments may be received by the faithful, that 'the unworthiness of the minister overthroweth not the nature of the sacrament', much more is the unworthy life of a lay Christian no invalidation of the correctness of his beliefs.

We are left therefore with two related problems in our judgement of Marlowe's beliefs: first, that there are ambiguities and imponderables in the structure of orthodoxy itself and for a poet or dramatist to explore the strains and incongruities involved in belief is a necessary part of intellectual health; and second that Marlowe's highly exploratory intelligence has frequently been overshadowed by the wilfulness of his expression and the alleged irregularity of his life. With the second of these matters we need no longer concern ourselves but deal more profitably with the tensions of his own thought within the plays as he handles three dominant concepts, knowledge, authority and beauty, which have provided teasing problems for traditional theology. That they were matters to which Marlowe frequently returned, in concrete symbols and in abstract speculation, provides us with a convenient point of entry to his thinking.

Human knowledge as either the source or the consequence of the Fall has produced a complex of ambiguities for both theologians and myth makers. 'Ye shall be as gods, knowing good and evil' is a seductive and a lying promise and in complicated ways. Knowledge is a necessary ingredient in maturity and the aspiration for greater knowledge one of the differentiae of the human condition. But the devil's promise has a dual falsity: first, the phrase 'as gods' involves inordinate aspiration, the desire to know beyond the natural terms of the human state; the fulfilment of this aspiration thus leads to the desire for magic and other forms of intellectual violence arising from the sin of curiosity. For Faustus it involved both demonism and necromancy, leading ultimately to a knowledge that, so far from being divine, involved the negation of human dignity itself and ultimately damnation; second, the phrase 'knowing good and evil' equates disparate qualities. The knowledge of good is a positive aspiration and is obtained by legitimate means (Faustus in fact lists some of them, though with ironic denial of their quality, as he recapitulates the areas of human learning in which he was master); the knowledge of evil is a negative state, involving loss of innocence. Marlowe nowhere shows himself more characteristically at the meeting-point of medieval and Renaissance values than in his constant examination of man's 'striving after knowledge infinite' and his continuous awareness that inordinate aspiration leads perversely to triviality. One of the most powerful contrasts in *Doctor Faustus* lies between the gravity of Mephostophilis' warnings on the condition of damnation in hell and the levity of Faustus' use of his demonic powers, not in compassing superhuman ends which he had formerly envisaged, but in mere conjuring tricks available to the common charlatan. To this intuition, that knowledge may be inordinate, can be attributed the consistency of Marlowe's *Faustus* which assumes throughout, before it is finally formulated in the closing chorus, that man may aspire to 'more than heavenly power permits'. This revelation of Marlowe's central orthodoxy may be shocking to those who regard him as a 'free-ranging intelligence' released from the fetters of medieval obscurantism but we shall find it to be a consistent attitude throughout his dramatic work.

Of authority as a concept in Marlowe's work we may feel his acceptance to be almost oppressively orthodox by contrast with the more complex ironies with which Shakespeare explores it. The paradigms of orthodoxy are established by the Homily on Obedience, echoing St Paul's exhortation to prayer even for those who exercise authority with tyrannous injustice. This pattern, the universal 'world order' by which the operation of natural law pervades the whole cosmic hierarchy, has been assumed almost excessively to be the unexamined assumption of all the dramatists. Indeed, the focal point of this order, 'the sweet fruition of an earthly crown', is so uniformly a theme of Shakespeare's contemporaries, that one might at this distance assume it to be a commonplace. The awe surrounding the symbols of regality, the crown and the chair royal, is most succinctly expressed in the words and actions of the English coronation rite, a sacramental ceremony involving the sovereign in divine functions. Hooker summarises the complexity of the status there conferred:

Crowned we see they are, and enthroned, and anointed; the crown
a sign of military, the throne of judicial, and oil of religious power.[3]

The harsh, the tragic dilemma in which the heroes of Renaissance
English drama are involved, is the measure of the disparity between this
noble quasi-priestly status of majesty and the frequently unworthy
person in whom the status inheres. This makes the superficial resemblance between Marlowe's *Edward II* and Shakespeare's *Richard II*
particularly attractive as exemplars of the commonplace attitude
towards the status and person of majesty: each is hyper-conscious of
his role, of the rights and responsibilities which it involves; each is
tragically aware of his failure to fulfil his regal destiny and each clings
desperately to the external symbols of royalty. But in fact the more
valuable critical comparison is that between *Edward II* and *Henry V*.
Shakespeare's king has won through to majesty by a hard way and there
is no doubting his regal purpose; indeed, on the eve of Agincourt we
find that rare being, a king whose status and person are commensurate
with each other. In this respect Edward and Henry appear the simple
dramatic converse of each other. But this is to consider them too superficially; their attitudes to the royal state are in fact deeply opposed.
Edward is quite simply aware of majesty, its dignity, power and duties;
his tragedy lies in his own awareness that he cannot fulfil the demands
of the office to which he has been sacramentally dedicated. In this
respect Marlowe is wholly orthodox to the point of the commonplace.
Shakespeare's king is equally aware of the magnitude of his office and
he is even more aware of its compassionate demands—of the beneficent
'little touch of Harry in the night'. Like Edward he is also aware of his
own conceivable inadequacy and of the burden of dynastic guilt he has
inherited. But there the parallel ends. Within Henry the Fifth's self-
awareness there is an irony of which Marlowe's royal heroes are
incapable. It is not simply that Henry is aware of the limited regality
of 'the hollow crown'—a shocking enough phrase in itself—but that
in his conversation with the common soldier and in the soliloquy which
follows, Henry establishes limitations to royal responsibility which
establish a more mature and ironic perception than Marlowe was at this
time capable of: Henry the Fifth had no doubt that physically he was
his brother's keeper even in the teeth of death by battle; but spiritually
his brother keeps his own soul, alone.

The most ambiguous of these three concepts is that of beauty,

---

[3] *Of the Laws of Ecclesiastical Polity*, viii. ii. 13.

traditionally ambiguous for moral theologians and certainly elusive in its significance in Marlowe. If biblical theologians have been able to write with propriety of 'the beauty of holiness', the incarnation of beauty in the female form has been another matter. It is difficult to imagine a greater conjunction of ambiguities than that of Shakespeare's phrase, 'Helen's beauty in a brow of Egypt', and certainly Marlowe's invocation of Helen has a like ambivalence. Nor is the long rhetorical analysis of beauty in *Tamburlaine* ('What is beauty, saith my sufferings then. . . .') free of uneasy searching. Marlowe, at least as much as Shakespeare, is involved with the teasing problem that beauty has been, on the one hand, for orthodox thinking a manifestation of mere appearance as opposed to reality, a snare, a delusion, the 'goodly outside' of no necessary significance; on the other hand it has symbolised creative harmony, the ultimate revelation in sensual terms of the divine perfection.

In these fundamental and pervasive concepts then, of knowledge, authority and beauty, Marlowe follows orthodox lines, indebted to commonplaces, in these as in so many other topics the inheritor of medieval thinking.

Before considering one or two of the plays in some detail, we may venture a temporary conclusion on the nature of Marlowe's orthodoxy. I find this in the clarity of the final moral judgement reached by every one of the plays without exception. We may feel that this concluding judgement is reached contrary to the prevailing tone of the play itself (the final chorus in *Faustus* has troubled critics on this account) but the tenor of the judgement can scarcely be denied. Indeed, in this respect Marlowe is in marked contrast with Shakespeare who leaves his audience and critics in a condition of moral casuistry, presented with the raw material for moral judgement but with the issues so nicely poised that finality seems studiously avoided. (Is Cleopatra truly the 'lass unparalleled' of her waiting woman's spontaneous tribute, with the undertones of innocence the phrase contains?) No such casuistic moral poise is demanded by Marlowe (the term 'casuistic' here used in its technical and not in its vulgar sense).

Though the final issues of death appear to be clearest in the 'fiendful fortune' of Faustus, *Tamburlaine* shows on analysis the most extended, most consistent judgement of the values which to the central character seem the most desirable. This makes of *Tamburlaine* one of the most supple examinations of political commonplaces in the Elizabethan theatre.

In the precarious balance both of internal and external power in the sixteenth-century European states, all statesmen owed an acknowledged debt to Machiavelli's analysis of the nature of a successful prince. The nature of sovereignty, the type of personal character in which it inhered, and the relation of this ruler to his state were practical problems to which it appeared that the *Discourses over the first Decade of Titus Livy* and *The Prince* gave the most adequate answer. The concepts presented in these works became the commonplaces of statesmen before they were execrated by dramatists, and it is not surprising that Marlowe, who had met the Machiavellian system academically and was connected with a fair degree of intimacy with men who applied it to English politics, should have accepted some of its implications and submitted others to scrutiny. The first part of *Tamburlaine*, concerned as it is in one of its aspects with the rise to power of a man who had no 'legitimate' claim to rule except his own 'virtue' and power, presents the first aspect of this scrutiny.

It will be useful in drawing out the implications of the serious Machiavellian parallels in Tamburlaine to have the terms isolated in which Machiavelli conceives the adequate ruler. This has been done by Grattan Freyer in an important article, 'The Ideas of Machiavelli', in *Scrutiny*, June, 1939:

> In Machiavelli, the important terms are *virtù, la fortuna* and *la gloria. Virtù* has nothing to do with Dante's use of the same word, nor with the English 'virtue'. It might perhaps be rendered 'manliness': it is essentially a-moral, in fact it cuts clean across moral values. . . . *La fortuna* or Fortune, covers a quaint feeling of a pagan goddess of destiny: If a man has both *virtù* and Fortune with him he will achieve *la gloria.*

To a remarkable degree, both in the dramatic situations and in the words of Tamburlaine, the analysis of the qualities necessary for the control of political powers accounts for the rise of Tamburlaine in opposition to men who are devoid of these qualities, and at the same time provides the starting-point for the undercurrent of criticism from the second act of the play to the end.

The play opens with the hapless situation of Persia under the weak king Mycetes. In this scene, as in Act II, scs. ii and iv, the contrast stressed is between 'working words' and effective action. Mycetes, who declares that ' 'tis a pretty toy to be a poet', expects of Theridamas that his words will prove swords and of Meander that 'Thy wit will make us conquerors today'. By contrast, in the interposed scene Tamburlaine provides the foil of prompt and decisive action:

> Then shall we fight courageously with them?
> Or look you I should play the orator?

while to Zenocrate he declares while still a shepherd:

> I am a lord for so my deeds shall prove.

Meanwhile, Cosroe is singled out by personal qualities and by Fortune to be the temporary substitute for Mycetes on the Persian throne.

> This should entreat your highness to rejoice
> Since Fortune gives you opportunity
> To gain the title of a conqueror
> By curing of this maimed Empery.

In spite, however, of this beneficent result in restoring peace to a discordant state, which was the proper end of power in the sixteenth-century conception of the prince, Cosroe in turn is superseded by the more powerful personality of Tamburlaine.

But the contrast between words and effective action also becomes a tension in Tamburlaine himself. It is seen most clearly in the soliloquy in Act V: 'What is beauty saith my sufferings, then?', where the word 'virtue' interpreted in the Machiavellian sense provides a probable explanation for the obscure conclusion. For the first fourteen lines Tamburlaine meditates rhetorically upon the inability of poetry to express the aspirations of man. But this is broken by an impatient realisation of the incongruity of poetic meditation to a man of action:

> But how unseemly is it for my sex,
> My discipline of arms and chivalry,
> My nature and the terror of my name
> To harbour thoughts effeminate and faint.

The sole purpose of the poetic imagination, embodying beauty, is to define and make explicit the aspirations of the man of action.

> And every warrior that is rapt with love
> Of fame, of valour, and of victory
> Must needs have beauty beat on his conceits.

But apart from this concession, beauty is subordinated to the more active qualities which reward the man of *virtù* however humble his birth, for Tamburlaine

> Shall give the world to note, for all my birth,
> That virtue solely is the sum of glory,
> And fashions men with true nobility.

'Virtue' here can have no moral connotation; it is obvious from the implied contrast between meditation and action that it is rather the *virtù* of the Renaissance and of Machiavelli in particular which results, when pursued with the aid of Fortune, in glory.

Tamburlaine has also the second positive element necessary for success, Fortune, but with it is linked an interesting and complicated concept of Nature throughout the play. It is his control of Fortune which provides him with his surest confidence:

> I hold the Fates bound fast in iron chains
> And with my hand turn Fortune's wheel about;
> And sooner shall the sun fall from his sphere
> Than Tamburlaine be slain or overcome.   (I.ii. 174-7)

Marlowe however links this Fortune with another power. Cosroe comments upon Menaphon's description of Tamburlaine:

> Nature doth strive with Fortune and his stars
> To make him famous in accomplished worth:
> And well his merits show him to be made
> His fortune's master and the king of men.   (II.i. 33-6)

This *Natura* becomes a presiding concept in the play and soon provides the starting-point of the criticism of Tamburlaine. He himself is conscious of his place within the natural order. He attempts to justify his very aspiration by analogy with the processes of Nature:

> Nature, that fram'd us of four elements
> Warring within our breasts for regiment
> Doth teach us all to have aspiring minds.   (II.vii. 18-20)

The seeming bathos of the end of this passage, 'The sweet fruition of an earthly crown', has caused much comment. The bathos is of course there, particularly in the description of the earthly crown as 'that perfect bliss and sole felicity'. But it is more than that; it is this very appeal to the natural order which violates the traditional medieval function of the concept. As we shall see the chief criticism of Tamburlaine by the other characters lies in his attempt to transcend his station or degree; in this passage he employs the very natural order which enshrined the medieval concept of degree to justify his pursuit of the

Renaissance ideal, the man of *virtù*. The bathos therefore consists not merely in the descent to 'earthly crown', but is reinforced by the incongruity of the analogies which Tamburlaine employs. For the 'aspiring mind' is justified successively by analogy with man's balanced faculties, the 'four elements', with 'the wondrous architecture of the world' and the order of the 'wandering planet's course', all of them elements in that cosmic order which controlled man's 'vaulting ambition' and the breakdown of which gave rein to the man of *virtù*. In brief, Nature 'doth teach us' very precisely *not* to have 'aspiring minds' in Tamburlaine's sense but to maintain the equipoise of the natural order.

It is this moral content in the natural order in its opposition to Machiavellian *virtù* which accounts for the insecurity in the implied judgement of Tamburlaine during the greater part of the play. Judged by standards of sixteenth-century power, Tamburlaine is wholly justified in his imposition of order upon a divided and chaotic fourteenth-century Asia; it is interesting to note the stress which Marlowe's own sources place upon this beneficent order achieved through force; for he is in the fullest sense 'the scourge and wrath of God'. But the repeated criticisms of Tamburlaine in the first part arise mainly from a feeling that he violated the natural order. It is the charge of Cosroe that he is 'Barbarous and bloody', 'bloody and insatiate', that calls from Tamburlaine the defence of his 'aspiring mind' by analogies from the natural order. But this scene (II.vii) has already been placed in its perspective by the preceding one in which Cosroe and his comrades employ a moral, almost a theological, reference to define the unnatural presumption of Tamburlaine. For in the first place Tamburlaine is guilty of an impious defiance of degree and order:

> What means this devilish shepherd, to aspire
> With such a giantly presumption,
> To cast up hills against the face of heaven,
> And dare the force of angry Jupiter?

This is followed by a repetition of abhorrence at his *monstrous* conduct:

> So will I send this monstrous slave to hell,
> Where flames shall ever feed upon his soul,

and

> What god or fiend or spirit of the earth
> Or monster turned to a manly shape
> Or of what mould or mettle he be made

he is a 'devilish thief', 'he was never sprung of human race', and

> Some power divine or else infernal, mixed
> Their angry seeds at his conception.

The crux of the charge anticipates the tone of *Faustus*:

> Since with the spirit of his fearful pride,
> He dares so doubtlessly resolve of rule,
> And by profession be ambitious.

Against this complex of the sin of pride, the violation of degree, and the unnatural springs of power, Cosroe asserts the normal composition of those who will oppose Tamburlaine:

> And since we all have sucked one wholesome air,
> And with the same proportion of elements . . .

where the stress upon 'wholesome' and 'proportion of elements' refers back to the 'unwholesomeness' of Tamburlaine's action and forward to his presumptuous claim based upon this same composition from the four elements.

A similar criticism is taken up by the Soldan in Act IV, sc. iii, with an added point from its ironic echo of one of Tamburlaine's chief boasts:

> A monster of five hundred thousand heads,
> Compact of rapine, piracy and spoil,
> The scum of men, the hate and scourge of God.

Cosroe's pattern of criticism is again followed; he is 'a sturdy felon and a base-born thief', 'this presumptuous beast' has 'pride' and the violation of due order is again stressed:

> It is a blemish to the majesty
> And high estate of mighty emperors,
> That such a base usurping vagabond
> Should brave a king or wear a princely crown.

Yet all these criticisms might have been considered but dramatic foils to Tamburlaine's irresistible transcendence of all normal sanctions but for the fact that Zenocrate, the tone of whose speech is always moderate and credible and who supplies a conscious antithesis to Tamburlaine in both parts, provides the fullest criticism of mere a-moral force with her reiteration of the transitoriness of glory:

> Those that are proud of fickle empery
> And place their chiefest good in earthly pomp,
> Behold the Turk and his great empress!   (V.ii. 293-5)

A crown, the symbol throughout the play of fortunate power, now becomes 'slippery crowns'; success in battle gives way to 'the wavering turns of war' while in a passage which at once deflates his aspiring fortune, bringing it back to earth, and indicates the emptiness of his quest for mere conquest, she prays:

> O pardon his contempt
> Of earthly fortune and respect of pity;
> And let not conquest ruthlessly pursued,
> Be equally against his life incensed
> In this great Turk and hapless empress.   (V.ii. 305-9)

It would thus seem that with all the fascination of the career of Tamburlaine, behind the picturesque progress there has gone on a balanced consideration of one of the dominant political enquiries of the sixteenth century. On the one hand, Tamburlaine, conveniently distanced by his oriental origin, has elements of the a-moral yet ordering power of sixteenth-century 'virtue' backed by Fortune, the ideal of the Machiavellian powerful ruler. On the other hand, there is insistently asserted the older moral order by which the private virtues of pity and humility are relevant in statecraft. No conclusion is possible in the covert conflict in *Tamburlaine* since that was not the main purpose of the play, but it is significant that when in *Faustus*, within the sphere of the individual soul, the conflict between Renaissance *virtù* and the moral order is enacted, rebellion and self-assertion, both in the order of angels and of men, are called 'aspiring pride and insolence', while the issue of the conflict is never in doubt.

In *Doctor Faustus* the tensions within Marlowe's thinking are at their greatest. Miss Roma Gill has placed their quality within the texture of the verse:

> Marlowe's play demonstrates the fearful consequences of violating the Christian ethic, and for this it may be called a Christian document. But Marlowe's sympathies (if the energy of the verse means anything at all) are for the rebel, the man who is . . . frustrated in his efforts to assert his individuality.[4]

This is very true, so far as it goes, though I find a grave energy in the

---

[4] Introduction, New Mermaid edition (1965, 1967) p. xxvii.

warnings of Mephostophilis against Faustus' levity which tell on the orthodox side as powerfully as the exploration and curiosity also assert Marlowe's sympathies; while the full weight of gravity is given to the measured beat of the concluding chorus.

But the play is no simple debate, of medieval orthodoxy against Renaissance humanism (and indeed the ambivalences of Shakespeare, Jonson, Chapman should warn us against too easy an antithesis along those lines). More profitable is to see Marlowe as contributing richly to the most ambiguous myth of the modern consciousness in a series to which the *Faustbuch*, Goethe, and Thomas Mann contributed confoundingly diverse interpretations; it is significant that the Polish folk version, *Pan Twardowski*, finds a final redemption for his 'Faust' even in the toils of hell itself, a consummation to which no other version ventured.

Any perception of Marlowe's predominant orthodoxy of expression in this play must rest on the complexity of its ironies, a fact which Professor Brockbank (whether consciously or unconsciously) underlines by his citing a major heresy as its parallel:

As 'hell strives with grace' for conquest in Faustus' breast, the powers of light and darkness seem matched in the Manichean way. But to patient judgment it appears that Faustus' yielding to evil is voluntary, while the Old Man's resistance to it makes it assist in the perfection of virtue.[5]

This cosmic struggle of grace and evil pervades more than the plot of the drama. Mephostophilis gives a classical expression of Hell's quality as condition rather than location ('why this is hell nor am I out of it') with a clarity that approaches pedantry, while there is a deeper irony in a stylistic device which unites two climactic moments in the play: at the instant that Faustus signs away his soul to perdition, he does so with the words 'Consummatum est', the final expression of Christ's redemption of man on the Cross; when Hell finally claims Faustus' soul, his plea for delay is again in Latin, a recollection in 'O lente, lente . . .' of a passage from Ovid's *Amores*. Marlowe is sufficiently engaged with the issues and in command of them to be able to move with an assured flexibility of tone through their involutions of moral and theological argument.

The political orthodoxy of *Edward II* has been sufficiently noted. This

---

[5] *Marlowe: Doctor Faustus* (1962), quoted Clifford Leech, *Marlowe, Twentieth Century Views* (1964) p. 114.

argument may perhaps be best concluded by examining briefly one aspect of the moral issue in the play, the congruity with which Edward's punishment and death fits the crime. Public execution in Shakespeare's day elaborated with dramatic ceremony the nature of the misdeed in the form of death and there is a horrible wit in the decree of the Council of Zurich in 1526 that whereas heretics were usually burned to death, Anabaptists 'will be drowned without mercy'. King Edward's sufferings are prolonged through a two-fold trial. As king he is humiliated to a point of abasement where he recaptures a dignity he had never known in the exercise of his majesty:

> Yet stay awhile, forbear thy bloody hand
> And let me see the stroke before it comes
> That even then when I shall lose my life
> My mind may be more steadfast on my God.   (V.v. 74-7)

But this plea is addressed to Lightborn, whose name Professor Levin has very plausibly associated with Lucifer; the devil's spit is the punishment most nearly appropriate to Edward's inordinate and unnatural sexuality. The modern man finds this ritual propriety horrifying if not wholly incomprehensible, but the tradition was long-standing and the London theatre has seen a powerful moment in that tradition in the National Theatre production of Seneca's *Oedipus*. Jocasta debates the proper mode of her death, which shall most adequately punish her wrongs and play out the ritual atonement. Mr Martin Esslin (in *Plays and Players*, May 1968) describes the scene:

> Irene Worth, as Jocasta, in the enactment of the mode of suicide Seneca has prescribed for her (she stabs herself through the womb; Sophocles' Jocasta merely hanged herself) performs the ultimate in ritual symbolism: she has to suggest that her suicide is an act of deadly intercourse with the sword on which she impales herself.

Jocasta is aware of the rhythms of guilt and the demands of atonement, as she is aware in her own body of

> the place the gods hate
> where everything began.

Blake had a similar appalling insight into Dante's mind as he traversed the *Inferno*, exposing the variety of hell; Marlowe is never more in accord with the orthodoxy of his intellectual origins than when he explores the patterns of sin and of punishment in the cosmic order and to this pattern the plays all return at their conclusion.

Index

[Titles are italicised. Characters in Marlowe's works are indexed individually]

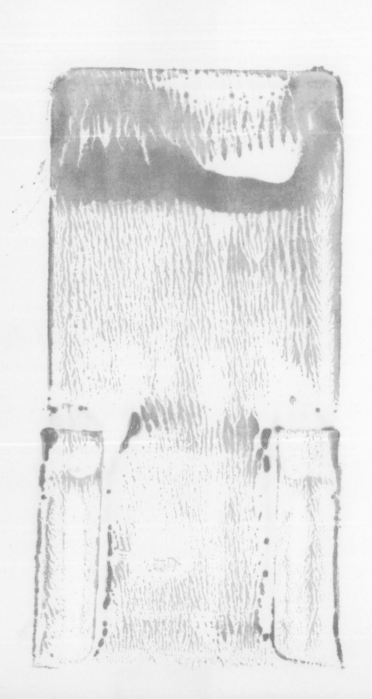